Ellen Tollet of
Journals and Letters from 1835

'....so large a family, not a family of quiet presence, able nonentities, but of active, stirring, talking beings...' Ellen 1835

'We know so little of each other's feelings...' Georgina 1836

Edited by
Mavis E. Smith

Betley Local History Society

Published by Mavis E. Smith, 3 Woodland Hills, Madeley, Crewe
Cheshire, CW3 9HN, UK
Tel: 01782 750176

© Mavis E. Smith 2008, except were otherwise stated and for illustrations.

The moral rights of the author have been asserted. All rights reserved. No part of this publication may be reproduced, stored or transmitted in any form or by any means without prior permission in writing of the publisher.

British Library Cataloguing in Publication Data
Data available

ISBN 978-0-9538151-3-5

Printed by: Delmar Press, Wall Lane, Nantwich, Cheshire, CW5 5LS

Contents

Preface *4*
Acknowledgements of the illustrations *7*
The Family Background *9*
Dramatis personae *16*
Journals One: January 1835-April 1836 *18*
    Introduction with a retrospective view of a marriage and a birth *18*
    The Betley social whirl in 1835 *22*
    Malvern and the return of the suitors *50*
    Return to Betley *60*
    Some disappointments *77*
    Georgina's parallel diary from 28th December 1835–19th June 1836 *96*
    A Birth *108*
    Return of normality after the birth *115*
    Deteriorating illness of Eliza *128*
Journal Two: April 1836-October 1836 *136*
    The closing family scene *141*
    Ellen goes to Welshpool *146*
    Georgina's journal only *148*
    Ellen resumes her pen *154*
    Liverpool, Venice of the North *161*
    A fortnight in Betley in July *166*
    Welshpool again, and the law *170*
    Summer in London *174*
    Betley in conclusion *180*
The period from 1836–1841 *183*
Journal Three 1841-1846 *193*
Ellen's life afterwards *211*
Appendix *231*
    1 Residents of Betley from White's Gazetteer, and the Journals *231*
    2 A short satirical sketch - untitled - by Ellen Tollet *232*
    3 Family Tree *236*
    4 Map of local halls visited in 1835-6 *237*
    5 Betley in the 1830s *238*
Notes and References *239*
Index *249*

Preface

About three years ago when I was writing an account of the occupants of Betley Hall, I discovered on the internet, among the Shropshire Archives, three diaries by Ellen Tollet, a short diary by Georgina Tollet and some correspondence. Now, with permission from Mrs Stacey and the Trustees of the Bridgeman Family Archive, and help from the staff in the Shropshire Archive, I have been able to study them in detail. Fortunately the enlightened policy of the Shropshire Libraries allowed copies to be taken of the precious diaries, to enable me to transcribe them at leisure.

On first seeing Ellen's journals, all three hundred pages, I realised that they said much more about the life of a young lady in the 1830s and also about life in the village than I had previously discovered. In them Jane Austen's world of fiction is brought back to reality almost twenty years later, in the life of a young woman in the North Midlands.

However there was a difficulty in reading what, at first glance, looked like beautiful, neat handwriting. The text provided a challenge. Words disappeared into the margins, were smudged, or were illegible because of the flow of the curves of u's, w's, m's, n's, and capital letters were sometimes indecipherable, and used frequently for common nouns, as was customary in the nineteenth century. Occasionally parts of pages could not be read because they had faded. Paragraphs were non-existent, and even the abbreviated date or merely the day was written in the middle or at the end of a line, so that there would be no waste of space. Some of Ellen's sentences flowed on for many lines without punctuation. Thus I have amended them for ease of reading, and I have used editorial licence to write abbreviations in full to avoid ambiguity. Where there is a question mark immediately in front of a word, it implies I am not entirely sure that my transcription is correct. Words that were incomprehensible have a comment in italics and in brackets to explain the problem. It may be that I have inadvertently misinterpreted a word or expression - such was the illegibility of the handwriting in some places. There is the odd spelling mistake, which remains unaltered.

Ellen was a writer! Her vocabulary was immense, her turn of phrase enjoyable and her use of imagery memorable at times. She seemed to experiment with words: her style varied from the rhetorical, or lyrical, or simple, or witty, bitterly satirical, to being simply convoluted in argument. Throughout Ellen's diary she creates suspense; the reader always wants to know more and is often frustrated because answers are not, or cannot, be given. Occasionally we learn from other sources the answers to the problem, but we are left to imagine what was the cryptic meaning of 'I had an amusing adventure on the stairs', or 'Mary Ann slept in my room for protection.' On one occasion a draft letter to Ellen's sister-in-law lay at the back of the first journal: on another occasion Georgina spills the beans. For Ellen they would be reminders of more intimate thoughts as she looked back over her life.

Journals I and II are one continuous piece of writing, from January 1835 to October 1836. They have a retrospective opening and a reflective ending with the major day by day section in between. At the end of the first journal there were a number of loose pages. Amongst them was a forty page journal by Georgina, Ellen's older sister. This covered a six month period from the beginning of 1836. It complements Ellen's thoughts at a critical period in the life of the whole family. What is more, the reader sees the same event from two points of view. I have included Georgina's diary at the end of Ellen's daily writing.

To attempt to keep the flow of the narrative, I have interspersed comments and explanations in the main text. They are written in italics. In addition, because Ellen referred so often to her current reading, I have used italics to give the title and date of publication to illustrate just how wide was her reading, and to illustrate the breadth of the famous Tollet library.

The third journal is totally different in content from the other two with a long time gap and covering a much longer period. It is made up of retrospective essays on one subject only. No further explanation is needed.

In the same Bridgeman Collection there were other items of interest which had a direct bearing on the life of Ellen Tollet. There was a sketch book of drawings of people with their names, and water colours, supposedly by Georgina but probably by Ellen, because it is difficult to see how Georgina with one arm could have drawn a likeness of herself in bed. Moreover there is no drawing of Ellen in the album. However we found elsewhere in the archive a silhouette of her when she was sixteen. Many of the drawings are relevant to the journals and have been included in the book. They are useful too, because

Ellen seldom mentions clothes in her writing, and we can discover the fashion of the provincial gentry at that time. There are amusing descriptions of one of their guests arriving for dinner in a ball gown and once Ellen wickedly spied the vivid coloured under garments of a little boy!

In addition there were hitherto unpublished letters belonging to Ellen and her sisters. Some of these have been incorporated after the section on the journals; the most notable were from Charles Darwin and Florence Nightingale.

A few of the letters, (of which there are more than forty) from the Wedgwood/Mosley collection, from Emma Darwin to her friend Ellen, have been included to show something of Ellen Tollet's later life. They are currently held in the archives of the Special Collection at Keele University and have been reproduced by kind permission of the Trustees of the Wedgwood Museum, Barlaston, Stoke-on-Trent. On this matter Helen Burton, the archivist at Keele University has been most helpful.

I am grateful to the committee of the Betley Local History Association, headed by David Thompson, and in particular to Gregor Shufflebotham, the librarian, for providing some information and illustrations about the Tollet family and their contemporaries in Betley in the nineteenth century. After a visit to Welshpool, I was kindly given some detail about the ministry of William Clive by Colin Rogers and Roger Brown, the retired vicar of Welshpool. To Paul and Anne Anderton, who have read the first draft and offered suggestions, I offer my warmest thanks.

Any attempt to make a transcription of the journals would have been impossible without the support of my husband, Peter. He accompanied me to Shrewsbury, photographed the manuscript and was always there to help and encourage, whether it was in deciphering almost illegible words, drawing the maps and family tree, proof reading, photographing halls visited by Ellen Tollet, or organizing computer files.

Acknowledgements of the Illustrations

I am most grateful to the following who have allowed me to use their material and images in this book.

Mrs Stacey and the Trustees of the Bridgeman Family Archive: the silhouette of Ellen Tollet (with the words 'Ellen aged 16, 1828,' written on the back), and, from the album of drawings by either Ellen or Georgina, numbers 6 Fanny, 7 Mr Bagot, 9 Mr Egerton, 11 Mr Haden, 12 Mary Wigley, 16 Mr Antony Whyte , 17 Mr Philips of the Heath, 23 Georgina, 24 Fanny Crewe, 26 Georgina's diary, 27 Charles Wicksted, 28 Ellen's sample page, 30 Unnamed lady, 35 Watercolour of a ship, 36 Mrs Earle, 37 Mr Tayleur and Miss E. Tayleur, 40 Mrs Dodsworth and Mrs Haden, 41 Mr Alington, 43 Caroline, 47 William Clive, 48 Miss Dunscombe, 54 Watercolour of a gate.

The Trustees of the Wedgwood /Mosley Collection, Barlaston, Stoke-on-Trent, held at Keele University: 34 Manchester School for the deaf and Dumb.

The Keele University Local Collection
a) *Ancestral Homes of Staffordshire*, compiled by William H. Bowers: 13 Maple Hayes, 15 Beaudesert Hall
b) *Shropshire Houses past and Present,* Stanley Leighton, London, George Bell 1901: 2 Buntingsdale, 39 Wallop.
c) *Sneyd Papers*, painting by Rev Lewis Sneyd 1810: 38 Keele Hall.

The Trustees of the William Salt Library
a) Betley Hall Staffordshire, south-west view from over the lake showing the bridge to the left, by Cornelius Varley, October 1820 - on the cover.
b) Betley Hall, an engraving, north-west view of the hall across the lake, based on Cornelius Varley's drawing, 1820: 10.
c) Betley Church, 1838 by Thomas Peploe Wood: 32 and on back cover.
d) Betley Church from Betley Hall, showing a distant view over the park from Betley Hall window, a drawing by C. Varley: 33.

Manchester Art Gallery Picture Library: the mezzotint of George Tollet, variously attributed to Ansdell and to S.W. Reynolds after Ansdell, about 1844: 49.

Mr E. A. Watkin who kindly let me use post-cards from his collection from the turn of the twentieth century: 1 Betley New Hall, 4 Whitmore Hall, 14 Lichfield Cathedral, 18 The Savings Bank , 20 Old Hall (Farm), 22 Centre of Betley, 25 Dorfold Hall, 31 Betley Court, 52 Betley Church and Vicarage, 53 Maer Hall.

Mr Severne who kindly let me use his photograph of Shakenhurst: 50.

The National Trust Powis
The East Front of Powis by Paul Sandby Munn, 1817: 44.

The Borough Museum and Art Gallery, Newcastle-under-Lyme
Newcastle, showing the Roebuck Inn, a painting by J. Hulse, about 1800: 42.

Hinchcliffe E. *Barthomley* (1856); 8 Crewe Hall.

Blagg C.J. *A History of the North Staffordshire Hounds* (1902): 3 William Wells, 29 Charles Wicksted.

The Family Background

Ellen Harriet Tollet was fortunate to be born in 1812 into a wealthy background, the sixth daughter of George and Frances Tollet. Their eldest child was Charles. On inheriting Betley Hall from Charles Tollet in 1796, George (born in 1767) was obliged to change his name from Embury. He took up residence after the death of Charles' widow in 1807. He was a barrister, a JP and significant land owner in the village and its environs. Locally he was a respected benefactor of charities and schools in the Potteries, Betley and Audley. Primarily he was regarded as an agricultural reformer, advising land owners throughout this area of the North Midlands. In politics he was active locally in North Staffordshire and South Cheshire as a Whig. He was a man eager to embrace modern developments.[1]

Ellen's mother was regarded by everyone as religious. In 1823 Elizabeth Wedgwood told her sister Jessie Sismondi that Mrs Tollet 'is exceedingly religious, and I think her duty to God is the first object of her thoughts. She is also so single hearted that it is a great pleasure to be with her and to read a heart so entirely without guile.' Elizabeth Wedgwood continued to discuss her religious beliefs on original sin and being born again. 'It seems to put good and evil out of our own power. Is this Calvinism? This is Mrs Tollet's doctrine and I believe that of the most evangelical clergy.' [2] Mrs Tollet had been described by her daughter-in-law, who was somewhat critical of her relations in Betley, as being rather naïve, by accepting only literal meanings - 'she is taken in by all the commonest artifices of a novel,' and accepted everything she read in newspapers as absolute fact.[3]

With seven daughters to care for, Mrs Tollet must have been an extremely good organiser to ensure they were taking suitable places in society. She had inherited a fortune from her mother, one of the Wicksted family from Nantwich. All eight children had been well educated, presumably by governesses and tutors, and probably the final part of their education was in a school, as was Ellen's. Music, drawing, literature, languages, needlework, and such subjects befitting respectable young ladies would have been undertaken in their privileged status. The only son, Charles, was treated differently; he went to Eton and Oxford. It was customary for young women in their position to marry well; the alternative for them would be to write, to enter a convent, or to remain old maids. It is not therefore surprising to find Ellen jokingly calling her mother a matchmaker. Obviously finding suitable husbands for seven daughters was an onerous task; in this matter she was not particularly successful. Her nerves, like Mrs Bennet's in *Pride and Prejudice*, were troublesome, causing her family much concern. That is where the literary analogy ends.

Charles, (born in 1796) changed his name to Wicksted whilst he was still at college, in order to inherit an estate from a great uncle in Cheshire. His greatest claim to fame was as a master of the hounds in the Woore country.[4] He rode with the Tarporley Hunt from 1817 and was claimed to be second to none in all fox-hunting knowledge.[5] His poems on the subject of hunting still survive. George Tollet, who managed Charles' financial affairs until he became of age, was rather concerned about the extravagance of his son, and in a letter written in 1825 warned him of developing his plans in the hunting scene.[6] It was a matter of concern for his father because Charles seemed to devote too much time to his sporting activities, as did other members of the landed gentry. This advice was not heeded because he continued to hunt into the 1830s. He was very wealthy. He became a JP, High Sheriff of Cheshire in 1822, and an officer in the Yeomanry, commissioned in 1831.[7] Local newspapers reveal that he attended local Whig political meetings with his father in Nantwich. Having seven younger sisters made him the centre of their attention. His popularity was noted by Florence Nightingale as a child, when she visited Betley Hall to be rowed by him with his sisters round the lake. Apparently he loved to amuse children.

However by the age of thirty-eight in 1834, Charles became engaged to marry Mary Meysey Wigley, an heiress from Shakenhurst in Worcestershire, a distance of about ninety miles from Betley. She was the youngest of a family of five. Her two older brothers died before they could inherit the estate, with the result that it was divided between the three daughters – Caroline, lively, vivacious, lame and always described as ugly, a writer, Anna, the second sister married to Mr Severne, and Mary, the youngest. Strangely to us, she was usually referred to as Mary Wicksted in the journals, just as Charles is given his new, full name.

Penelope was the eldest of the Tollet daughters and fifteen years older than Ellen. Little is said about her in the journals apart from her help with poor children, but what is said is always respectful. She was involved with local charities. Frances, the next daughter, and twelve years older than the diarist, seems to be rather sickly and is seldom referred to; Elizabeth (Eliza) a mere ten years older is loved by all. Her knowledge of geology was said to be impressive. Catherine Darwin wrote to her brother, Charles, in November 1833 saying, 'Poor Eliza Tollet is thought to be in a consumption. She has had a cough now for nine months and is gradually getting weaker.'[8] When the journal begins in 1834 we discover that she had improved to some extent.

The next in line and the only married daughter was Marianne. In 1829 she married the Rev William Clive, vicar of Welshpool. Educated at Eton and Cambridge, he was the second son of William Clive of Styche, a nephew of Clive of India and cousin of the first Earl of Powis. All reports stated that he was public spirited, kindly, wealthy and loved by all his parishioners. This was a good match for Marianne.[9] However, she seemed to be totally obsessed by her inability to produce an heir. Mrs Tollet was aware of this obsession and apparently arranged for her other daughters to keep Marianne happy. When Ellen began her journal in 1835, she was staying in Shrewsbury with Marianne and William. He was about twenty miles from his main parish in Welshpool, where his curate would be deputising for him; moreover Marianne was close to excellent medical support, namely Dr Darwin, father of Charles. The birth of a child was eagerly awaited.

Georgina (Georgy) was four years older than Ellen, and Caroline (Carry) three years younger. These three sisters were particularly close to one another, and Ellen called them by affectionate names, which are somewhat surprising to the modern reader. Ellen felt particularly protective of Georgina, probably because she had suffered the misfortune of having her arm amputated in 1826. Florence Nightingale stated that her arm hurt badly and she 'had concealed the fact because she did not want to have her music lessons stopped .... She had gone *all* alone to Chester and submitted to the operation.' [10] This must have been a piece of fiction because Catherine and Caroline gave a more reliable version of this terrible surgical procedure when they told their brother, Charles Darwin, that 'poor Georgina has had an abscess in her arm and, to save her life, has been obliged to have it cut off; she bore the operation without a scream or groan.'[11] In a letter written to Emma Wedgwood in 1826, Georgina made light of her loss and explained that she had not enjoyed the sea bathing on the Liverpool Coast at Crosby, which was deemed necessary for the healing of her arm, because 'unfortunately I have a great dislike to it.'[12] She had speedily learned to write and draw with her left hand. Indeed her handwriting is very much easier to read than that of her sister. In the journals Georgina's disability is rarely mentioned. She is fairly active, because she goes for longish walks with her sisters and drives the pony carriage – no mean achievement. She never attends the balls with them. Caroline (Carry) seemed to have an attractive, gentle personality, and was loved by all.

It seems that Ellen was the lively, noisy, boisterous, witty and really clever sister. Her ability to draw, do caricatures and paint was admired by her friends. She would act as their representative if need be. At times though, like her mother, she could feel low. She was devout in her religion and exacted very high standards of behaviour. Her real thoughts were not always included in her journal if she felt shame or great unhappiness. In a family of seven women there was occasionally sibling rivalry, particularly with the presence of the sister-in-law, which Ellen only occasionally refers to. Georgina commented that when Ellen left the house, the atmosphere was very dull. Physically the diarist was attractive, as shown by her profile, with slight build, being only five feet tall and weighing eight stone.

1. Betley New Hall.

The house where the Tolletts lived had been built in 1783 by Charles Tollet on the site of the black and white hall that was falling into disrepair, (not to be confused with the Old Hall, the manor house, on the other side of the road which Charles Tollet had bought from the Chetwynds in the late eighteenth century.) The Old Hall Farm is mentioned only once in the journals. The Tolletts' New Hall was large with all the attributes of the country houses being built at the time. It had large rooms for entertaining, with the drawing room and dining rooms overlooking the lakes. The library was 27 feet by 19 and probably housed many rare books from George Tollet I, the naval commissioner, from Elizabeth Tollet, the poet, and from George Tollet III, the scholar, as well as many books of the period, judging by the reading of Ellen. The ceiling of this room had plaster figures of Cupid and Psyche, known as the boys, so perhaps we can assume the other main rooms had elegant ceilings too. The beautiful, small Morris Dancers' Window must have been part of the background and consequently never referred to in the journals. The house was set in attractive grounds with a walled garden, stables, flower gardens, gravelled walks, woods and an impressive drive-way to the centre of the village of Betley.

During the nineteenth century the beautiful Old Hall, which still exists, was made into the experimental farm for the agriculturalist, George Tollet. Like his predecessor he was buying up land in the village, so that he owned more than half the property by the time he died. Many of his servants who worked in the hall lived in the village. They are mentioned in the journal only on a few occasions when something unusual occurred; they must have worked very hard to cater for a family of ten and all their guests. The fact that a former servant revisited the household implies that the Tolletts were considerate employers.

The other landed proprietors in Betley were Miss Fletcher and Sir T.F. Fletcher of the Court and the Earl of Wilton in Wrinehill, an absentee landlord. The church was a perpetual curacy, in the impropriation of George Tollet. The vicar was the Rev Henry Turton, who frequently dined at the Hall and the Court. There was also a small Methodist chapel, not mentioned in Ellen's journals.

The two main houses provided much employment for the Betley population of 870. In 1834 there were 163 inhabited houses containing 166 families.[13] Betley was fairly self-sufficient in an area of mixed farming. The village had its own surgeons, shopkeepers, blacksmith, publicans, shoe-makers, a weaver, builders, maltsters, painters, plumbers, tailors, and farmers, etc. There were numerous places to consume alcohol – The Black Horse Inn, The Hand and Trumpet, The Red Lion, The Swan Inn and the Three Anchors, as well as beer houses.[14] Drunkenness was a problem in the village in 1835, as Ellen points out in the journal. The closest the industrial revolution had impacted on the village would have been through the nearby North Staffordshire coal mines which provided work for a few men. The post office was housed in part of The Black Horse. In several acres of land was a school, with a small library of 200 volumes, now known as the Reading Room. A savings bank was held there once a month. Georgina was proud to write in her diary in 1836 that few other village schools could hold a public lecture. The day school was never mentioned by Ellen, but she often helped at the school on Sunday. The ladies of the hall visited the poor and sick in the community, including the inmates of the work house in Wrinehill.

The occupants of the hall were privileged particularly in receiving medical help, such as it was in 1835. They could afford to send Georgina to Chester for surgery or to have doctors in attendance in childbirth. To bleed a woman in labour would have been acceptable! Dr Brady from Nantwich was frequently called for his expertise, whether it was for bleeding, leeches or blistering. Once in the journals Ellen mentioned that Georgina had received dental treatment in Chester. Some of the medicines given would have been frightening to us. It is a miracle that anyone survived.

Food did not play a significant part of Ellen's life. It was only the unusual foods that were mentioned such as oysters and partridge, iced brandy cherries, raw mutton, or wedding cake with cocoa. To us it seems most peculiar to eat uncooked meat: Ellen makes it seem like a delicacy. It was customary to have evening tea parties at this time, as we discover when Ellen goes to Malvern and London.

The Tollets were most hospitable to their friends and acquaintances. It seems as though the landed gentry used one another's houses as staging posts or hotels. House parties were very frequent and popular. Caroline Clive said of them, 'The Tollets are so many and various, and so given to talk, that conversation scarce ever goes down.'[15] They mixed with the intelligentsia of the North Staffordshire and the immediate area, and were regarded as a group of clever spirited girls. They were close friends especially of the Wedgwoods of Maer. In 1824 when Emma Wedgwood was sixteen there were no fewer than fifteen visits between the houses.[16] Their frequency was such that Emma's mother felt as if she knew 'every stock and stone on the road' between Maer and Betley. In 1832 Mrs Tollet and three daughters went to tea on 21st March when the young ladies were in such high spirits and 'Ellen Tollet made such a noise laughing and chattering that Uncle Jos grew quite cross and left the room.' (This was Josiah Wedgwood II.) Emma Wedgwood said that she had never seen anything more pleasant than the ways of going on in this family: 'one reason is the freedom of speech upon every subject; there is no difference in politics.'[17]

At this period of time, when Ellen opens her journal, relations between the Hall and the Court in Betley were most amicable. What is more, they had numerous, mutual friends; they frequently called on one another, dined together, and before they left the village, they made their formal farewells. Earlier George Tollet had used his diplomatic skills to mend the rift between the two houses, as there must have been a difficult situation when he succeeded to the title of Lord of the Manor on the death of Charles Tollet in 1796. Charles had married Catherine Cradock from the Court, thereby joining the two Betley houses. Unfortunately their three children died in their teens, thus leaving Charles without an heir to the title. Charles' widow continued to live in the hall until her death in 1807. Subsequently there were complicated negotiations to prove George Tollet's entitlement to the hall. For a number of years at the turn of the century, the Tollets were living in Swynnerton Hall, rented from the Fitzherberts. Ellen and Caroline were the only two children to be baptised in Betley, after the family moved to the hall.

Ellen Tollet, at the age of twenty-two, began her journal in 1835 with a retrospective view of the previous months. After a few pages she continued with a daily account. It seems strange to us that she had difficulty in obtaining a suitable notebook; we have to realise that the nearest book shop was about eight miles away either in Newcastle or in Nantwich. Before the building of the railway, Crewe, which is nearer, was only a tiny village.

Dramatis Personae

Family
George Tollet (born 1767) father, né Embury. He changed his name to inherit the Tollet estate.
Frances Tollet (b 1775) mother, née Joliffe. She was from the Wicksted family of Nantwich.
Charles Wicksted (b 1796) son, changed his name in order to inherit from his mother's relatives.
Penelope Margaret (b 1797) daughter.
Frances (Fanny) Elizabeth (b 1800) daughter.
Elizabeth (Eliza) (b 1802) daughter.
Marianne (b 1804) daughter, married to Rev William Clive of Welshpool, cousin of Lord Powis.
Georgina (Georgy) (b 1808) daughter.
Ellen Harriet (b 1812) daughter.
Caroline (Carry) Octavia (b 1815) daughter.
Mary Wigley Wicksted, from Shakenhurst, wife of Charles Wicksted.
Anna Severne, elder married sister of Mary. She has two children.
Caroline Wigley, eldest sister of Mary, later married to Rev Archer Clive, cousin of William Clive. She became a well known Victorian novelist and minor poet.

Friends
- Hugh Woodhouse Acland, (b 1818), son of Sir Hugh Dyke Acland of Killerton and Ellen Jane. Woodhouse, daughter of the Dean of Lichfield Cathedral. His cousin was William Woodhouse.
- Lord Robert Clive of Styche Hall, brother of William and Henry, and cousin of Lord Powis.
- Hungerford Crewe was the third Baron Crewe. His elder sisters were the Hon. Henrietta and Annabella, both of whom correspond with Ellen. Their father Lord John Crewe died in 1836.
- Dr Robert Darwin from Shrewsbury (b 1766) married Susannah Wedgwood. They had six children. Charles Darwin (b 1809) was the fifth child. His

younger sister was Catherine, and Caroline and Susan were also mentioned. Charles Darwin married his cousin, Emma Wedgwood, from Maer.
- Egertons in Madeley. Mary-Anne was the 6th daughter of Sir Philip Grey-Egerton, and Rebecca du Pré. Lady Eglantine was a younger sister. Of her older brothers, William was liked by Georgina, and John, who was described as Mr Patent Paragon, was a clergyman.
- Miss Fletcher (1782) owner of the Court and her younger sister, Elizabeth (b 1785) née Fletcher, was married to Francis Twemlow.
- Captain Justice and his brothers were often mentioned in the company of the Clives. No record has been found of them.
- Joseph Sykes (Psyche), probably born in 1811, a writer.
- The Tayleurs of Buntingsdale were very wealthy family friends.
- The Tomkinsons lived in Dorfold Hall, near Nantwich. A relation, Major Tomkinson, came from Willington Hall. (The Tomlinsons were probably George Tollet's friends from the Potteries.)
- Rev Henry Turton, formerly of Sugnall Hall, the perpetual curate of Betley, was married to Harriet Northen, the daughter of a prominent Newcastle doctor. She had three sisters, Frances, Mary Ann and Ellen.
- Josiah Wedgwood II of Maer (b 1769) married Bessy Allen. They had nine children: 1 Sarah Elizabeth, 2 Josiah, 3 Mary Anne, 4 Charlotte married to Charles Langton, 5 Henry Allen (b 1799) married to Jessie Wedgwood, a cousin, 6 Francis married Frances Mosley, 7 Hensleigh (b 1803), the seventh child married to Frances Mackintosh, 8 Frances, 9 Emma Wedgwood (b 1808) married Charles Darwin.

Robert Wedgwood (b 1806), the seventh child of John Wedgwood and Louisa Jane Allen, was Emma Wedgwood's cousin. He married Frances (Fanny) Crewe in 1835.

Lancelot Baugh Allen (b 1774) older brother of Jessie (née Allen) Sismondi and related to the Maer Wedgwoods.

Please note that any italicised comments, together with subheadings, in my transcript of the Journals are editorial.

Journal One: January 1835-April 1836

Introduction with a retrospective view of a marriage and a birth

January 15th 1835 I had intended to have begun this year with keeping a journal but owing to the delay of the book seller, I have been prevented until now. The later months of this past year were marked by some very interesting events. I must look back on them and record them.

All this summer and autumn we had the most unspeakable blessing of witnessing the gradual restoration of health of dearest Eliza and also of Mamma's gradual improvement from one of her nervous illnesses. These were the greatest mercies, and on the 28th October another happy event was the marriage of my brother to Mary Wigley, one of our dearest friends. It seldom happens that sisters are entirely satisfied by their brother's choice, but in this case it was a desire of our hearts accomplished, to know her to be in every respect exactly calculated to make him happy. As it was decided that they were at present to live with us, we had not even the selfish aspect of parting with Charles to interfere with our rejoicings.

Yet a wedding is always melancholy, and anyone, who had seen the tears which flowed when Carry and I with Captain Hartford left in the family coach, attended the bride and groom to the church from Shakenhurst, would hardly have thought it the joyful occasion it really was.

The wedding rejoicings were kept up with great spirit both at Betley and at Shakenhurst. No one was ever more beloved than Mary among her poor neighbours. Ringing of bells, sheep roasting, dancing, illuminations, nothing was left undone, and when, a fortnight after their marriage, the dear pair came home to Betley, a very fair scene was acted. Another troop of Yeomanry gentry met their carriage at Keel and escorted them home. At Wrine Hill, all the parish joined them with music, flags - garlands were decorating the houses. Twelve men were harnessed and drew them to the house. I never shall forget the very striking and very tear affecting sight when we saw the procession coming along the coach road, the crowd before and round the carriage, and the troop in their beautiful uniforms with the plumes waving the air – then the stopping and alighting and entering the house - it was so overcoming.

Mary was perfectly composed and really seemed to enjoy the time. She is not afflicted with that foolish Tollet name which makes us very unsure when anything excites us much.

It was a beautiful, clear, autumnal evening so that the troop drew up in front of the house, and tables were speedily set out and laid with good cheer, of which the yeomen heartily partook. After many speeches, toasts etc, they all took their departure, leaving us to our dinner.

The marriage took place in the pretty little church at Bayton, standing on a steep hill overlooking Shakenhurst. Descriptions of the wedding celebrations of Charles Wicksted and Mary Wigley have been narrated before in the local press and in a personal account by Mary to her mother.[1] Apparently Charles protested in vain, about being pulled by thirty men. One man swore and was soon called to order and, on the way from Wrinehill, another soldier fell under the carriage wheels, 'but most providentially was not much hurt'. Perhaps, knowing how sensitive the ladies of the house were, Charles and Mary had excluded these facts.

The first week was very happy but my nerves and fear lest anyone should do or say anything that might annoy the dear little bride quite fidgeted me. I felt a keen sense of the awfulness of her situation in coming into the midst of so large a family, and not a family of quiet presence, able nonentities, but of active, stirring, talking beings, but I soon found that she was completely suited to her new situation and the kindly devotion of her husband. All our parental and sisterly feelings seemed to make her happy.

We had soon after a delightful visit from Mrs Lister, Harriet and little Isobel. We found Harriet a very charming companion, and Georgy and I set up a new friendship with our old friend.

We had a good deal of company, and we enjoyed ourselves very much with only a little anxiety as to the level of Marianne's confinement at the end of December.

It was settled that I should come to Shrewsbury and would be with her on the 20th. Charles and Mary brought me here on their way to Wallop [2]*(to the west of Shrewsbury)*. I found Marianne in very good spirits and very well. Her spirits raised mine which had been low, but on the 22nd a sad piece of news reached us, which to me was a very dreadful shock. Poor dear Mrs Turton, our nearest neighbour and warm friend, had died in the most awfully sudden manner after only an hour's illness. She had been confined more than three weeks, and the day before I left home I had sat an hour with her. She was sitting up, looking pretty well, and talking just as usual. The next morning she was a corpse. Her loss is most distressing to think of her four little children and her poor husband; it rends my heart to think of them.

The Rev Turton was the vicar of Betley. Ellen's friend, who had died on 20th December 1834, twelve days after the birth of her son, was Harriet (née Northen), the daughter of a well known and respected Newcastle doctor, the first physician of the North Staffordshire Infirmary. She had married in 1830 and had four children, two sons and two daughters. In the 'Staffordshire Advertiser' her death was said to be after a complication of childbirth and possibly affected by an epidemic of 'Asiatic cholera'. Harriet's three sisters, Frances, Mary Anne and Ellen, seemed to spend time in Betley helping Henry Turton with his small family. It is interesting to note how, during the course of 1835, Ellen's attitude towards him changed significantly.

February 9th 1835 I was interrupted in my writing by circumstances which I explain in their natural place, continuing my account from where I left off. After our spirits had recovered from the sad shock on the 22nd, William, Marianne and I all endeavoured as much as possible to be cheerful and to support each other, and we were enabled to do so and to look forward to the confinement with a degree of hope. Each day almost she, poor soul, became more wearied, and anxious to have it over. I don't know what we should have done without the Darwins,[3] and Catherine was most kind in coming frequently to see us, and cheered us always. Mr and Mrs Cotton were very pleasant and constant visitors, and Capt Justice and Henry Clive also came, so we were not dull. But each week that passed brought additional anxiety and Marianne's discomforts increased, but her spirits kept up. She felt certain she must be confined before December was out: we found ourselves a week in January with disappointment.

There was to be a ball on the 15th to which, expecting all to be over, I was to have gone with a little party and were to have to dinner, Charles and Mary coming to Mr S. Owens, Condover, for it. A day or two before Allen Wedgwood, who came to Dr Darwin's, called on us and announced what we could hardly believe, viz the intended marriage of his brother with Miss Fanny

Crewe of Nuneaton, to whose father he went as curate about three quarters of a year ago. She is fifty and he is twenty eight, and is a particularly boyish person of his age. He has been handsome but has lost one eye so looks quite as old as she really is. Of course, this match occasioned a great deal of gossiping and much regret among her friends. Such infatuation is really just unfortunate. For myself, my feelings towards her are very harsh indeed. I know she must have coaxed the poor youth into it, and I am heartily angry with her. Our interest in this affair had one good effect - it directed our minds a little from our own anxiety, which was now becoming intense. I saw that the nurse, Mrs Chidley, was getting uncomfortable, and I grew very nervous, but my spirits never much failed till Wednesday 14th when Charles and Mary came on their way to Condover and brought with them Carry, who, hoping all was over, thought she should come for the ball.

BUNTINGSDALE
(John Tayleur, Esq.)

2. Buntingsdale, the home of the Tayleurs.

I felt melancholy to a degree that night and went to bed with a heart-ache. About three in the morning, we heard by the stir overhead that Marianne was ill. At six we lay in anxiety, but were not allowed to get up. At eight Mrs Chidley came and told us all was very prosperous. We got up to breakfast, saw Mr Sutton who said all was well but slow, and at ten I went to the dear sufferer and was sadly distressed to see her, but was full of hope and so came to William and Carry. We determined to employ ourselves as much as possible and I wrote the first part of this journal, not without many a horrid anxiety and dread coming over me. But I was now in good spirits. At about two o'clock, when I began to fear that all was not quite right, Mrs Tayleur [4] and her little girls called and persuaded me to go out a little, but every moment I got more and more fidgety and soon came in.

Then I heard that Marianne was certainly not doing well and my anxiety became misery. Dear Carry was not so much alarmed as I. Five o'clock came and Mr Sutton came in to dinner, looking ill and downcast and not speaking a word. We were all silent-like. William got up and ran out of the room. I sincerely said, "Oh, Mr S., I am sure she is going on dreadfully ill." He then told me, what gave me great comfort about my dear sister, but which convinced me he must give up the dear child. From that time until after seven, when we heard she was delivered of a dead girl, our state is beyond description. Dear William bore it like a true Christian, but the sorrow was bitter. Carry and I did not see Marianne that night. She was very ill, but a good account in the morning relieved us much. Poor Carry, after seeing both the poor mother and the infant, set off home with Charles and Mary. My poor little niece was a noble looking child, very fat and like Marianne.

A fortnight after this, I staid with M. She improved as heart could wish and bore her deep sorrow with great submission. This second loss is indeed grievous. God only knows the grief it is to her, and the fear of a repetition of the trial is much distressing to her and to us all. I had great comfort in being of use to her and William, and felt quite sorry to lose my patient on the 28th January when I joined Charles, Mary and Carry at Peatswood[5], and Georgy took my place.

The Betley social whirl in 1835

For the next few months there is a relatively happy insight into Ellen's life in the hall, and a glimpse of happenings in the village. The most important visitor to Ellen was Hugh Acland, who took on a major role in Ellen's life during the following year. However there was a significant age difference between them: he was seventeen years old, very well connected, and a student at Oxford: she was twenty-two. They seemed to share many interests.[6]

On arriving home on the **29th January** we found Mrs Acland and Hugh still here. She was looking well but not in high spirits - rather depressed, perhaps by the ideas of what the world says of her intended third marriage, which is certainly to my mind a very lowering step so very soon after her last husband's death. Hugh is a very clever boy and if he is kept from evil ways will be a delightful man. I found them all here, mad upon acting charades and very amusing it was. Hugh is a capital actor and we got up some excellent scenes. The party dispersed on Saturday 31st, and on Monday 2nd Charles and Mary went to Aqualate[7] for the Newport *?illegible word*, since which time we have been very quiet.

Poor Anne Tomkinson was with us at the end of last week. She is in low spirits and her nerves are much shaken. We heard of the death of poor Fanny Egerton.

I went over soon as I came, to see the poor darlings at the parsonage. I can't express my feelings on entering that house, where we so often went to see my poor dear friend, and in passing the rooms where I last saw her, and where, twenty-four hours after, she was laid a corpse. The sight of those four dear children in their black drapes, more particularly of that poor dear baby, to whom I was godmother by her request, was trying indeed. We have had the two older children with us one morning since. They were perfectly good and not at all shy. How I wish we could do more for them, and if I had the power to be of any use to that baby, either in childhood or manhood, I promise never to forget it!

Carry brought yesterday, from the village, the news that the intended bridegroom of Miss Short, Capt Mackenzie, was ill with a fit. He has always been a confirmed invalid and not very sane, but notwithstanding this, Miss S. is determined to take him for better or worse on Thursday next, but now the old man is likely to die without being married, and the kind gossips in the village say that some time ago Miss S. announced that she'd have much ado to keep the captain alive till he was married! All the wedding clothes he's bought! It will be a sad pecuniary loss.

Sunday 8th Charles and Mary arrived home from Aqualate yesterday. They were full of gossip and in high spirits. Today went to church twice. Mr ? Garnett preached the afternoon.

Monday 9th Called on M.A. Northen. Heard that all was over between Fanny N. and Mr Dicken. Poor Old Wells came home from hunting with a broken jaw - much hurt.[8]

WILLIAM WELLS.

3. The keeper of Charles Wicksted's kennels.

Tuesday 10th February Wrote to Jane Lawrence, *(whom Ellen visits the following year)*. Charles dined at Dorfold *(near Nantwich)* to meet the Grosvenors.

Wednesday 11th Mrs Wigley and Caroline arrived at seven in the morning. Brought a good amount of news about dear Marianne, whom they saw on the way.

Thursday 12th Mr Turton and Mr Northen called. Nothing of interest happened. Read the review of Coleridge's 'Table Talk'.

Friday 13th Frank and Julia Turton came to dinner at seven o'clock. Went to Madeley. They were not at home. Mr and Mrs Tollemache came on their way to Leamington. We all thought her excessively pretty, very pleasing and open in manner.

Saturday 14th A wet day. Mr J. Sykes[9] arrived in the morning. We acted a charade for Mrs Wigley to see – 'Roman tick'. Charles looked capitally as Pompey's statue. I was Caesar, Mary and Carry - Brutus and Cassius.

Sunday February 15th School and church twice. Mr Sutcliffe *(the curate)* preached a very good sermon on a future state.

Monday 16th Carry set off at nine o'clock to Shrewsbury. Poor Capt Mackenzie died in the night *(aged forty-three)*. Late in the morning my wife, Georgina, came home. We have been separated since the 20th January except for four hours. A great happiness indeed it is to be together again.

Here, as elsewhere in the journals, Georgina is described in a similar way, to show the deep bond between the sisters.

Tuesday 17th Charles, Mary and Caroline W. and Mr Sykes went to hunt at Crewe. The latter, as was expected, got a fall. In the evening we played question and answer, and had some very brilliant 'jeux d'esprit' *(witticisms)*.

Wednesday 18th Walked in the grounds. The little Turtons came. Reading Madame Junot's 'Memoirs', 'Review of Coleridge's Table Talk' etc, etc. A short time ago we read 'Philip van Artevelde', a poem by Taylor *(1790-1837)*. The first volume is quite charming but the second is, I think, very disappointing. The imitation of Shakespeare is very evident throughout, but, as a young poet cannot find a better model, perhaps this is not a fault, and there is enough originality in the characters to redeem it, if it were one.

Thursday 19th A wet day. Read, drew, worked and practised all day. Mr Turton and Mr Sutcliffe dined here. The latter, we all pronounced, to be very clever and wonderfully original and independent. I was full of painful recollections of poor dear Mrs Turton, but why should we sorrow for those who are removed from what we call the happiness and pleasures of life to a state in which they view us (if at all) with compassion?

Friday 20th February Mrs Wigley, Caroline and Mary went to Manchester to see the hounds. The Twemlows and Miss Fletcher dined here. The latter was highly delighted with Mrs Wigley's playing.

The news came that Mr Abercromby was elected Speaker by a majority of ten over Sir C.M. Sutton.

I did not mention in the right place that Mr Sykes brought with him some notes from dear Mrs Bentley from his mother. The warmth of that dear creature's heart and her unbounded love for all our family are beyond anything I have known. We shall never have a more affectionate friend, but we must not, cannot regret her having joined that blessed society she has long appeared fit for. *(She has entered a convent.)*

Saturday 21st We amused ourselves as best we could, and in the evening sang comic songs and wrote questions and answers - and very brilliant we were, and very personal and expert.

Sunday 22nd School and church in the morning, and church in the evening. Read Jones' sermons.

Monday 23rd Mr Turton, Mr ?Beathy and Mr Ford dined here. Henry Tomkinson came over in the morning.

Tuesday 24th Drew three sketches till twelve, then went and called at Madeley Manor.[10] Saw Lady Egerton and Mary Ann and the young Lady Eglantine and two very nice children. Practised 'Caller' very industriously with Caroline Wigley.[11] She is more a favourite with us than ever. We played at 'bouts-rimés'.[12] The best words were: 'tart', 'smart', 'bush', 'blush'. My own I put down, not on account of its merit, but for curiosity in the future:

> Rather had I my wife could make a tart
> Or pudding well, than dress so very smart.
> For rouge or feathers, I don't care a bush,
> And Beauty's best adornment is a blush.

We heard that Capt Mackenzie has left his little all to Miss Short.

Wednesday 25th February Worked hard at my sketches. Mamma and Mrs Wigley played duets together, to our surprise and admiration. This day we were particularly mad - Mary and I playing and skipping about like babies. I am sure I feel very old, notwithstanding, but still I can't help being riotous sometimes. The servants danced in the evening and we went to see them. I danced with Billy Pollard *(a gardener)*. Afterwards we played at questions and answers.

Thursday 26th Coming downstairs to breakfast, I had an amusing adventure. *(What happened?)* Mrs Tayleur, Emma and Lucy arrived. The hunters went to Heleigh Castle. Had a dullish evening and quantities of music.

Friday 27th Went in a party to Crewe - Lucy T. and I in the phaeton, saw the dear old house, the first time since Lord Crewe's death. The poor old housemaid was very pathetic.[13]

Before dinner we, that is, Georgy, Mr Sykes and I, had a long poetical conversation. In the evening we determined to be very gay and act a charade, so we fixed upon the words 'courtship' and 'infanticide'. Charles, Mary, Mr S. and I were the actors. I think our two best scenes were 'tie' in 'infanticide'. The first was a scene in which Charles consulted his valet, Mr S., upon the state of his neck-cloth, whereupon the latter read a chapter from 'Necksclothiana', which was admirable. The last was 'The Babes in the Wood'. Charles and Mr S. were babes, Papa the cruel uncle, and Mary and I as babes with red hearts and paper beaks. This was received with unbounded applause.

This was my dearest Georgy's birthday. Alas, she was twenty-seven actually!

Saturday 28th The Tayleurs went. In the evening we had a turn of 'bouts-rimés'.

March 1st 1835 In the morning Mr Sutcliffe preached a most admirable sermon on the text, 'When I was a child I spoke like a child' etc. It is indeed too true that the pursuits which give us all much delight are in fact childish ones – childish as regards their importance and worth, as regards their innocence, yet how eagerly we seek them even while we know their worthlessness.

Monday 2nd Free in the morning. In the afternoon went a long walk to Balterley Heath, saw Farmer E. Yoxall. In the evening acted two charades, rather dull ones - discovered that the celebrated Mr Northen is a correspondent of Mr Sykes.

Tuesday 3rd I forgot how the morning passed but we were rather melancholy at the thoughts of losing our dear, delightful Caroline Wigley the next day.

Wednesday 4th At half past eight, Mrs Wigley and Caroline departed. It was a horrid windy, stormy day indeed, but Georgy and I got to Miss Short's, who was not able to see us. *(Were they going to commiserate with her about Capt Mackenzie's death?)* We had a cheerful evening, building castles about going to Harrogate or Brighton this summer. I felt internally low but was externally very high. Began to read Boswell's 'Life of Johnson' again.

Thursday 5th March G. and I were all in readiness to go to Maer, *(the home of Josiah Wedgwood II)*[14] for two days but were put off, Emma being poorly. Charles and Mr Sykes went to dine and sleep at Styche. We had a cosy evening, not without some strokes of wit. That night had a very amusing dream about the Duke of Louchtenberg and the Queen of Portugal.

Friday 6th Employed in the morning in making a new edition of my famous caricature of 'Making a Treaty on Eg-wall terms', and execute a new one 'of the eleven gigs going to a picnic'. *(The allusion is now lost.)*

Mr S. and Charles came home, and Mr Ford dined here.

Saturday 7th A very wet, bad day. Drew all the morning: played, read and talked nonsense all the rest of the day. We had a long argument as to how great a proportion of persons are useful and how many useless. Poor Charles had a tooth drawn.

Sunday 8th Church and school twice.

Monday 9th Georgy and I went in a horrid snowstorm to Maer. Mr S. and Charles started at the same time to Aqualate. At Maer we found Susan Darwin, Jessie and the colonel. We had a very quiet, snug evening - much gossiping.

From the 'Diaries of Emma Darwin', we can see that the relationship between the Wedgwoods of Maer and The Tollets was long standing. There were many interchanges in the previous year, and in 1835 Penelope Tollet had visited Maer earlier in the year, but this seems to be the first time Ellen has been there.

Tuesday 10th March Staid in the house. Read the first volume of 'The Collegians' *(by G. Griffin)*. In the evening played at Questions and Answers, passed many jokes about Allan, Robert and his grandmother, heard a story of Mr Sismondi *(husband of Jessie)* seeing some people plunging a boy in the river on a cold day. Mr Sismondi remonstrated and they replied - *(in French, that the cold water would make him catch cold so that his voice would be deep.)*

Wednesday 11th Came home and found Mr Sykes returned from Aqualate. We compared our adventure - each party highly satisfied.

Thursday 12th Mr S. hunted with the Cheshires, returned early and we walked. Then Georgy and I went to see Eliza Yoxall *(of Balterley?)* and read to her. Charles had a very long run and came home very late.

Friday 13th A nice, lovely, warm day. Poor Psyche *(Mr Joe Sykes' nick-name)* departed and very sorry we were to lose him, in spite of his oddities of manner and appearance. He was a very entertaining companion and we shall be sure to miss him.

4. Whitmore Hall

Mr and Mrs Tarleton came here. Mary, Charles and I went to Whitmore.[15] The party at Whitmore – Mr and Mrs Adderly, Mr Bagot, Col Wedgwood, Mrs Russell and her daughter. We played at commerce. Mr Adderly was sad – sad - and his grave wife obliged to keep checking him. Sat up till twelve. Weary, weary.

Saturday 14th Walked about the pretty grounds and came home for luncheon. Nothing happened. Read 'O'Hara Tales' aloud *(by John and Michael Banim, 1828)*. Evening - very quiet and sleepy. Discussed Psyche.

Sometime this week I was much struck by an anecdote of General Wolfe the evening before his last battle. He was shown for the first time a MS copy of Gray's 'Elegy'. He was full of admiration, and said he had rather have written that, than succeed in his engagement of the morrow. I wish anyone would write a poem on the subject.

Sunday 15th March School and church a.m. Read a very excellent paper in Sheppard on preoccupation, which is the destruction to devotion.

Monday 16th Not well. Staid in the house, wrote to Jane Lawrence. Colonel Wedgwood, Henry Clive, Mr Powys and Mr F. Tomlinson dined here. They played at whist - rather dull.

Tuesday 17th Nothing at all happened. Col W. staid and played at chess in the evening.

Wednesday 18th Walked to Wrine Hill. Charles and Mary went to Dorfold.[16] Felt very dull. Eliza beat me at chess.

Thursday 19th A beautiful day, gathered violets, had a letter from Carry, beat Eliza at chess. I came to the conclusion that I am not a very domestic character because, after having a great deal of company and a cheerful time sitting in the drawing room, I did not feel to enjoy returning to rusticate, and 'fusticate' and masticate in the old breakfast room with a small party. However I must confess our small party is not a very dull one. I do think I should soon lose my spirits if I were to live with only one or two quiet souls.

Friday 20th March Walked with my dear wife in the morning. Lady Egerton and Mary Ann called and took me back to Madeley with them. Mr H. Legh there. We had a very pleasant, quiet evening there, and I felt very glad to be some comfort to poor M.A. who has had much to try her.

Saturday 21st M.A. and I walked to the village. She is very kind to the poor people. Mamma fetched me home. Charles and Mary returned from Dorfold - brought the news that Maria Cotes at thirty-nine marries Col ?Gley at fifty-two. Everyone seems to marry sooner or later.

5. Madeley Manor.

Sunday 22nd Two good sermons from Mr Sutcliffe - 2 Hosea 14, 15 and the other - the Prodigal Son. A letter from Mrs Lister announcing the intended marriage of Lady Ribblesdale to Lord John Russell. It seems but a short time since we were crying over her heartfelt misfortune of Ld R. and now we are called on for congratulations, and well it is that it is ordained that the most dreadful news are those recovered from. I hope and trust Ld R. will prove a worthy successor of that most excellent and delightful man!

Monday 23rd Total oblivion.

Tuesday 24th Carry came home from Welshpool, from which she brought a good account of Marianne. We had great fun telling her all the news of the late visitors etc.

Wednesday 25th March Mr, Mrs and Miss Davenport and Miss Hunt came. A dullish evening, but Mrs D. is a very clever woman and her profile is beautiful, but still, because she married him and because she is such a very strong character, I don't feel to love her. Miss D. is fifteen, in a white frock - totally inanimate.

Thursday 26th Mr Sneyd called *(from Keele)[17]*, went a horrid dawdle round the gardens, put entirely out of humour by seeing him because I can't abide him - an old, heartily worldly, impertinent, clever coxcomb. M.A. Egerton came - a dullish evening again.

Friday 27th Horrid feelings, headaches and M.A.E. ditto. I attribute mine to east wind and prolific ice brandy cherries. *(Was this the effect of greed at the previous meal? Such iced desserts were made possible by the ice-house just beyond the walled garden.)* Did nothing - but talked, read a little poetry with M.A.E. and went to bed in her room. We did not sleep for talking, drank tea together upstairs, instead of dining at table. Misses Tomkinson, C. Ford, H. Mainwaring, and Tollemache dined here and Mrs Twemlow and Charlotte Massie called.

Saturday 28th M.A.E. and I called early at the Court. She went home. I walked with my wife.

Sunday 29th Church but no school. Had a long talk in the library - many associations connected with these Sunday evening sittings.

Whilst Ellen is with Mary Ann Egerton, her behaviour seems distinctly immature.

Monday 30th Went to Madeley. The Miss Sneyds called there. Walked with M.A. who came and slept with me for protection. *(Why?)*

Tuesday 31st Read 'Life of Boccaccio' and Shakespeare. Did not stir out. Rain came at last.

April 1st 1835 Heard it was April Fool Day at breakfast but quite forgot to make any. I don't think I ever missed the ceremony before. This must be a sign of increasing gravity. Talked with M.A.E. and read Werner *(who was an astronomer, or more likely, a play of the same name by Byron)*. Mr Patent Paragon, alias Mr J. Egerton called. Felt quite awkward from having talked so much about him and his 'paragonism'. If I were considered a paragon, I wonder how far in the path of conceit my vain heart would carry me. I am sure one has every reason to bless God for every humiliation one experiences for many circumstances, however trivial and however painful, which make one feel of one's own deficiency, whether it be in religious, moral or intellectual qualities or external attractions.

Came home. A letter from Henrietta Crewe, written as if she were low and rather less affectionate than usual for the poor dear creature.

Thursday 2nd The party returned from Wales *(Welshpool)*. A most lovely, warm spring day. Went with Carry to gather moss in the wood. Georgy sat by so we felt very rural and romantic.

Friday 3rd That good girl Emma Wedgwood came to breakfast in spite of the rain, and we talked all the morning. Dr and Mrs T. and M.A. Northen and Mr D. Hill dined here. M.A. very pleasant and the poor 'abandonata' wearing less willow than we expected. *(Ellen was expecting Mary Anne to be in mourning for her sister, the late Mrs Turton.)*

Saturday 4th Went to see the little Turtons, and Henrietta was very loving to me. How I would adore a nice child that loved me, for which reason I suppose I am never to be an aunt, and the trouble of being a mother is too great for one to desire it very vehemently, I think. But alas, poor Mary does not seem to think so, nor does Marianne!

Sunday 5th April Church twice. School once. An excellent sermon: 'Except ye repent ye shall all likewise perish'. The only fault was that Mr S. dwelling long on conviction and contrition and not enough on the renunciation of it.

Monday 6th A nice letter from Mrs Lister and Harriet. They seem happy in this mourning, though selfishly it is a great loss to them.

Tuesday 7th Miss Humberston and Sophy arrived. I began with a cold and felt poorly and stupid.

Wednesday 8th Staid in the house. Read 'Mathilde' and German. Charles and Mary, who went to Tilston yesterday, returned - they met the Tomkinsons and Capt Walpole.

Thursday 9th The news of Sir Robert Peel's resignation arrived in consequence of a large majority on the Irish Church Bill and the king having sent to Lord Grey who recommended Ld Melbourne.[18] Mamma talks politics to everyone and I am really sick of them. We are amused to hear that Harriet Lister and Lady Ribblesdale were speedily converted to Whiggism.

We saw in the paper the marriage of Mrs Acland and Mr Hinckley, and the wedding cake arrived. *(Is this an early record of this practice of sending wedding cake to friends?)*

Friday 10th April About ten o'clock a phaeton full of gentlemen drew up quite unexpectedly to see the hounds. It contained Mr Applewaite, Mr P. Shaw, Mr Saunderson and Mr Trent. The four strangers came in to luncheon - rather awkward it was, and I felt strongly disposed to laugh at what I imagined their horror must be, at suddenly being inundated by at least ten ladies. They all were asked to stay for dinner after visiting the kennels, and they turned out to be very good specimens of the rare fox hunter. Mr S. was very deaf but a clever old fellow. I played chess with him and beat him. He is said to be a crack player.

Saturday 11th Played another game at chess after breakfast and had the glory of beating *(him)*. They all went away. Miss Mainwaring came and announced the marriage of Miss ?M and Mr Farquhar. Mr Hargreaves of Toft Malpas and sister arrived.

Sunday 12th Church twice and no school. A Mr Smith from Audlem did his duty very well. Mrs Humberston and her daughter and the Leycesters came. Penelope, Georgina and Carry sang a great deal of sacred music. Ralph Leycester is a nice amiable boy but Emma is very good, but her little childish manner is to me extremely tiresome. I can hardly admit to talk to her as much as I ought.

Monday 13th Passion Week. Did not go to church, not being well. Wrote to Mrs Lister. Eliza and Fanny went to Nantwich to be under Dr Brady's care. I hope he will be able to do good to dear E., though I think time is the only thing for her.

This is the first time that Ellen's sister, Frances, has been mentioned by name. She is twelve years older than Ellen who appears to be closer to the younger sisters. It is to be assumed that all the family take part in the visits to church and dining together, since she tends to comment when members of the family leave the hall. Presumably the two sisters are going to Nantwich to have their illnesses diagnosed. It does seem rather strange that the activities of her father in the local scene of politics and agriculture are not referred to.

6. Frances (Fanny) Tollet, the second daughter.

Had a letter from Marianne – rather out of spirits apparently. I cannot help dreading her visit and feeling melancholy at the thoughts of how happy we should be now, if God had blessed her with a baby, but regret is akin to mourning, which I must repress, and may He help now.

Mr Sneyd dined here. He was full of conversation and held forth to Papa and Mr Leycester, but did not condescend to the ladies.

Tuesday 14th Went to church. The Leycesters and Mr Sneyd went. Quiet evening.

Wednesday 15th April Nothing happened. Read Shakespeare to Sophy Humberston, which she had had never read nor seen before. She is a very nice girl, but quite too quiet for anything, and we were disappointed to find her not come out any more now we are all so well acquainted. I am sure my wife, whom I consider a very quiet person, is quite a riotous character in comparison.

Thursday 16th Mamma, Mary and I went a journey to Newcastle in a snow storm, called on the Northens and saw the little Turtons. A very hard frost this night, the potatoes and peonies pinched, and the damsons expected to be so.

Friday 17th Good Friday. Church - a most excellent and affecting sermon on the text in 'Lamentations': 'Is it nothing to you, Oh, ye passers by.' Alas! I feel to hate myself when I think how dark and cold have my feelings been throughout this blessed day - though so forcibly reminded of those sufferings, which were induced for me, and to which alone I look for the remission of my sins now at this moment when, by my carelessness and evilness, I act as if I despised them. Am I not one of those who would attempt to make Christ this salvation, without this being their sanctification?

Saturday 18th Eliza and Fanny returned from Nantwich. Dr Brady thinks he has discovered the cause of Eliza's continued weakness, and want of walking power, to be a slight inflammation of the spinal chord, for which he applied leeches and blisters. Sophy Humberston went and poor dear Marianne arrived. She was much agitated just at first, particularly in consequence of Dr Darwin's having been very angry with her for having consulted Sir Charles Clarke. This was most unjustifiable and showed bad feeling in him. Mr Tomkinson dined here.

Sunday 19th Church and sacrament. A great many people at the latter for Betley. What a blessed thing it would be if one could see here religion increasing in the village, considering the advantages. Ours is, I fear, a demoralised population. Sermon in the afternoon on the character of the Jew – carried too far, but very good.

The news came of the formation of a new Ministry under Lord Melbourne: Lord Russell - Secretary, Home Department. It is now six months since this same man was dismissed by the king - the latter must have felt awkward – poor man!

Monday 20th April Marianne very well. Charles and Mary went to Baddiley *(which he owned)*.

Tuesday 21st Marianne, Mary and I went a journey to call on the Butts.[19] Saw the beautiful vase (Etruscan), for which Mr Edwards gave £1200. Called on

Mrs MacDermott yesterday. She gave us some interesting accounts of her residence in Ireland.

Wednesday 22nd Wrote to Jane Lawrence. Messrs Green and Darlington came. Had a letter from C. Bury *(Ellen's schoolfriend)*. Eliza thinks herself better but seems much lowered by the discipline. Rather low myself today. I began Aikin's *(1781-1864)* 'Life of Charles I'. Had a very comfortable conversation with Mary before going to bed.

Thursday 23rd Dear Charles and Mary left us, to our great sorrow. We had passed a happy winter together without any of those disagreements which are generally said to hurt, because sisters-in-law and Mr Wicksted's affection is increased instead of decreased by five months' companionship.

Mr and Mrs Tomkinson, Anne and Julia, Mr and Mrs Buchanon and Mr Bagot came. A tolerably pleasant evening. Miss Fletcher and Thomas Twemlow dined here.

7. Mr Bagot.

Friday 24th A cold disagreeable day. Walked about the grounds, and shewed the pansies to Mrs Twemlow and C. Massie, who called. William Egerton and Mr H. Legh dined here. The latter prophesied a revolution in five months. A pleasant evening, though we disgraced ourselves by singing a trio very ill *(inserted in very tiny writing)* and I by a ridiculous laugh when looking at drawings and asking Georgy to show her 'Interior' *(one of Georgina's sketches?)*

Saturday 25th April All the company went. I wrote to M.A. Egerton. Removed from the drawing room to the breakfast room with every prospect of a long continuance of quiet retirement. *(Was this because they had behaved inappropriately on the previous evening?)*

Sunday 26th Church twice; school once. Horrid, cold day with snow storms and a hard frost at night.

Monday 27th Cold day. Heard that Mrs Brady had died suddenly at Nantwich on Saturday, which was the reason Dr B. could not come to see Eliza.[20] Reading Inglis's 'Ireland', which seems a very impartial book, but it is not made as entertaining as it might be if he gave more of the manners of the people. The account of the wretched poverty is really heart-rending.

Tuesday 28th Walked to Wrine Hill. Had a nice letter from Mary, giving an account of their triumphal entry to Shakenhurst. Mrs Holle was there - poet laureate *(?)*

I am much interested in the Court of Charles 1. I don't think Miss Aikin an impartial writer, but certainly the simple facts she relates are such as to give me a great horror of Charles's conduct in the early part of his reign. His love of arbitrary power, his want of honesty, and his cruel treatment of those who had no crime but their animosity to Buckingham are very striking.

Wednesday 29th Went to see B. Hinckley. *(Is this Hugh Acland's mother, who has just got married?)* Had a very nice letter from Harriet Lister describing Lord and Lady J. Russell's wedding. Charles Lister is going to be an artist, having no taste for the church or law.

Thursday 30th A very high E. wind, bitter cold. Did not go out. Read a good deal.

May Day 1835 Very wet and disagreeable. Read, sang.

Saturday 2nd Carry and I went in the phaeton to Dorfold, and called on Mrs Wicksted, heard all the particulars of poor Mrs Brady's having hanged herself.

Sunday 3rd Church twice.

Monday 4th Georgy and Carry went to Cranage *(near Holmes Chapel)*. We were very quiet at home. Dr Brady came and ordered more blistering.

Tuesday 5th May Walked all around the grounds with the little Turtons, who were full of delight at getting into the country among the flowers again. *(They were last mentioned staying with their grandparents and aunts, the Northens, in Newcastle.)*

Wednesday 6th G. and C. came home. Talked over this visit. Messrs Jos Wedgwood, Turton and Sutcliffe dined here, and Allen W. Read Bernard Bayley's 'Mr S.'

Thursday 7th Mr J. Wedgwood *(father)* came. I beat the son at chess. Very nice day, not very warm. Sorry to hear of D.J. Russell's defeat in Devonshire.

Friday 8th Georgina, Carry and I went to spend the day with the Northens, a take leave visit. We were much edified by the sight of a Highland Regiment in kilts. *(To see a highland regiment so attired would have been an amusing sight for the residents of Newcastle. The men would probably have belonged to the Seaforth Highlanders, involved in the Kaffir War of 1835.)* Emma Wedgwood, Jos, Mr Butt and Mr Bagot dined. Everybody full of the marriage of Miss Heathcote and Mr W. Taylor. It is said his rich father has cast him off. If so, the young lady has sadly overshot her mark. Very warm day. Rather dull and lazy altogether, very glad to come home at night.

Saturday 9th Gardened. Eliza seems very much better. If she can but be well enough to go to London in July, I am sure it would do her good.

Sunday 10th May A rainy day.

Monday 11th Papa and I went to visit the Butts at Trentham. Met Mr Locke, the railway engineer, in Newcastle.[21] The party was only the family, and Mr Barlow and Mr Cotterill. A pleasant, quiet evening.

Tuesday 12th Walked to see the gigantic flower garden at the Duke of Sutherland's. It is ten acres - all actual flower beds and turf.[22] Read Lyttleton's 'Letters' *(1735)*, amused with an anecdote of a fashionable widow who said she was trying to rub their father out of her children as fast as she could. Mrs and the Misses ?Chides dined here. The youngest, a very pleasing girl, is to be married to Mr Blunt, a clever and excellent man, author of 'The Veracity of the Gospels' etc, etc. Dr Howard, Mr Smith and Mr Parker of Park Hall. A very long chat with the Edwards.

Wednesday 13th Begged several new flowers to take home. A letter from Mary and from Mr R. Egerton. The latter hopes to be here on the 20th. Planted my flowers.

Thursday 14th A most cold, wet day. Papa, Georgy, and I went to Tilston *(west of Bickerton)* to visit the Tollemaches. Found only Mr Aldersey, Mr J. Thorneycroft and a Mr Dewhurst there. Sweet little boy of three years of age, and a pleasant, quiet evening. They had prayers. Mr Thorneycroft read a chapter in the Bible and a prayer of the church.

Friday 15th May Prayers at nine o'clock. Mr Dewhurst read and expounded. This part I did not like - the passage of scripture was perfectly clear and required no explanation, and is quite tedious. His extempore prayer too was rather long and not much to the purpose.

Mr Tollemache drove us in his curricle [23]round Beeston Castle and to see Cholmondley Castle - and a very beautiful place. This evening we were quite quiet - Georgy and I were not quite pleased with Mrs Tollemache's manners: she is pretty and childish, but she has taken up very strong religious opinions, and this no doubt has improved her speech, but it cannot make her sensible. She amused us by the light, playful way she told us she was a Methodist, quite out and out. Mr Tollemache is the most amiable creature I ever saw.

Saturday 16th Dr Brady had put Eliza on a new system – no meat, only milk and farinaceous *(cereal, nuts etc)* foods by way of subduing irritation.

Sunday 17th Church and schools.

Monday 18th We began to think Eliza improved by her present diet, in spite of a provoking little cold she caught. Called with Marianne on Fanny Northen and played with the children *(of Mr Turton)*. Mamma went to Madeley and heard an indifferent account of Eglantine, *(the sister of Mary Anne Egerton)*. They don't return till next week. A fine, warm day.

Tuesday 19th Charles arrived looking fairly well and brought a letter from Mary, the contents of which disappointed us much. William Clive arrived unexpectedly, dear soul, and very happy we were to see him.

Wednesday 20th May A warm wet day. Emma Wedgwood arrived. A comfortable evening.

Thursday 21st A letter from M.A. Egerton. A good account of Eglantine. Hopes to be home this week. Fanny Northen and Mr Turton dined here. I attempted to sketch and made a mess of it.

Friday 22nd Very fine day. The gardeners from the Duke of Sutherland came to see the pansies. Charles caught six trout. We went to Crewe to see the tulips Hungerford had bought.

8. The Jacobean home of Lord Crewe, with Annabella, Henrietta and Hungerford.

We and Emma had a very droll talk about marrying Hungerford Crewe. I was very mercenary and said I had rather marry him than a vulgar, though sensible, curate. Georgina took the other side. Eliza backed me. Better, say I, to marry for situation or money, than for neither love nor money. All the party in with headaches in the evening. Had a figurative note from Mrs ?Buller.

I don't feel very good in spirits about Eliza. How ungrateful have I been for the freedom from anxiety which we have enjoyed until lately!

Saturday 23rd Charles and William caught thirteen trout – some very big. Emma went.

Sunday 24th William Clive preached in the morning a very good sermon, and Mr Sutcliffe in the afternoon.

Monday 25th May Mr Gratton came, and Mr Short and Captain MacDermottt dined. Miss Short and Mrs M. in the evening. Played at chess. Miss Short was in deep mourning but apparently good spirits.

Tuesday 26th *(Lord)* Robert Clive arrived early. They fished all day. Miss Jolly and Miss E. Heathcote came, the first a tiresome woman of forty-five with feathers and red roses etc, the latter a nice hearty girl of fourteen. Mamma likes to be kind to her for the sake of her poor mother, Lady Elizabeth, who after a life of misery left this only child.

Wednesday 27th A beautiful summer day. Mrs Buchanon and four children arrived directly after breakfast to spend a rural day, and very pleasant it was. The dear children seemed to enjoy it so thoroughly I'd wished to be a child myself; then thought it quite as good to witness their ecstasies. Mary Anne Egerton arrived and this evening, as we expected, a grand flirtation between her and Robert - great fun!

Penelope and Georgy were at the Missionary Meeting at Newcastle. It was most interesting. Mr Gate, a missionary from New Zealand, brought the most delightful accounts of the progress of the blessed cause there. The first fifteen years the missionaries had no converts. How incomprehensible this is! Now they have hundreds.

Thursday 28th Miss Jolly and Elizabeth went. Fine morning but wet afternoon. Played at bagatelle. Mamma heard of the death of her uncle, R. Wicksted, aged 92. Dr Brady came. Found E's throat bad but thinks the milk diet agrees. A letter from Lady Bloomfield offering to come here in August. A most amusing scene this evening which, provoked laughter, though we were low, thinking of the parting tomorrow. Flirtation extraordinary.

Friday 29th A sad day. Parted with dear William and Marianne, after having her for five weeks. R. Clive and M.A. Egerton went too. This day I am twenty-three. Many extreme thoughts occur and I pray for assistance to enable to make them useful. Oh, that I were less occupied with the things that belong to this world, and more devoted to the all important work of preparing myself for eternity, of cultivating all those qualities which alone can make me happy here and hereafter. Have I improved in any aspect since I was twenty-two? I feel that my experience has much increased the last two years but is my heart improved? *(There was no celebration of the birthday.)*

Saturday 30th At ten o'clock Charles, Carry and I set out in the phaeton to Newcastle. They were to join the coach to go to Shakenhurst: I to buy mourning for Mr Wicksted. I felt very sorry to part with Carry, and had a great qualm when I saw her step into the coach, her first debut to carry her on her way to the great city. I do hope she will enjoy herself.

Newcastle-under-Lyme was strategically situated as one of the main coaching routes from London and Birmingham to Liverpool and Manchester. At this period the traffic of stage-coaches was at a peak. Once the railways were developed, it declined rapidly, and Whitmore station became the junction for Newcastle.

We are reading Balaver's 'Student', an interesting paper on the difference between authors and their writings. He argues that the characters of authors are more consistent with and evinced by writing than is often imagined. We may perhaps be well able to judge of their imaginations, but certainly their conduct in life is often quite opposite from the spirit of their writings. We also began to read 'The Mayor of Windgap' *(1835 Banim - an Irish family of writers)* by the author of 'The O'Hara Tales', and it promises to be interesting.

Sunday 31st Mr Cooper who married Miss Bickerstill preached a good but very long sermon. School twice and church.

A nice letter from Mary on **Monday June 1st 1835** Showery morning. Went out gardening in the afternoon. Mr Tayleur of Buntingsdale and Miss E. arrived unexpectedly. He played at chess with me and beat me giving me a castle but, I must say, with difficulty. *(Superimposed above this entry were mainly illegible words about the butterfly mind of* Betty Hinckley who amused me by discoursing about Penelope's being shy' *and immediately continuing with the topic of the* 'creation of the world until the present day prophets'.)

Tuesday 2nd Georgy and I drove over to Madeley. Found Eglantine no better. What heavy trials poor dear Lady Egerton has! We had a long chat with Mary Anne in her room on many subjects particularly upon that of her flirtation with Robert C. I really think she would marry him, and he is a goose if he doesn't try. She has qualities which would make him happy. However I must leave off match-making, for Mamma says she won't have them meet any more *(in her house)*. Rainy afternoon.

Wednesday 3rd Mr Tayleur went and Papa set off for Ingestre, [24] where he has some hopes of meeting D. Spencer. A severe thunderstorm with furious hail. The stones the size of large marbles, but the glass was not broken, surprising to relate. Warm evening. A nice letter from Marianne - a little gossip about the flirtation. Read a great deal of 'The Student' and like it, though one feels there is something not quite right in the writer. This elevating Scott's poetry above his prose does surprise me. He puts a curious sentiment in the life of a dying Christian, viz that one of the greatest pleasures he anticipates in heaven is in seeing Plato.

Thursday 4th Nothing happened that I can remember.

Friday 5th June A letter from J. Lawrence. Georgy and I dined at Betley Court and met two Northens only. Of course, the gardener there called the 'Quatre Saisons' rose the 'Quarter Sessions.' It was dull and very hot.

Saturday 6th Had a letter from William *(Clive)* intimating that a domestic misfortune had befallen them in the misconduct of their accounts.

Sunday 7th Went to church twice but did not go to school, as I have been all the week poorly with a pain in my shoulder. Very tolerably satisfied with Eliza's progress. Hot day.

Monday 8th A long and melancholy letter from poor Marianne. She now feels her misfortune, but it is truly distressing to be so grievously deceived by those we had trusted, and such vice under her roof is disgusting. How humiliating are the falls of our fellow creatures and how often their great sins make us commit lesser ones by giving way to wrath against the sinner more than the sin!

Elizabeth Wedgwood came. She brought some entertaining letters from Charlotte from Teneriffe. Very hot day. *(This is Emma's sister. At that time the wealthy could afford to seek better climes.)*

Tuesday 9th The dear little deaf and dumb child came again after several days' naughtiness.

Such a child was Mary Gater, the daughter of a poor widow living in neighbouring Balterley with five other children. The Tollets decided to help her and for the next year she lived in the hall, taught by Penelope (and Ellen, in her sister's absence). George Tollet was a founder member and chairman of a branch in the Potteries area to enable children with loss of hearing and speech to attend the Manchester School for the Deaf and Dumb. His eldest daughter, Penelope, was very much concerned about the education of these children and throughout her life donated money to its cause. As a woman she could not attend meetings to decide policy, but she could give practical help by finding out how many children should be supported in the various areas surrounding Stoke-on-Trent. Charles Wicksted also made contributions to the society.[25]

Papa, Mamma and I went to Peatswood in a roasting heat. The party – Mr and Mrs Corbett of ?Darnhall, Mr and Mrs W. Buchanon, the Miss Townshends, Mr John Justice and Mrs Corbett's very unaffected, nice girls - rather a dullish evening but not at all disagreeable.

Wednesday 10th June The morning overcome with heat. Went down to the pretty pool and log house where Mrs Twemlow *(related to the Twemlows from Betley Court)* keeps a visiting book. Papa wrote some verses. Mr J. Egerton, this 'paragon', came and was agreeable at dinner, and told he had been to lay a ghost at Stoke Lacy in the evening.

Thursday 11th Came home in spite of Mrs T.'s kind and earnest entreaties to stay and meet M.A. Egerton – a good deal tempted, but I thought I should be wanted at home.

9. Col Egerton.

Friday 12th Dr Brady came and gave a very good report of Eliza. He thinks she has made decided progress. This is an impossible comfort for which we cannot be too grateful. We now talk seriously of going to Malvern early next month. *(Originally they had planned to go to London, Harrogate or Brighton for the season.)*

Saturday 13th Thought a great deal of dear Carry, who would make her first entrée into London today. I am amazingly busy watering the gardens and hurting my back, but I think it is quite a matter of humanity to cool the poor little burnt darlings.

Sunday 14th Very hot. Church twice. A sermon preached by Sir W. Dumbar. We were rather disappointed with his preaching. The collection was £8 -0s-5d. Francis Turton went with us to church.

Monday 15th June Drew in the morning. A hot, idle day. Began the hay.

Tuesday 16th Had a letter from Carry written in great ecstasies, full of gaiety and enjoyment. This is the great luck of being at such a gay hotel, with such a gay chaperon as dear Mary. I hope she will have the health, strength, and spirits to enjoy it.

Wednesday 17th The weather changed to cold, but no rain to signify. Harry *(Allen and his wife)* Jessie *(Wedgwood),* Susan and Catherine Darwin arrive. *(They* *are sisters of Charles.)* Harry has a great garden, or rather flower mania in him just now, and he and I had much sweet communion on the subject. A pleasant evening.

Thursday 18th Went into the hay-field, not intending to be very rural, but all except myself found it too cold to read and sit. I read Campbell's poems for an hour and enjoyed my solitude.

The Burslem Wedgwoods came. She is a very nice woman but I complain that she ought to make herself more entertaining than she does - the daughter of such a man as Sir J. Mackintosh, herself clever and having lived in the best and most literary society. How might she amuse and instruct if she would! But I fancy an indifference to shining, and indolence often attacks young married women, and prevents their being as agreeable as they ought.

The Darwins and ourselves had a conversation in which we divided ourselves and the world into the adorers and the adored. Catherine *(Darwin)* and I declared ourselves of the first class: Georgy and Susan of the second.

Friday 19th Harry and Jessie W. and Darwins went. Sat in the hay-field with the Hensleighs *(Wedgwoods)*. The little Turtons came up. In the evening we discussed the merits of single or double life - most astonished to hear Mrs H. W., who looks the picture of happiness, declare that she believes the balance to be in favour of the single.

Saturday 20th The Hensleighs went. Read, and walked in the afternoon and wrote to Carry. We were in fits of laughter in the evening reading aloud Banim's 'Tale of Canvassing' *(Here the handwriting becomes so small that it is illegible.)* ... Eliza groaned heartily over it.

Sunday 21st June School and church, each twice. Brought Frank Turton home and amused him. Took him home and saw the two little children put to bed. A letter from Carry, who is enjoying herself - been to the opera etc, very glad they did not go to Ascot. Letter from Mrs Hill about Malvern - a house likely to suit.

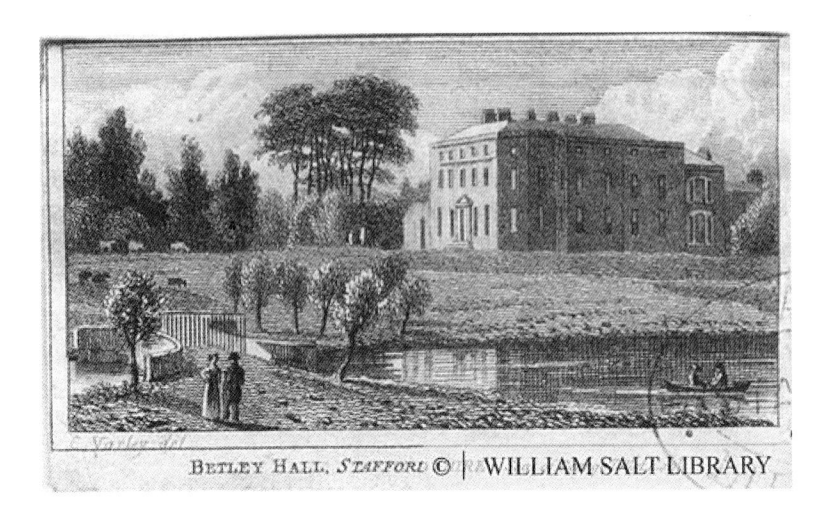

10. Betley Hall, 1820

Monday 22ˢᵗ Went with Mamma to call at Maer and Whitmore. Saw the daughter and the Hensleigh children who are very nice. Chatted with old Mrs Wedgwood in bed. Went on to Whitmore.

The Wedgwoods, Darwins and Allens, all related to Josiah Wedgwood 1, have long been associated socially with the Tollets. The families all owned impressive estates and were known to be public spirited, trying to improve the lot of the poor, especially in the Potteries.

Tuesday 23ʳᵈ Showering day. Drew, gardened in the afternoon.

Wednesday 24ᵗʰ Regular wet day. Mr and Mrs B. Philips came, but the Longtons did not, to our great disappointment. The Twemlows dined here.

Thursday 25ᵗʰ June A letter arrived from Mary giving the joyful intelligence of her having a <u>little</u> prospect of an heir. Truly thankful for this great blessing. I am sure much of her and Charles' happiness depended on this.

Friday 26ᵗʰ The Philips went. She was very pleasant to us but is evidently a most unhappy, discontented creature, and has a great contempt for her husband, as well she may, for he is a sad fool though an amiable one. She married not for a companion: the tree she planted she must gather the fruit of it. She is sadly too often letting everyone see her feelings. How wretched I should be if I were she - a silly husband would be a perpetual distress and give me a feeling of degradation!

Saturday 27th A long call from the two Northens. A very melancholy letter from poor dear Marianne, who is sadly distressed by the iniquity of her servants.

Sunday 28th Church and school as usual.

Monday 29th Georgy and I went to Buntingsdale, spent a very quiet comfortable evening. Of course, the chief topic of discourse was the approaching marriage of R. Wedgwood and Fanny Crewe. Mr Tayleur was very eloquent thereupon.

Tuesday 30th Spent the morning in drawing and talking. Read old Boswell and in the evening there came to Maer – Mr Carr Colburn, W. Egerton and Mr Upton. Talked geology with W.E., who says Eliza *(Ellen's sister)*, is the best lady geologist he knows, and better than many men. A great deal of chat with the Tayleurs on divers subjects.

July 1st 1835 Returned home. ?A Wedgwood, the Northens and Mr Turton dined. We heard the particulars of a most horrid murder committed at Doddington. The poor girl Mary Malpas was buried here today.[26]

It has taken a long time for this local information to reach the ladies of the hall; it must have been common knowledge in the village. In the Betley church yard a stone was erected to Mary's memory with an unusual inscription that on the night of June 20th 1835 Mary Malpas was 'cruelly murdered in Chapel field, Hunsterton.' The alleged murderer took his own life shortly afterwards, thereby 'escaping the punishment of the law.'

Thursday 2nd Mr Langton, Charlotte *(an older sister of Emma Wedgwood)* and Mr Bagot came. Saw some nice drawings of Madeira and Teneriffe.

Friday 3rd Went to the hay-field. Mr and Mrs?Inge and two children came. I put them to bed.

Saturday 4th A delightful day. I sketched in the Bowhill field. Drank tea at the parsonage. Saw the dear children going to bed.

Sunday 5th July School and church. Sermon was on 'Behold I stand at the door' etc. Another melancholy letter from Marianne. Oh, that it please God to give her peace of mind for her own sake and dearest William's! Oh, if her mind could dwell more on the life to come and less on the trials of this present! She has many, many of blessings, and of what advantage are all the higher and better powers of overseeing all our spiritual enjoyments and glorious hopes for eternity, if they do not in some manner rise above the influence of what may certainly be considered as minor misfortunes and grievances?

Monday 6th A very unsettled day. Packed up our drawing ?materials. The Northens and dear little Turtons came to take leave. Frank and Julia *(Turton)* dined. I took them home - afterwards called at the Court. Look forward to our journey with some anxiety, though I am sanguine.

Malvern and the return of suitors

Like the other spa towns of Buxton, Bath, Brighton and Harrogate, Malvern was a popular holiday centre for the wealthy to take the spa waters for health reasons. Certainly the country air would have been more conducive to Eliza's condition than that of London. On 4th March Ellen mentioned that the family had considered a holiday in Brighton or Harrogate. Perhaps Malvern was chosen because it was nearer. The journey along poor, unmade roads was of approximately seventy miles. It took three days with a little sight-seeing. Once they arrived they were able to restore former friendships, presumably made on other such holidays. The Bloomfields were some of the first of these friends. Lord Bloomfield was a diplomat in overseas posts for a number of years. Lady Bloomfield had two daughters mentioned here - Georgina who married Henry Trench the following year, and Mrs Kingscote married to Colonel Thomas Henry Kingscote.

Tuesday 7th We set off about half past ten – Mamma, Georgy, Eliza and I and Moreton *(a servant?)* inside. Rested and dined at Stafford and arrived at Mr Haden's about seven o'clock. Much comforted to find dear E. not a bit more tired now than when we got to Stone. Found the Hadens settled in a delightful small house and pretty garden.

11. Mr Haden.

Wednesday 8th G. and I went a nice walk with Mr Haden, saw the church at Brewood and some very old monuments in the good preservation or rather restoration belonging to the Gifford family. Drove in an open carriage to Somerford, (not pretty) and then to the avenue to Chillington,[27] a most imposing entrance two miles of this and back. Heard of the misfortunes of Mr H's sister who has had her house set fire to five times in three months by a house-maid.

Thursday 9th Left Beansfield after breakfast and after dining at Kidderminster and meeting with no adventures, arrived about seven o'clock at our house in Malvern. We had only just entered the drawing room and peeped at the view and Eliza had seated herself in an armchair, when dear Georgina Bloomfield and Mrs Kingscote ran into our arms. Lady Bloomfield soon followed. We had just a few moments' chat, and then they ran away, leaving us to tea. Fanny and the house-maid came later than expected and we had begun to fidget.

Friday 10th July Dear E. not the least the worse for the journey - indeed very well for her. G. and I went to walk to the Bloomfields, but met them and returned. Went to the bakers, library etc. and then Lady B. drove us to the Chalybeate Spa where G. drank some nasty water. Went to sketch in the afternoon. Mrs ?Hening came and took lodgings next door. Hugh Acland called - very nice as usual. Went house hunting for Mrs Sykes.

Saturday 11th Wrote to Mrs Sykes and drew. Lady B. came and fetched G. and me up to Essington's Hotel. There we found Mrs Shapland. The dear Bloomfields were kind and dear as ever. Mrs K. is an excellent little creature, not so fascinating as Georgina Bloomfield, but so open hearted. Mr K. is five foot nine ins, handsome but heavy in appearance and manner; his little boy of five is a charming creature. Walked up to the top of the hill, dined, chatted, and then Lady B. and Georgy brought us by a beautiful drive of some miles back home into the valley.

Sunday 12th Went to the church of the abbey. Dr Card preached – don't like him.

Hugh Acland came and walked us to St Ann's Well, where we drank and came down again. He amuses us with accounts of the people at the boarding house. The great heroine is a Miss Pinkorn, who is seeming a rather dangerous damsel. In the rain, in afternoon church, Mr Thrupp, the curate, preached an excellent sermon. Miss H. and Fanny went to Lady Huntingdon's chapel. Letters from Marianne and Carry, the former rather better.

Monday 13th At twelve o'clock we, that is Mamma, Eliza, Georgina and I set off in the carriage to take leave of the Bloomfields at Essingtons. We saw them all except Mr Kingscote. Dear, beautiful Nigel was much admired by Mamma and Eliza. Mrs K. seems a delightful and happy stepmother, indeed to such children she must be a great addition to anyone's happiness. After parting with the B's we went to the well, and then down to call on Mrs Parker, whom we found in a pretty house on a lovely common, over a mile from Malvern. Really amused at our footman's jumping over the gate instead of ringing at it.

Mamma, G. and I took a long walk and sketched in the evening.

Tuesday 14th Drew all the morning. A letter from Mary giving us the good news that their trial is safely and happily over, costs being given to them. *(Why, we wonder, were the Wicksteds in court?)*

Walked to the well in the evening. The weather here has been charming, neither hot nor wet as is usual in July. This has made us enjoy ourselves very much, and I feel that these days have been among those sweet and smooth spots in one's life, which should be enjoyed and remembered with gratitude, and which ought to be used as reasons for strengthening and refreshing the mind as well as body, and endeavouring to prepare it for its less peaceful days.

Wednesday 15th July Spent our time in walking and looking about us. Fine with one shower.

Thursday 16th Drew and walked. Mrs Henry, a young widow, a friend of the Bloomfields, called upon us. Heard from Carry to say they come here from Friday.

Friday 17th In the evening Georgy and I walked on the Worcester road to look out for our travellers, staid a long time, and then returned, when just as we got near home who did we spy but Charles and Mary were arrived at the Belle View *(a hotel)*, and Carry was at the house. They came by Cheltenham. We were delighted to see them again.

Saturday 18th Rather showery. Mary sat with us. Charles went with Hugh to call on Mr Hockenhull. Mr and Mrs Sykes and son arrived. After dinner Charles, Mr Sykes*(Psyche)*, Hugh, Carry and I went to the hills and saw the splendid view to perfection. It was very enjoyable. A tea party in the evening.

Sunday 19th Breakfasted with the Wicksteds. Went to church twice. Walked to the Witch in the evening

Monday 20th July Mr and Mrs Collet came. Charles and Mary went, alas! Walked with Psyche to the common. Miss Hill drank tea. *(Is she the daughter of the owner?)*

12. Mary Wigley (Mrs Charles Wicksted).

Tuesday 21st A grand expedition to Herefordshire Beacons. Georgy, Carry and I had three donkeys to ride, and Psyche for an attendant! The weather and views were perfectly delightful but the donkey's saddle was very agonising. The wind being very high at the top of the hill, our figures assumed the appearance of balloons and all our exertions were insufficient to keep our ankles covered. Carry's draperies became unmanageable that she was obliged to sit down to hold them. Returning homeward we were overtaken by H. Acland and Mr Thrupp.

Wednesday 22nd Dawdled, read and drew all the morning. Walked to the link in the evening.

Thursday 23rd A very large luncheon party. Mrs Dillon just eighty, as fresh as a cabbage, Miss Darke sixty-five, a perfect rose, and a nice Mr Platt, Mr Maxwell and sister and a Miss Bannister all from Tewkesbury. We did our duty and sat to be admired and cooed over, having likenesses found for us, our ages guessed at - not very successfully. Drank tea with the Sykes. Sang our glees and saw Miss Blayden's drawings.

Friday 24th A larger party went to lunch with Miss Hill. I began to read Lord Brougham's 'Discourse on Natural Theology' - found it interesting, but I think not very new. A very hot day, we were very languid and only stirred a little in the evening.

Saturday 25th July Read Lord Brougham and German all the morning. In the evening went on donkeys to Cradley Woods. Our faithful cavalier *(Hugh Acland)* was not able to set out with us, but followed us but did not overtake us till we were nearly home again. He was in a terrible stew, both in mind and body, rather above temperate. He assured us by giving us a history of the contrary love affairs at Aberdovey, where the young ladies and the Oxonians were always at cross purposes, though with the kindest intentions.

Sunday 26th Went to church and were half suffocated with heat – an excellent sermon on 'The blessed receiving light' from Mr Thrupp. His fault is being too diffuse, touching on too many topics in one sermon.

Monday 27th At two o'clock went with Carry, Eliza and Mamma to Worcester, calling at Pilmaston on our way in a roasting heat. Called on Mrs Shepland. She told us a great deal about Mrs Sherwood, who has taken up the doctrine of the final salvation of all. She is quite strong in her belief of it and wishes every one to believe it too. Mr and Mrs and Joe Sykes went too. Drank tea at the inn and shopped. Charles, Mary and Caroline Wigley arrived at half past eight, and then Mamma and I returned home, having sent Eliza home with Mr and Mrs Sykes. Parted with dear Carry with great regret.

Tuesday 28th Caroline Wigley came and spent the day with us – very dear, as usual. *(She was the literary sister of Mary Wicksted.)* To our great surprise, the Twemlows of Peatswood came on their way from Cheltenham. Very glad to see her and enjoyed chatting with her in the evening.

Wednesday 29th Went with the Twemlows in the evening to Little Malvern. It was very pleasant.

Thursday 30th July Colonel and Mrs Parker called and were very agreeable and asked me to go with them to Worcester the next day.

Friday 31st Went to hear Mr Benson preach for the propagation of the Gospel. Delighted with his manner, but perhaps from the subject, taking one, which is though most interesting yet exhausted, I was disappointed. There appeared to me a little want of spirituality in his handling of the subject, but while I write these remarks I accuse myself of presumption. I enjoyed the cathedral music. Finished our morning by a grand luncheon at the guildhall with the bishop and the clergy. Came home and drank tea at Mrs Henry's.

August 1st 1835 Went to a tea drinking in a field at Col Parker's. Met Mr and Mrs Leckmere and three nice children, Lady Haddington, Miss Moresby and Miss Cook. Found it very pleasant. It was a lovely evening and everyone was agreeable and happy, particularly the merriest little darling of six years, also Lucy Leckmere.

Sunday 2nd Church in the morning and received the sacrament. A very good sermon in the afternoon on 'I am the way, the truth and the light.' I enjoyed the services very much today, but I always fear my feelings are only the temporary excitement and I doubt and tremble but they leave no good permanent effects. In the evening G. and I walked up the hill, met Mr Thrupp, who took us to the Ivy Rock which we had never seen. Found him a very agreeable companion and formed a very pleasing idea of his character. Delighted to find him very fond of poor dear Hugh, and discussed the different degrees of capability of happiness in men and women.

Monday 3rd Went all over the church which is very curious and beautiful. Mrs Shapland called. 'Nice cordial things' she calls G. and me! Georgy and I dined alone and then took a long walk all round by Ivy Rock (which we drew), and down North Hill to visit a poor dear woman of the name of Borough, who is only waiting till after her confinement to lose her precious right arm. Saw the case was particularly affecting to us, and if sympathy could have done her good, God knows she had ours! What a lesson against discontent to see her cheerfulness – never can I forget my feelings at seeing my darling Georgy comforting her poor fellow sufferer and instructing her in many little useful acts with her dear left hand.

Tuesday 4th Mrs Henry called. Walked to St Ann in the evening in search of a screw pin-cushion for poor Borough.

The two sisters were trying to find a pin-cushion that could be screwed into the side of a chair or table so that sewing could be done with one hand. During her Journal, Ellen has so far only made this one reference to her sister's handicap.

Mr, Mrs and Miss Terry and Mrs Dukes of Hull and the Sykes called. Mr Thrupp drank tea. A good deal of interesting conversation with the latter on divers topics. Gave my pin-cushion for poor Borough.

Wednesday 5th August Our last day at dear, dear Malvern - very melancholy. Heard of the death of poor dear Eglantine. *(She was referring to Lady Eglantine of Madeley Manor.)* May God comfort her mother and my poor friend too!

Mr Thrupp called afterwards and took us to see Dr Garlis' garden, which is very pretty. Georgy and I breakfasted with the Sykes and went to the home of Mrs Parker.

Thursday 6th A sad, unsettled, sorrowful morning, wishing goodbye to many whom we may never meet again. We drove out of that dear place with heavy hearts.

The change from thence to Birmingham was most striking: cleanliness, cheerfulness and beauty for dirt, dullness and frightfulness. I shall ever look back on our stay at Malvern as a period of great enjoyment - and of such enjoyment as, I trust, has not been unproductive of improvement. I do think it is the least worldly place that can be, and whether it is only that our society there was not of a worldly kind I know not, but the effect on myself I do know. Dear, dear Malvern, how often shall I think of you with gratitude, also with respect.

We arrived this day at Sutton Coldfield. Miss Perkins has produced great effects on her spirits. *(Who is she? Did they stay with her? Mr Perkins went to Betley Hall a little later.)*

Friday 7th The morning was wet and I felt very low, but it cleared up and we went to Sutton Park, where we had the delight again of seeing the dear Bloomfields, who were with W. Hartness and Sir Edmund Ackerly. Mr and Mrs Redford dined. Dull evening rather.

Saturday 8th Walked to the rectory, a nice place. Mrs Bloomfield ought to be very happy. She has five lovely boys – rather too many to be sure. She always gives me the idea of not caring much about Mr B. and that is enough to prevent anyone being an admirer. Arrived to dinner at Maple Hayes[28] and were introduced to Mr Hinckley, our friend's new husband, *(the stepfather of Hugh Acland)*.

13. Maple Hayes, the new home of Hugh's mother.

Mr Hinckley is very kind and agreeable and, I think, sensible, but there are many reasons why it would have been far, far better for her not to have married him. I do think at an advanced age, an only son *(Hugh)* would be a companion and interest enough for one. I should have thought her whole happiness would have been to devote herself to him and to his interests, temporal and eternal.

Sunday 9th Went twice to the cathedral *(Lichfield)*, the music very exquisite, but alas the service not very profitable. The twanging *(of)* the sentences annoy me so. The dean preached a very good sermon. Lunched at Mr Hinckley's house – all very nice.

Monday 10th August Very hot day. Went in the boat with Hugh Acland. He showed me some of his poetical effusions - a great deal of talent and good feeling in them. Heaven grant his may not be a religion of feeling only.

Mrs Tollet must have approved of this arrangement, as Ellen went alone in the boat with Mr Acland! Unfortunately for us, Ellen did not elaborate her opinions about Hugh. However he did not give up hope.

William Woodhouse *(Hugh's cousin)* dined – he amused us in the evening with most admirable imitations of the Dean of Lichfield, Mr Hodgson etc.

14. Lichfield Cathedral.

Tuesday 11th Georgy, Hugh and I drove in Mrs Hinckley's britzka[29] to see Beaudesert Hall. It's a fine, melancholy, deserted place – view and extravagance have contributed to make it so. W*e saw* a very fine picture of Lord A. *(Is this Lord Anglesey?)* by Lawrence.[30] A very fine view of Camp Hill at the top of the park, looking over Cannock Chase. We saw Malvern Hills in the distance, dear, happy Malvern. We had a great deal of chat with dear Hugh. I do think he has one of the most amiable, natural dispositions I ever know.

15. Beaudesert Hall.

General and Miss Dyott and Mrs Charles Hayes dined. Miss D. played a most powerful march on a most powerful pianoforte, with the most powerful fingers, and a most powerful effect it had on the drums of our ears, like being in a steeple when its bells are set ringing. A dull evening - just one of those which make one feel as if one disliked society.

Return to Betley

Ellen writes her journal from home until June 1835. At first she becomes quite philosophical and then shows signs of suffering mild depression. Later problems arise ... .

Wednesday 12th August Left Maple Hayes after a pleasant visit and arrived at home in good time. Delighted to see dear Carry again, but disappointed to find myself not so charmed to come home as usual, but this must not be, and I hope I shall soon get settled.

Thursday 13th Read Mrs Butler (F Kemble's) clever, vulgar first journal and the review of MSS *(Shakespearen manuscripts)* which makes one not long to read the Quarto. Hungerford Crewe dined. He is grown much handsome, and his manners are good, but he is still and ever must be an odd soul.

Friday 14th Called at the Court and had Julia Fenton for two or three hours.

Sat under the trees and read. Found amidst all the tiresome stuff in Mrs Butler's Journal a passage which pleased me on a subject which always interested me. I write the substance in my own words. There are many reasons why women are more religious than men, moral reasons and physical ones. Among the first, that nature of their minds which renders them more inclined to simple, confiding faith than to investigating the abstract meanings of a metaphysical subject than their having warmer and deeper affections - affections which are so capricious that not even the tenderest ties on earth are sufficient to exhaust, or even to call them forth entirely, thus leading them to the belief which is a religion of love and which discovers to them the most worthy objects of devotion, admiration and trusting confidence. The physical existence of women is also one of such much greater weakness and endurance than that of men; this induces a necessity of patience, a seeking for strength and support. "The fragile form, the sensitive imagination, and the large capacity of loving are the sources of religious faith in us." We cannot doubt that the piety of women is of great use to the rest of the world, however retired they may live; this secret influence is very, very great and important, but still we must look to men, for producing under God's blessing that change in public general opinion and feeling which will only make our country happy and prosperous. *(Does this make sense?)*

Saturday 15th August Emma Wedgwood and Charlotte Langton *(an older sister)* came to dinner. We rowed in the boat in the evening and enjoyed their company very much.

Georgy, Carry and I were agreeing that we were surprised often to find what an effect the casual society of some people has on our feelings afterwards. There are some persons, whose conversation always makes me feel low and unsettled and discontented afterwards, and this I attribute to their being in some measure worldly, and worldliness of feeling is very infectious. If one hears wealth, rank, beauty or fashion spoken of as of importance, one immediately has an uncomfortable desire to profess them a sort of ?restless sense of their value, if not to our own individual happiness, to no consequence in the sight of others. But is not this a wholesome trick? Ought we to shun entirely such society? I think it should be declared as a temporary evil, but carefully avoided as a lasting one, for the mind that is weak and susceptible enough to feel its effects so quickly would, too rarely, be easily corrupted by it. *(Another rambling argument!)*

Sunday 16th Read for an hour and went to church. Poor dear Mr Turton seemed to present his sermon so unknowingly that I thought even one of Dr Card's 'Grammar Discourses' would have been more profitable, but I try to remember the duty of gleaning good from everything. Alas, how do I succeed?

Mr Turton was not Ellen's favourite person. She mocked him. She did not like Dr Card either. He had written not 'Grammar Discourses' but novels, and a 'Dissertation on the Sacrament of the Lord's Supper', 'Thoughts on Domestic or Private Education', 'Papal Power' etc

In the afternoon poor dearest Hill gave us a flowery discourse. He is certainly much improved owing to Mamma's kind admonition. *(This is an unusual reference to one of the servants.)*

Saw in the paper with much concern that Mrs B. had a stillborn child. From my heart I pity her. I know too well what an anxious, afflicting disappointment this is. Very anxious about Mrs Kingscote. *(Presumably Ellen is thinking about the last confinement of Marianne as well.)*

Monday 17th Drew, walked, and so heard the history of my poor little patient, Hannah Moore, who died during my absence. She put her arms round her mother's neck and said, "Mother I love you," stretched herself out and died instantly - poor little, dear lamb!

Tuesday 18th Gave the dear little deaf and dumb girl her first lesson in drawing. She is wonderfully improved and it is astonishing to see how the enlightenment of her mind has affected her continuance which is now radiant with happiness.

The last two days have shown a different side of Ellen's nature: namely that she does show compassion for the sick girl, who lived locally, and she enjoys teaching the deaf and dumb child, Mary Gater.

The weather is so hot that we did not go out till evening, drove in the pony carriage and then had a row in the boat. The Pool was like glass and the deep, still shadow of the trees with their outlines were delicately defined against the warm, yellow-tinted sky, only broken by the gentle splash of the oars and the occasional rising of a wild duck. The rooks were settling on the tall trees in the Old Wood and sent forth a murmuring call. Oh, how sweet it was!

Wednesday 19th Still very hot. Drew, and worked at the baby's coat. *(Another accomplishment for a lady!)* Read German and 'Romeo and Juliet'. Took Julia Turton in the fly-cart and then another late row in the boat, accompanied by Carry. Came in at dark and stewed till bedtime.

Thursday 20th August Drew and worked. Mr Tomkinson called. Gave us a hint that made us think there is something between Henry and Miss Vyse.

Dr Brady came. He seemed to think Eliza a great deal better and so I really hope she is, but her complete restoration, I fear, is but a very distant hope. God grant it may be perfected in time!

In the evening I went to fetch Julia Turton and brought her here to play. We had a little row in the boat, and the little soul was as happy as possible.

We have been speculating a great deal on the chance of our being old maids, and having to provide for ourselves. Our imaginations have now found a home near Malvern about two miles off. I think there are only two alternatives for an old maid: one is an entire seclusion and retirement, which in the case of bad health, is the only plan; the other is a life of acting hourglass - surrounding oneself with the objects of interest, compassion, tending the sick, teaching the ignorant, feeding the hungry and having all sorts of young things that require care and attention – children, chickens, ducks, rearing delicate flowers, striking cuttings, sowing seeds. Even if one's health were good these plans would certainly be preferable to the life of contemplation and sitting in arm-chairs, dressing gowns and slippers, which Georgy and I formerly determined upon. As to mixing with 'the world' properly so called, it would be misery. How desolate, how solitary would we feel, how empty how tasteless its joys, how worthless its advantages would appear! Mothers, who have to watch and steer their children through it, may endure it, but not those who stand alone.

Friday 21st Wrote to William and Marianne. A great deal of very bad thunder and lightning – it caused so many awful feelings as usual. I always feel both the power and the mercy of the Almighty brought very strongly before me and wish the effect were less transitory.

Very much surprised by the appearance of our old housekeeper, nice Tunnicliffe. Since leaving us she has been left a widdow *(sic)* by the death of drunken Brown and is sole but safer, of the present day remarrying a young man. She looks very happy and flourishing and seemed happy to see us all again.

Saturday 22nd Penelope departed for Welshpool. *(Was it her turn to keep up the spirits of Marianne?)*

We were curious to see whether the little deaf and dumb child would show signs of sorrow at her going. It was evident that, when she went to the door with us, the physical delight of seeing the carriage and horses etc quite overcame her - moral feeling, prospect at losing her friend - but when we brought her into the breakfast room and I sat down in Penelope's place to teach her lessons and write on the slate 'Lady go', the poor little soul turned her face in her hands and cried for five or ten minutes. We comforted her in every way by writing 'Lady come,' and this we showed and explained to Mamma afterwards with evident delight.

A little more rain in the evening.

Sunday 23rd Church and school twice. Received the sacrament. Mr Sutcliffe preached an excellent sermon on 'This is life eternal to know God, the father, and Jesus.'

Very much rejoiced by a letter from Lord Bloomfield announcing the birth of a little girl to Mrs Kingscote. My own reference to dear Marianne's case has opened up all my sympathies on that subject.

A long letter from Harriet Lister.

Monday 24th A very wet day. Drew and worked at my coat and determined to do battle with the enemy.

Was this the family weakness, depression, mentioned on the first page of Ellen's journal? Certainly we have seen signs of this illness in Marianne after the still-birth, where it is understandable to us.

Tuesday 25th August Wet day again. Drew, worked and read. Very cheerful on the whole in this trying weather, but have occasional battles against too much thought, too many fancies, too much imagination, and see reason.

Wednesday 26th Not so very wet but quite cloudy. Mrs Tomkinson and Julia called and, alas, Hungerford Crewe. *(Another suitor?)*

Little Mary Gater is a great source of interest and amusement. It is very beautiful to see the drawings of her mind and very delightful to see her so happy.

We discussed among ourselves divers topics on vulgarity and refinement in their different degrees, causes and effects, etc, etc. I fear I set more value on refinement than I ought, but still I think it comprises more than is generally supposed, and more valuable qualities are included in it, according to my ideas, than we generally fancy. How many there are, whom birth and education have preserved from vulgarity who still are totally devoid of that refinement of feeling and manner which constitute the greatest charm a person can possess, and certainly possessed oftener by women than men, and this I think proves that feeling, and susceptibility of impressions have a great deal to do with it. We also all agreed that we, and I am now, I may say I most particularly, are often amused by people having such entirely matter of fact understandings, and after being indulged in the least flight of imagination or exaggeration of expression in this company, one discovers great reason to report of it, by finding that they seriously sigh and literally interpret all one's words and actions. I feel sure these people are very honest, upright-minded people and that this fault is perhaps near "to virtue's side", but their society does not please me. I don't think it is necessary for people to have very lively imaginations themselves to enable them than to understand those who have. I think it is a peculiar quality of the mind which enables men to understand and appreciate slightly the characters and feelings of those who one sometimes see persons of the most opposite dispositions, thoroughly comprehending and valuing each other. *(This is a long rambling argument that birth and education may not always improve a person's ability to be sensitive to others.)*

Thursday 27th Very wet day. Did not get out till the evening. Read and worked all day. Read German and 'Peveril of the Peak' *(by Sir Walter Scott 1822).* Heard from Penelope and from Mary Ann Egerton. Lady Egerton has taken the house at Highlegh *(Heighley near Madeley?)* for five years from April next. I hope they are all much better. They are sure to be supported in this town for they are very submissive.

Friday 28th Very fine. Mamma and Eliza went to Maer. Georgy and I walked and called on Mrs Meek. *(We discover later that she is almost blind.)* Papa dined at Butterton.

Saturday 29th Mrs Northen and two daughters called. Worked all day at my coat. In the morning called on ?A. Eardley and Mrs Wells, *(the wife of Charles Wicksted's kennel huntsman in Balterley?)* The former amused us by her interpretation of the Gater signs she fancies that she expressed to her – something about dying and being a good girl and going to heaven. Poor little soul! It will be long before she makes such an advance as that. *(Ellen was right: Mary Gater lived to the age of seventy-two.)*

Went in the boat with Carry, a charming, calm evening, noticed such a pretty effect of a swan's feather shining along the gently rippled surface of the water – like a tiny sail.

Sunday 30th Church and school twice. Read some of ?J's 'Remembrances', which is a delightful book about God's power to enable me to look forward with more hope and joy to the time when my soul may be a permanent one and my happiness and holiness immutable.

Monday 31st Mamma and Carry went to Longton, and Charles arrived at home. Mr H. and Miss Hobhouse came with him from Shakenhurst on a visit to Mr Turton. Carry and I drove to Balterley Heath in the evening.

September 1st 1835 Charles and Mr H. went shooting. Mr Turton and Miss H. came here and we took her in the boat and lionised her. They and Henry Wedgwood dined here.

Poor dear Charles had a violent attack of pain in his side, which often makes me very low, for I often think how he would bear the deprivations, which an increase of that complaint might bring upon him. How much more the illness of a man affects, more than a woman's! It appears as if our frames were to suffer: theirs to enjoy. Our natures are adapted to different states. Oh, how necessary it is that everyone should provide themselves with a store of those enjoyments (which can exist even with a state of bodily privations), those refined and elevated pleasures which sickness cannot weaken nor pain destroy.

In June 1826 Georgina had written to Emma Wedgwood saying that Charles thought he had cured the recurrent pain in his side by taking rhubarb pills. Apparently they were not effective.[31]

Wednesday 2nd Worked hard and practised. Mary Gater had the great treat of riding on a donkey. We dined at Mr Turtons. The Northens and T. Twemlow were there. The only fun of the evening was my laying *('making a loud noise' or 'diminishing')* the latter, which I did thoroughly. If I had not been quite certain there was no fear of hurting his feelings, I would not have done it. A sad melancholy came over me many times this evening, thinking of the wife and mother whose mortal remains lay so near. I felt as if all the relations ought to be so unhappy. How little real consequence we are, even to those we love best. Perhaps well it is that it could be so. Yet surely in such cases it would not be, as in this; all are so soon forgotten, but still we must not blame those to whom Providence has given no strong capabilities of either expressing or suffering.

Thursday 3rd Catherine Hobhouse came and we walked with her. Mrs H. Tomkinson called, and at three I went to the christening. Mr Twemlow and Mr Hobhouse were the godfathers. *(Ellen was a godmother.)* Mr Turton performed the ceremony himself. Oh, how affecting it was to see that poor baby, unconscious of its loss, receiving admission into Christ's church, immediately beneath the mother's monument! I dined at the parsonage in the evening and brought the Northens to sleep here. Poor girls, I was very sorry for them, for they felt themselves neglected by Mr Turton's niece and nephews, and certainly it was not amicable in Catherine Hobhouse to take more pains to be kind and civil to the sisters of her uncle's departed wife. Any use of tender feelings would have been naturally inclined to do it.

Friday 4th G. and I called at the Court. Mr T. Twemlow quite civil and civilized by his bowing, so I have really done some good.

Saturday 5th I went to Madeley. Poor Lady Egerton and Mary Anne tolerably well. M.A. and I went on to Newcastle. Heard the particulars of poor Eglantine's happy end.

Sunday 6th Two very good sermons from Mr Sutcliffe. Very much comforted by dearest Eliza. Very miserable all day, full of self-reproach and wretchedness. *(Was she now troubled by her reaction to Mr Turton and his relative?)*

Monday 7th Mr John Wedgwood called and staid for dinner. Mr Butt came, the latter very agreeable and full of conversation as usual.

Tuesday 8th Very wet day, got out a very little. A great deal of interesting conversation, Mr B. always tells a thousand new things. Mr Davenport came. Much amused at seeing him and Mr B. together - both clever, both fond of leading conversation and both hot tempered, but Mr B. has besides being a much better man, the advantage of much more thorough going information. Mr D. is a comparative dabbler.

Wednesday 9th A capital breakfast. Both the great men had their opportunities and each gave a long lecture. Mentally well pleased, I'm sure. It was amusing to hear and see them each trying to cut in with his own speech the moment the other stopped, but each often baffled by the other setting off again immediately. Talked of language - a curious fact that the Biscayans and Irish can make each other understand – which proves the truth that Ireland was peopled from Spain, though some deny it.

Dined at the Court. Met Sir T. and Lady Boughey, and was weary, weary.

Thursday 10th September Wet morning. Mrs Twemlow and Maryline called. Mr Sneyd talked about trees, and explained to us why the idea, that the closer an oak tree grows, the better the timber, is now thought erroneous. After each year's growth there is a flaw; consequently the longer between those flaws the better.

Papa, Frances and Caroline dined at the Court. Quiet evening.

Friday 11th Drew and, in spite of the weather, went to call at the Court.

It is melancholy to think that dear sweet summer is gone. Even if fine weather returns it will be autumn weather, delicious in itself, but sad in its associations. Thank God, for this glorious summer. I am sure it has added much to my happiness, and the pleasures of the fine weather are such sweet pleasures, they leave no sting behind. Surely one is filled with higher and better feelings and enjoyments in summer than winter, and yet I fear the purity of feeling, which only depends on a clear sky, in the warmth of a heart which is produced by a glowing sunshine, our emotions of too romantic and too transient a nature to do much good to one's character - still there may be a little gained by these temporary elevations of mind, though we may fall down again, yet we may not fall quite so low as the point we came from. Heaven knows the smallest step is precious to our souls.

Eliza and Frances went to Maer. Mr Tomlinson dined here.

Saturday 12th Called on Fanny Northen. The Miss Parkers arrived – nice and agreeable, good women, a very becoming old age indeed! Messrs Turton and Sutcliffe dined.

Sunday 13th Church and school only once, not very well. Miss Eliza very much to complain to. Hope her trip will do her good. Bless her!

16. Mr Anthony White (probably the Mr Whyte referred to).

Monday 14th Left Georgy all alone and went with Papa, Mamma, and Carry in pilgrimage to Heath House *(in Tean)*.³² The E. Bullers and Mrs Hart dined. Messrs C. Broughton, E. Kynersley and Gregg in the house and a tolerably pleasant evening.

Tuesday 15th September A boring day, passed tolerably thanks to some patchwork. The Whytes of Barrow Hill came and Mr R. Philips and Miss P. The children here are very nice, the little girl quite out of the common way, so natural and amiable. Much amused yesterday by Mrs P's devoted attentions to Mrs Buller, and her contemptuous way of speaking of her dullish evening.

17. Mr Philips of the Heath.

Wednesday 16th Came home. Found G. quite well and Charles and Mary soon came, the latter looking quite plump. Very happy to have her again.

Thursday 17th Miss M.A. Egerton came. Charles brought home the news that he had asked an officer to breakfast, whose name he did not know.

Friday 18th Great fun, expecting the unknown. He came and was introduced without his name. As soon as they went out we sent to ask his servant, who declared him to be Mr Keagan of Cafn. I said as soon as I saw him that I had seen his sisters, and so it proved. Soon discovered him to be unco *(remarkably)* dull. Hungerford Crewe, Mr Tomkinson, and Devereux Hill dined.

A great deal of chat with M.A. on her affairs, gave her all the good advice I could, and told her how inconsistent I thought time past of her manner and conduct which relate to men – her flirtations both shallow and deep are with her religious professions and with, what I am sure, sincere wishes to become a pious minded Christian.

Saturday 19th Mr Henry Legh called and took M.A. back with him to Madeley. Repented that I did not advise her to not to stay for him but to go home with the governess. Had a long letter from J. Lawrence. M.A. gave me a sweet little Bible and Prayer Book. *(Was the advice of the previous day resented?)*

Sunday 20th September Very showery. Church and school once. Excellent sermon: 'Here we have no abiding love'. How easy it is to acknowledge this truth! How difficult to act as if we believed it. That delightful woman who wrote 'Memorials of a departed friend' seems to have professed to an extraordinary degree the faculty of enjoying this life so thoroughly, yet never losing sight of that which is to come.

Monday 21st Called at Madeley with Mamma. Saw Lady Egerton, M.A. and Mr Legh. I am very anxious about poor dear M.A. She is, I think, engaged in a puzzling affair. Thank goodness, I don't think her a person likely to be made unhappy by anything. Certainly those who are conscious they would suffer more seriously are more cautious how they involve themselves in 'affaires de coeur'.

Mr Severne and John and Arthur called. *(Mary Wicksted's's brother-in-law and nephews)* Two dearer boys I never saw, so pleasant, so good and so pretty. Played at cat's cradle with them.

Tuesday 22nd Boys went fishing. Brought the little deaf and dumb girl to see them. Their manner to her was so lovely that I was quite charmed with them. This dear child has been rather naughty recently and I have had one or two struggles with her. It is so painful to see the afflicted little darling cry, that I cannot help suffering more than she does, but still I shall regret when Carry and I have to resign her in great ?succour to Penelope.

Papa and Mamma dined at the Court. Mr T. and J. Northen dined with us. Mr Severne is an excellent but insignificant man who seems as if he was only made to be the devoted servant of his wife and children.

Wednesday 23rd Hunting at home. Did not go out, except against my will to dine at the Court with Caroline and Mary. I am getting wonderfully domestic.

Thursday 24th The Severnes went. Drew violently for some hours. Went with Mamma and Georgina to Hales. The Tayleurs and Northens and Mr ?Ryder and the ?Carrics were the party. A headache - dullish.

Friday 25th September Sewed and helped the children all morning. The Twemlows dine. Tolerable evening.

Saturday 26th Called on our way home on the bride, Mrs R. Wedgwood. I bore it very well without even a vinaigrette. *(Robert Wedgwood has married Fanny Crewe. We learn later that Penelope was once admired by him.)*

Found Charles gave bit the head of Potters *(his horse)* to Lichfield. Reposed quietly this evening.

Sunday 27th Church and school twice. Mr Sutcliffe's brother preached two excellent sermons on: 'Doth it seem a thing incredible that God should raise the dead?' and Paul before Felix 'What advantages we have.' Thank God, I do believe some little improvement takes place in my sinful life, but oh, in what a miserably small proportion does it bear to my opportunities and means of grace! Alas, I fear my temper and manners are not improved, even in proportion to my increased delight in religious subjects.

From this point in the journal it is obvious that Ellen is becoming more and more introspective and self critical of her failings.

Monday 28th Miss Clive came. Mary heard of the dangerous illness of her cousin Mr Greenwood. Poor young man – he was to be married in November. Miss C's society is always depressing, so we had a sombre evening.

Tuesday 29th Went to the Savings Bank,[33] read 'Richard III' and walked Miss Clive about. Mrs Massie, two Miss ?Harvers and Mr Short, *(a Betley surgeon?)* dined – beat the latter three games at chess in a breath.

18. The Savings Bank now known as the Reading Room, visible as the small building behind the tree.

Wednesday 30th Miss Clive took her departure.

October 1st 1835 Mary set off for Maple Hayes for the gay Yeomanry Ball and Review at Lichfield. Very much disappointed that some of us weren't asked to go with her. It would have been such a pleasure to see Charles at the head of his Potters charging before. P. Anglesey called at the Court and condoled with M.A. Twemlow, who like ourselves would fain have gone. One never should be disappointed at this sort of want of kindness even in one's family or friends, unless one really believes them to be neither selfish nor designing, which is not so in this case.

Papa and Mamma went to Buntingsdale. Went with M. Gater to the fir plantation to gather blackberries for a pudding. We were very happy home birds- snoozed away our evening over Scott, Shakespeare and chess.

Friday 2nd Drew and walked out with Mary Gater, a considerable resource. Grew a little dull in the evening, and Georgy and I tried to play at casino on our knees for a table, but found the cards all wrong. Explained with success that Penelope was coming home tomorrow.

Saturday 3rd Misfortune – Mary Gater had a fit of obstinacy and sulks, which occupied an hour or more. She begged pardon and seemed contrite. She was delighted to see Penelope.

A better account of Marianne, as regards the present, but the past has been very bad. It is really distressing to hear how sadly she has given way in uttering sentiments and using expressions which, if she could remember when in her usual health and spirits, would surely strike her with horror and remorse. Oh, if she could, besides sinfulness to God, remember how she is undermining the happiness of her whole life, by lessening if not losing, the esteem, the best part of the love of her invaluable husband. Poor, dear soul, she is to be pitied and gently blamed.

Sunday 4th Wet day. Church twice. Mr Sutcliffe preached on 'And they made light of it.' I did not think he made so much of the subject as he might.

Charles and Mary returned at night from Lichfield.

Monday 5th October A full account of the gaieties. The Duchess of Sutherland seems to have been the great lady there. Her speech on presenting the colours was much admired. Got over all my longings to have seen the review tolerably well.

Tuesday 6th Drew. Miss Coape expected - did not come. Patched assiduously. *(Emma Wedgwood wrote in her diary on this day that she had heard of Eliza's illness.)*

Wednesday 7th Drew and went in the pony carriage. Set off at half past eight with Charles and Carry to the Newcastle Ball. (Charles was very communicative and sentimental all through this week.) It was pleasant enough though not very brilliant. I had only one waltz - agreeable partner - Mr Butler. I procured two partners for M.A. Twemlow (of whom I am inclined to be a wee bit jealous for Carry) - Mr Emery. I am glad I was so good-natured. Oh! I procured one for Julia Russell, whom I don't like. And this was the only part of the ball to look back upon with any satisfaction, though I was in very good spirits all the time.

Thursday 8th Rather inactive as usual after dissipation. This is really a strong objection to it, particularly for those who have important actions/duties to perform. Wrote to J. Lawrence. Allen Wedgwood came. Sleepy evening.

Friday 9th I did not mention in its proper place that on Wednesday morning Charles declared to Mamma and Georgina that he actually has ideas of giving up the hounds. This of course was a delightful astonishment to all, but they forbore expressing it, knowing that from the nature of man, that would produce a bad effect!

We talked a good deal to Allen Wedgwood about the arrival of Miss Coape, till the frisky thought struck Mary of dressing me up to personate her and to torment him with questions etc. So about three o'clock I was attired in a riding habit, dirty old shawl and had my eyebrows blacked and my hair frizzed. The disguise was so perfect they all declared I might personate whom I pleased, so it was agreed that I should first be Miss Coape to Allen, and then on Mamma's return from a drive turn into a housekeeper come to offer for a vacant place. To our infinite delight Allen was completely taken in, and I kept him in talk for an hour. When Mamma arrived I had to be ready to receive her. Again everything answered; I talked so sensibly that every moment she got to like me better, till at last on her beginning to know about Morison's Pills,[34] which my supposed mistress, Lady Sophia Grey, had been taking, she laughed and I, fancying that I had been discovered, mistakenly threw up the game. The laughing this occasioned was great. More ludicrous than all was Allen's face by perplexity when Miss Coape re-entered the drawing room with a rain of laughers behind her. The veritable Miss Coape came to dinner and was very amusing and theatrical all evening.

This sounds like a passage from 'Jane Eyre', published in 1847. Mr Rochester had dressed up himself as a gipsy to question Jane in front of his guests.

Saturday 10th October Wrote and read etc, as usual –Yates' 'New Zealand' and Lamartine's poems. Don't remember anything particular.

Sunday 11th Wake Sunday. No school, two excellent sermons. 'Now we look not at the things which are seen' etc. Evening – normal.

Monday 12th Drew and read. Some fun with Mrs Pollard who left her house wide open, while she went out. *(It was not safe to leave the house open in Betley even in 1835!)*

Miss Coape amuses us all very much with her stories, her funny ways of ordering us all about, but she is a good, kind-hearted woman in spite of her oddities.

Tuesday 13th Carry and I went a pilgrimage to dine at Whitmore. We met the bride, Mrs Farquher, and her husband. He is one of the most disagreeable men I ever saw. Oh! How much happier to be single and poor, than rich and his wife. This thought I: she thought differently!

Wednesday 14th Heard from Hungerford Crewe, who dined here yesterday, that Mrs Cunniliffe is coming to winter at Paris. Papa came back from Ingestre. He says Mrs A. Talbot talks much of Annabel's charms. The little Turtons came up. Baby so very nice and good.

Thursday 15th October Drew. Very much interested in Yates' 'New Zealand'. The letters from the converted natives are most interesting, the style so simple and peculiar and their affection for their teachers so beautifully expressed.

Every day passes just like its predecessor just now. Miss Coape likes us to drive every evening, and we sing to her, work and talk etc.

Friday 16th A very nice letter from Annabel. *(This was the older sister of Lord Hungerford Crewe.)* She says she has read Mrs Butler's journal and thinks of it just as I do. She says she thinks her residence in America will not be very pleasant if it is true, as a Yankee told her, that they cannot realise an actress as being respectable!

Saturday 17th Charles and Mary returned from Hales, where they went yesterday.

Sunday 18th Church twice. We are all full of the Temperance Meeting which is to be here on Monday 26th. The great discussion is where it is to be held.

Monday 19th Went to see some poor people at Wrine Hill. Mr and Mrs R. Wedgwood called. She looked very neat and he seems cheerful, though we thought rather ?glum in his attitude to us.

Tuesday 20th October Miss Coape went and very sorry I am for it. She and I have a great deal of fun about my marriage. She evidently thinks much of a rich match, and I pretend to be determined on poverty and tallow candles, though I promise her one wax for her own use.

Reading Venn's 'Life' *(Henry Venn 1725-1797 wrote on religious themes)* - very beautiful letters, especially one to a lady declining on religious grounds a legacy she intended to leave him. The lady was one he had influenced very much in religious affairs, and he feared lest any should think he had used his influence to get her money, thus enemies of religion might rejoice.

Mr Perkins arrived. *(The Tollets had previously seen Miss Perkins on their way back from Malvern.)* He brought word that it was reported strongly that Hugh Acland was engaged to Miss Pinkorn, who was at the boarding house at Malvern with him. Much grieved at this.

Mr Perkins and the Twemlows dined here.

Some disappointments

Just at this point for the next few days, the script becomes faded and written in tiny writing which has been inserted above the regular lines. Much of it is very difficult to read. Ellen has been clearly shocked by the current news about Hugh Acland.

Wednesday 21st Mr Turton dined.

Thursday 22nd The little Turtons came and the Northens called. Also Hungerford Crewe, Mr ? of Butterton and Capt Manning, the hero of the Wolverhampton riots,[34]who also came to dinner (a fine looking man with blunt manner). He shewed his talents for attack on a Cheshire cheese which speedily surrendered. We think the Fates have been most favourable to Piggy Perkins!

Friday 23rd Called on Ellen Northen and heard the news that M.A. Northen is going to marry Dr Wilson of Newcastle. All parties highly satisfied – a very good thing.

Saturday 24th Mr Perkins departed. Quiet day.

Sunday 25th October Two very good sermons; then I fear too general to do so much good as they might.

Monday 26th This eventful day began by the appearance of Mr Gilpin, the landscape gardener, at breakfast. [36] We walked out with him and heard all his suggestions as to the place they appear very easy to be acted upon – in almost all instances they were what we had sometime or other proposed ourselves.

A very distressing thing happened to me today - I hope I did not act wrongly. I did pray for guidance, but I suffered very much. I don't know when I have shed better tears. Alas, never for my own sins!

What did she do? We now discover the tension that exists between Mary Wicksted and her sisters-in-law in a draft letter, full of alterations, found at the back of the first diary written by Ellen. This partially explains her anxiety for the rest of the week.

Monday 25th October 1835

My Dear Mary,

A feeling of pride prevented me last night from solemnly denying the truth of the charge that 'we considered that Papa had spent too much money upon Charles,' which was the only part of what you said in haste that you did not thoroughly retract. I felt that after knowing us as you have, you could be capable of suspecting us of this meanness, which was no use my making declarations to the contrary. But now I feel in justice to my sisters that I ought to declare, if it is required, our entire freedom from any such thought or feeling.

I can safely swear that such a notion has never entered any of our hearts, as it has long been our thoroughly satisfied conviction that Papa did not intend to leave us one single shilling; all our fear, if fear we had, when we thought him laying out too much on coal mines etc, was lest he should really injure the interests of those he meant to serve, and his own credit with them.

Dear Mary, you have mistaken us - and very, very, much grieved I am, but I assure you on the word of a true woman that I have no feeling of resentment. I am quite convinced that true increased knowledge of our characters and your own amiable feeling will, in the end, convince you that however otherwise faulty, we are all immeasurably above the slightest hopes of the feelings you confess you have suspected us of. I will try never to think of this again. My affection for you will not be diminished one grain, nor my gratitude for all the love and kindness you have shown me. God bless you, dearest M.,
Your very affectionate sister,
(signed) EHT

We do not know whether this letter was sent.

Miss Wedgwood dined and the excellent, delightful Mr Chapman came from Birmingham to speak at a meeting for the formation of a Temperance Society here. There was a good attendance. Four men from Nantwich, reclaimed from drunkenness, spoke most interestingly of their past guilt and suffering and present enjoyments. In the evening we fell into conversation and found that Mr Chapman's brother is a missionary in New Zealand. He gave such an interesting and simple account of his going out, I went up to bed wishing to be the wife of a missionary in New Zealand!!!!

Tuesday 27th More delightful conversation from Mr C. He entirely devotes his life to doing good. Happy, happy man! He saw dear little Mary Gater and promises to be interested in her when she goes to the asylum at Birmingham, which he says is admirably conducted – the master being a truly excellent man.

Set out in the afternoon with Charles and Mary to Cloverley *(three miles north-west of Market Drayton)*. We met there Mrs Dod's sister, Mrs Cayley and her husband. She is a particularly plain but agreeable woman, and he a handsome but heavy man. They appear to do very well together. Mr Robert Hill and his daughter, Mr Upton and Mr Eyton were the party. The evening on the whole was rather dull though the ladies were more than usually brilliant.

Wednesday 28th Charles and Mary - William and Marianne's wedding day. *(anniversary)*. How many serious and interesting reflections this thought brought! Felt rather uncomfortable bodily, not having yet recovering my sleep, which tormenting thoughts have destroyed these three nights. *(Is this the guilt of the event which took place on Monday, when she wrote on behalf of her sisters, or is she upset by Hugh Acland's supposed engagement?)*

Read Washington Irving's 'Abbotsford and Newstead *(Abbey)*'. Walter Scott, in speaking of a magnificent tree which he had seen arrived from America, said it reminded him of one of those mighty obelisks which now and then arrived from other lands to show us what pigmies our own performances are.

The hounds met at Cloverley. Dull walk with the ladies. Entertaining dinner with Mr Justice. Heard of a new machine or engine in which magnetism is to supersede steam.

Thursday 29th Left Cloverley for Styche *(the home of Robert Clive, Marianne's brother-in-law)*, where we saw all Robert's birds, beasts and fishes, and very interesting it was. He and Charles played billiards. Then we saw their fine dairy. Ate oysters and partridge for luncheon.

We continued en route to Brand Hall,[37] a house Charles is thinking of taking. We were received by Mrs Davison, a most flourishing mannered woman, who

19. Brand Hall (recent photograph).

after showing us the house, had her four children in, playing what she asked us whether we had heard before - the overture to 'Babylon' and the 'Hallelujah Chorus'. It was really most amusing. She fussed and ?stewed and praised them, just as if she never in her life had heard a mother laughed at for doing so. In a book the scene would have been declared exaggerated.

We came home just in time for dinner and I felt very happy to be again with my own darling, blessed sisters. I found that they had been enjoying themselves in our absence by the unexpected arrival of a very agreeable Mr Locke, the engineer, and dear old Mr Saunderson, who was so delighted with his last visit to us that he came eighteen miles out of his way for our evening. Papa, Mamma, Penelope and Frances dined at the Court, so Eliza, Georgina and Carry entertained them most delightfully. He tells us that he reads one verse of scripture a day only!

We talked over interesting subjects before we went to bed. We confessed that we all strongly felt the truth of the text 'Money is the root of all evil.' At this moment we see a most amiable character clouded and defaced by it and we hope only for a time, God grant it may not be lasting! It will, however, be a long time before I can recover from the shock and surprise of Monday. A hitherto unknown mortification has come upon me. I hope it may be useful, but for the time not joyous but grievous.

Mamma received a letter from Mrs Hinckley in answer to one she wrote to have a report from Malvern. Immediately on its receipt, off she posted to Oxford and desired to know the truth from Hugh. He says there is nothing like engagement, but owns to folly being excusable at seventeen. I felt she was a dangerous girl at Malvern from an anecdote he told me. I wish we had warned him! But we could not think from his way of speaking that he cared for her. He made me draw a caricature of her weeping over the departure of her flirts!

This seems to be reminiscent of episodes in Jane Austen's novels. The theme of Ellen's thoughts on suitable matches and the references to her action on the previous Monday are obviously connected. Did she put pressure on Mamma to discover Hugh's feelings for her by writing to Mrs Hinckley? She has been experiencing sleepless nights as befits someone in love.

Friday 30th Found myself possessed of a sore throat and cold. A letter from Mrs Kingscote – the Bloomfields don't come till the end of November. They have had a grievous disappointment in Mr B's being sent back almost as soon as he arrived from Stockholm.

Charles and Mary dined at the Court. I drank tea upstairs instead.

Saturday 31st Poorly with a cold. Mary has given up going to Olton for her lying in; the question is now between Ludlow and this place. She must make up her own mind – whatever she likes but we shall like best. *(Olton Hall was a house belonging to Mary's family.)*

November 1st 1835 Staid at home alone this morning. Read the Bible and Venn's 'Letters'. Thought over the little troubles that now perplex and distress me - almost came to the conclusion that it was best entirely to resign oneself to God's will, and unless positively and clearly called upon, not to let any pains to arrive at that hopefully unattainable object – making other people think as we do ourselves, or inducing persons to see and judge clearly, in cases where their own interests are concerned. My own business is to watch and pray, lest irritation and resentment mingle in my feelings about what is really considerable in others, in which case I sin myself as much as they do.

Monday 2nd The Bougheys did not come in consequence of Lord Grey's death. Then the Tomkinsons, Mr Bagot and Hill were the party. Pleasant evening enough.

Tuesday 3rd Such a wet day. The Tomkinsons were so delighted with Mary Gater, who indeed was most enchanting. I shall never forget the sweet way in which she implored me not to do such violence to her feelings as to play at ball with her before company, getting 'No' on her fingers.

The Court came to dinner and ?Darnford Childwell, the latter very sweet on the ladies as usual.

Wednesday 4th All the company departed and we were left to our own devices. Don't remember anything that happened.

Thursday 5th November Charles, Mary and Carry went to Dorfold. Mary Gater very entertaining looking at pictures, beating the bad people, stroking the good and imitating all their faces. Quiet evening.

Friday 6th Mamma, Fanny and Eliza departed for Welshpool. No-one more missed, I think, than an invalid in the family. They are each fixtures, always to be found in their own arm-chair, ready to be amused or consulted. I am sure Eliza has been to me too often comfort, instruction and reproof not to be very much missed. Mary and Carry returned. Misses Short, Rose, Robson and Daltry dined here - the two country nieces were much thrown into the shade by the Londoners.

Saturday 7th Wrote a very long letter to Annabel Crewe. Mary Gater rather naughty. She requires a very firm hand in her education, dear child. I hope she may turn out well but I fear there are many chances against her. One can only hope and pray.

Sunday 8th A hazy, pretty looking morning. I stood on the gravel walk looking at the water, which was perfectly smooth and dotted all over with wild ducks, coots and moor hens. Barthomley bells began to ring and the sound came so musically from behind the Old Wood. I could not help feeling distressed, however, at reflecting how often such opportunities for useful and interesting reflection are wasted by our inner searching into confused reverie, which is hardly to be called thought. What a useful lesson it would be to learn to exercise a strong and wholesome government over our thoughts.

Two excellent sermons : one on 'We all do fade as doth a leaf' and the other 'What meanest thou, the sleeper, and arise' etc. We could not help thinking of those poor miserable people, Mr and Mrs ?Haston, of whose sins we heard such a truly miserable account yesterday. It really quite haunts me – this description of their sin and wretchedness. I can't help thinking that if I were a clergyman I should call and endeavour to set their state before them and entreat and influence them to think a little. To see them coming here to church on a Sunday and to hear of them, the unhappy woman drinking, and immorality, and his rage and swearing – it is truly frightful.

Monday 9th Drew for Mrs H.Tomkinson's bazaar *(to raise money for a local charity)*. Went to see Martha, the cook, and had a very good account of her husband's sobriety since he signed the temperance promise. She told us she never begged him to sign because she thought that might prevent him. So in all ranks it is the same – men are dreadfully afraid of being supposed to be governed by their wives.

Tuesday 10th November Charles and Mary went to Withington for the Knutsford Ball. A letter from Mamma – no good account of poor Marianne. This is a real trial. It is an inexpressibly bitter feeling to think that our dear sister is making our excellent, beloved William unhappy by her ill regulated grief and anxiety about children.

At this time there was no understanding of post-natal depression. We must remember that Marianne has suffered at least two still-births.

Began doing Indian sketches.

Wednesday 11th The hounds met here. Charles came with Mr Cholmondley; Annabel was there. He says he thinks it 'mauvais ton' to talk to young ladies, and perhaps if he'd gone, I should not have been able to speak of Acland. Quiet evening. No want of employment.

Thursday 12th Beautiful morning. Went in the pony carriage to the Stone quarry, which is a very picturesque place. Georgina and Papa went on to see the rail road.

This is the first time the railway has been mentioned in the journal. Several years before George Tollet had written a letter in 1830 in which he stated his Quaker friend, David Hodgson, had travelled on the trial train from Liverpool to Manchester, where he was able to sit and read in comfort whilst travelling at 27 miles per hour! This was faster 'than human beings ever before moved upon the surface of the earth', and George Tollet tried to persuade the gentry to allow the railways to come through 'the whole length of Staffordshire', because he knew they would revolutionise the whole economy of the country.[38]

Read Abdy's 'Journal of the United States'. He is ultra liberal in his views, I think. *(The tour from 1833-1834 by E.S.Abdy gives an account of the time spent with various groups of freed slaves in Ohio and New York State. It is an indictment of American* attitudes to other races. *The book was published in 1835, thereby showing the speed at which the Tollets' library was kept up to date.)*

Friday 13th Charles and Mary returned. Georgina and I went to wish poor Mrs Hewitt farewell. She was very melancholy, and all the poor old people in mourning over her departure. *(Note the euphemistic way of saying she was dying.)*

Amused ourselves this evening with making charades and 'jeux de mots' etc to send to Hugh Acland, and I propose, as a vignette, his lady love weeping and he standing over her to be called 'Great Hue and Cry at Malvern.' Then as a charade :
    My first will prick you;
    My second will stick you;
    My third will trick Hugh.
Charles had a fine poem, beginning 'This is the youth neither shame nor storm /who wooed the maiden called Pinkorn' and such-like follies - beguiled us half an hour.

Is Ellen recovering from her infatuation with the help of her family?

Saturday 14th Heard of the shocking death of Henry Davenport out hunting. How such news make one tremble! Began to read aloud the 'Life of Mackintosh' *(edited by his son in 1835)*, and like it very much. He tells a droll anecdote of himself, when as a boy he wrote a forged account of his own death to his late school fellows that he might know how much they loved him!!

Sunday 15th **November** Dear Marianne's birthday; thought much of her. Heaven send her comfort. A very excellent sermon from Mr Sutcliffe: 'We who believe have rest.'

Monday 16th A headache in consequence of our agitating conversation last night with my wife and daughter. *(If Georgina is the wife, is Carry the daughter?)* We were talking over our anxieties and annoyances to each other. One cannot help it occasionally because it is so sweet to find how much our hearts answer to each other's, but I do believe it is better to resist the indulgence.

Visit to Newcastle and called on Jessie – not at home – bought a doll for Mary Gater.

Tuesday 17th Kept house. Read Coleridge's 'Table Talk' *(1835)*, like it very much. He seems to have been a good man.

Wednesday 18th Read as usual, and at eight o' clock the Welshpool travellers arrived, Eliza happily none the worse for her exertions.

Thursday 19th Mr ?Bank and Mr Hollins, who afterwards proved to be an artist, called. Mr B. invited two of us to accompany Charles to his house for a Cheadle Ball. But as Mrs B. does not go we are afraid of being without chaperon and so we hesitate about going. Caroline Wigley arrived late this evening and very glad we all are to see her.

Friday 20th November Mary, Caroline, Georgina and I went about the farm. *(The Hall Farm was used by George Tollet to experiment with the new ideas on farming, ideas which he was advising his friends to try. He was a significant agricultural innovator.)*

20. Old Hall Farm taken from the west.

Saturday 21st I don't recollect what happened, but we were very comfortable.

Papa and Carry went hunting. The latter got a fall, but happily was not the least hurt. Dear Caroline Wigley is very agreeable and a great comfort to and enlivenment to us all.

Sunday 22nd School, church. A most delightful sermon on 'Blessed are they that mourn for they shall be comforted.' Mr S. explained what were the legitimate and most wholesome mournings: the sorrow for our own sins; the sorrow for the sufferings caused by our sins to the Saviour and the sorrow for the sins of others.

Monday 23rd Reading and drawing as usual. Pleased with a remark in the Preface to Coleridge's 'Table Talk'. The editor speaks of the every day evils of society, in which the literary and scientific society and the rest never break through the spell of personality where anecdote reigns and everlastingly paramount and exclusive, and the mildest attempt to generalise the babel of facts and to control temporary and individual phenomena by the application of eternal and overruling principles is unintelligible to many, and disagreeable to more.

Tuesday 24th The dear little baby at the parsonage very ill indeed. I am alarmed about it, poor little lamb. It looks so pretty and affecting, and the nurse suffers just like a mother. Mr Turton, *(the father)*, dined with us.

Wednesday 25th November Baby better. I have good hopes. Went to see the poor people at the workhouse.[39]

21. The Summer House of the Egertons, which may have been the workhouse.

Sir James Mackintosh's life has inspired me with a wish to read Bacon's 'Essays', and I am perfectly charmed. They are so comprehensible and yet so full of beautiful thoughts. Other essays would appear so diluted after them. He says prosperity is the blessing of the Old Testament, and adversity the blessing of the New.[40]

In the evening Carry, Georgy and I acted a charade on 'Firebrand'.

Thursday 26th Went to see some poor people. Took Mary Gater to see the funeral of a navigator go by. *(Probably the navigator was working on the railway construction nearby.)* She was quite oppressed, with a sense of the awfulness of death. She enquired whether Eliza was going to die! She cried yesterday when told that that her father was dead.

Messrs Beech, Bagot, Clive and Captain Justice came, the former is an enormous young man with quiet, unassuming manner though his possible brilliancy is his diamond ring. Pleasant evening enough.

Friday 27th The gentlemen went shooting in the family coach to our amusement. Miss Twemlow and Miss Fletcher *(from the Court)* called. Invited M.A. Twemlow to dinner because she thought she would like to share our beaux, and Georgy gave up her share in Mr B.'s conversation in the evening!

Saturday 28th They all departed. Rev John Armistead called. *(He was related by marriage to Charles Tollet, the previous owner of Betley Hall.)* Penelope went to Nantwich, and met with a very interesting poor woman, who had by great exertions, got her boy into the Deaf and Dumb Asylum at Manchester. He was a delightful child, and as he was dying he spelt on his fingers, "I have never heard on earth, but I shall hear in heaven!"

Sunday 29th Sermon from Romans. Very wet afternoon and did not go out.

Monday 30th Not particularly joyous at the thoughts of our company. They, Sir T. and Lady Boughey arrived in the evening - went off better than was expected. Lady B. was attired as if for a ball in brocade satin with gold and silver flowers, but she was in high good humour.

This day Papa and Mamma have been married forty years. We wished them joy and many years more together. I hope and pray they may never long be separated.

December 1st 1835 The morning spent in trying to write a letter while Lady Boughey was chattering in her incoherent, flighty way. Quite weary, and Mary and I went to the Shorts, saw a most sweet baby of Mrs Rose. Evening much the same as the last.

Wednesday 2nd Caroline and Mary went to Ludlow viewing Brand Hall on their way. I only wish she might be taken by surprise and bring forth at Ludlow.

This is the first time Ellen has indicated in her journal that perhaps relationships between her sisters and Mary are not quite as smooth as they were at first. Earlier she said it was immaterial to them whether Mary had the child in Betley or elsewhere.

Lady Boughey more rational this morning. Walked with her and dined at the Court. Met ?Fielding. She is sadly altered, still very interesting - perhaps more so. M.A. Twemlow in the seventh heaven at the thoughts of the Cheadle Ball, *(which the Tollets decided would be unbecoming to attend without a chaperon.)*

22. View from the centre of the village towards Betley Court.

Thursday 3rd Penelope and I went to Maer. We talked a great deal to Emma about Sir James Mackintosh. She told us an anecdote illustrative of the extraordinary prejudice and injustice and fickle hatred which Coleridge had against him. He held forth before Mrs Wedgwood saying, "Ah, Mackintosh, nobody loves him; God does not love him or he would have given him a mask instead of a face!" They talked a great deal of Sir James, as very much attached to him, and they all were agreed he must have been a charming man.

Friday 4th Read Charles Lamb – don't much like his writing.

Jessie *(Wedgwood, daughter of John Wedgwood)* and Mrs Frank came. Heard a good story of a lady's maid who went to see the improvements at Trentham. She inquired what the new building was, and on being told it was a conservatory exclaimed, "Dear me, I thought the duke was quite on the other side." *(The Duke of Sutherland was a Whig. There were important reconstructions to Trentham Hall at this time, employing the architect Barry. Pillars from his conservatory survive.)*

Caroline Wigley told me one of the clerk at Solihull giving out in church, when small pox was in the place, that all the children were to be 'evacuated'.

I played at casino with dear old Mr Wedgwood in the evening. I told Elizabeth what Mrs Shepland told us of the new doctrine that Mrs Sherwood had newly taken up of the final retribution of all. She surprised me very much by saying it was the only belief that could make her love God. Quite distressed to find what a heathen she is. Oh, that so sweet, almost perfect a person should be so sadly wrong. It is really mysterious, for surely she seeks the truth. *(See the entry for July 27th.)*

Heard of the intended marriage of Major Tomkinson *(of Willington Hall)* and Susan Tarleton. She is four or five years younger and handsome. It surprises me very much and well it may – a handsome young girl, marrying Penelope's cast off. *(Susan Tarleton was related to Mary Anne Egerton.)*

Came home and heard what they had been doing. Mr Sneyd had made himself very agreeable; his sister Charlotte was staying with Lady Salisbury at the time of that dreadful fire. It is to be feared the poor old dowager was in a very unprepared state and a horrible end it was to anyone! *(News of the death on 27th November of the Dowager Marchioness of Salisbury has spread quickly.)*

Sunday 6th Mr S. preached one of Cooper's sermons. Mr T. - one for the Society for the Propagation of the Gospel.

Monday 7th Miss A. Tomkinson and Miss Cotton came - she is on her way to see Mr Hodson about her leg.

Tuesday 8th Georgina and I set off to Dorfold, where we found an immense party – Lord and Lady Robert Grosvenor, Sir ?Hussey Vivien, Misses G.Hopwood and Kingscote, Captain Lancaster, Mr Ford, Mr and Mrs Dixon. Lady Robert is a lovely looking woman, not perhaps a decided beauty, and very pleasant on the whole. Mr Hopwood was the person I spoke to most. He is entertaining but very flippant.

Wednesday 9th We were sewing all the morning and talking. Went to call on Mr and Mrs Dermott at Acton. Lord Delamere, Mr Aston, and Mr Glegg were added to the party. Lord D. came with each separate button of his red coat enveloped in silver paper, which Lady R. and Mrs Tomkinson kindly picked off. Mrs Aston at dinner - a good humoured young lady.

Heard the news that Lord Crewe was dead. *(He died on 4th December, 1835.)* It will make a great change in our neighbourhood of Hungerford Crewe to Crewe *(as the new owner of the estates)*.

Thursday 10th December A pleasant breakfast party. Lord R., Mr Hopwood, A Tomkinson and I were all weighed. I was of stone eight. Pleasant evening, talked to Lady R. about books. Talked to Mrs Kingscote whom we found was mother to H. Bloomfield's husband - he is very different. I suspect rather a wild youth.

Friday 11th Came home, and soon after Lord and Lady Bloomfield and Georgina and Ellen Sheppard arrived, the latter not prepossessing, the others as nice as ever.

Saturday 12th Chatted all the morning and walked etc. Poor M.A. Twemlow's manners appeared to peculiar disadvantage.

Sunday 13th Mr Turton preached from   *(left blank for Ellen to complete later.)* Mr Sutcliffe - a most excellent sermon on "Strive to enter the strait gate for I cry, 'Many shall seek to enter in and shall not be able'." It was a striking and impressive sermon and I hope and trust I shall remember it.

Monday 14th Walked to Mary Dod's, and Mrs Wilson, Jessie Wedgwood and her baby – and a very nice child she is - and Mr Turton dined here.

Tuesday 15th December We persuaded Jessie to stay and had a pleasant day indoors for it rained. A nice talk between G. Bloomfield, Georgy and myself on some 'affaires de famille'. This evening dearest G.B. gave me her opinions on the subject of ball-going at length. I could not agree with her as to their sinfulness, though I entirely respect her conscientious feelings, and she expressed herself so sweetly, and I gently argued that there was no more sin in balls than in dinner parties or any other amusement which led you into general society. I felt it would be perfectly inconsistent in me to give them up while I continue doing, thinking, and saying perpetually what I know to be immeasurably less innocent. She brought scripture forward, of course, but it is difficult to agree on such texts as 'Present your bodies a living sacrifice.'

Wednesday 16th Grieved to part with them all, and *?merry* about our visit. Dear Lord Bloomfield kissed our hands, a tender parting with us all, including Mary Gater, who is going to Manchester on a canvassing expedition.

Rather a long drive to Shaw *(House, near Alton Towers)* where, when we arrived, we were shown into an empty drawing room and left there half an hour – very much puzzled we were. At last through a side door in skipped an extraordinary looking woman with a very bad squint, masses of black ringlets and 'frenchified' manners. This we found to be Mrs B.'s humble companion or rather, I should think, the case was vice versa. Well, at last, we dressed, then we found assembled the clergyman of the parish with a thin little wife and a fat little sister, and Mr and Mrs Bradon and Mr Ingleby and these were for dinner only. Staying in the house were a Mr Hicks and Mr Prior. In the last, not least, I beheld a peculiarly gentlemanlike, interesting looking man of about twenty six or twenty seven, and him I had the luck to be consigned to at dinner. I soon found that though Mr B. was more brilliant than usual and though he had £10,000 a year, that I liked my other neighbour much the best.

In the evening we sang and talked and found Mr P. very agreeable – there was something so uncommon, elevated about him, and Carry was fascinated though he talked chiefly to me.

Next morning **Thursday 17th** we did duty all morning in talking to Mrs B. and Miss Ledwich. The former is evidently a most amicable woman, depressed by sorrow and not very sensible. After luncheon, walked with the men. Charles came to dinner, after which we dressed and went to the ball. Both Carry and I had the satisfaction of each thinking the other looked lovely. The ball was very pleasant: my two pleasantest partners were Mr Prior and, of course, Edmund Kinnersley, a very nice young man. (I ought not to omit Hugh Acland, who was very nice and affectionate.) Mr P.'s conversation was most agreeable though entirely free from the smallest degree of flirtation, which is a peculiarity I think I never met with before with the same quantity of conversation.

Ellen clearly is still obsessed by her former suitor, Hugh Acland.

Friday 18th Carry, Miss Ledwich and I went to see Alton with Mr Hicks who became our guide, after much apologising and some incomprehensibility from Mr Prior. We had much laughing about this in the evening and as a joke, we presented Mr H. with a piece of a broken plate, with an inscription expressing our high sense of his monotonous and painful sacrifice in giving up a day's shooting. The evening spent by me entirely in listening to my agreeable lawyer, (and added who was enough to disgust one for life, with all our backwardly men.)

Saturday 19th Wished all farewell, never to meet again with some. Found some middling verses from that merry, ugly boy, Mr A., which charmed Mrs Buck and off we drove home. We spent the whole evening retailing, not only all our adventures, but all our conversations to the great amusement of dearest G. and E.

Sunday 20th December Tried all I could to struggle against the feeling of flatness and even a little discontent, which involuntarily attacked me. I did something, but not so much as I might if I had never the habit of exercising power of my thoughts. A very good sermon on 'These things that I have told you that you might have peace.'

Monday 21st G. and I go to Trentham today. We were so reminded of Mr Butt the other day by a remark in the 'Life of Mackintosh' that though his memory was most accurate, he did not make it an 'Engine of colloquial oppression'. Is not this exactly what our Lord does?

I forgot to note in the proper place a charming story in Coleridge of some great man, not Johnson, who when a young man told him he never believed anything he could not understand, replied, "Then, sir, your creed will be shorter than that of anyone I know."

Waited an hour at the Roe Buck, *(a coaching inn in Newcastle)* for Mrs B's carriage. Watched the coaches, which is to me always interesting and melancholy. Only Mrs Morgan dined.

Pleasant evening. A long talk with Mr Butt upon matrimony. He is very lenient on the delinquencies: I am violent against such a charming and sensible woman with imagination to understand and heart to love, uniting themselves to those who can neither call forth nor appreciate any of their higher qualities. I daresay he has reason or Christian kindness on his side, but I have high feeling of refinement on mine.

Do you think Mamma has asked Mr Butt to discuss this matter with Ellen, as she seems unable to forgive Hugh Acland for his flirtatious behaviour in Malvern with the young girl in his boarding house? She condemns the way in which young women do not have the same rights as men.

He says with great truth that we must not attribute our unwise or strange action to any one bad or foolish feeling but to a mixture of circumstances, inclinations etc, which are only to be comprehended by the person herself. He quite agreed with me about the miserably fallen and vulgar state of general opinions on the subject of celibacy which drives many a poor woman to marry for fear of being an old maid. This stigma will, however, never be removed. I know, because men who guide public opinion know it is much for their interest it should continue, for it is by this which enables almost every ugly, dull, uninteresting man to provide himself with a nice, pretty, pleasant wife! The colloquial oppressor *(Mr Butt)* was more merciful than usual.

Tuesday 22nd Talked, walked, read 'Mme de Maintenon'. Mr and Mrs Tomlinson dined - also Misses Rhoyds, H. and F. Smith and Adderley. Mr B.- a good, tiresome old man just like Oakes, the schoolmaster *(in Betley)* - too dull to be wicked and too good to be entirely disagreeable. I laughed at him when we went to bed, for which heaven forgive me! Hard frost.

Wednesday 23rd Hard frost. We were amused by many entertaining histories from our friends who are just returned from Paris. They told us many characteristic anecdotes of a French family they got acquainted with. Messrs Jos and Allen Wedgwood, Robinson Russell and ? dined. I played and we sang badly enough - not having practised together.

Thursday 24th Took leave of Trentham and returned home in the phaeton. Hard frost. Found them newsless and humdrumish.

Friday Christmas Day Woke at two o'clock by the singers. Church and Christmas dinner as usual. Two girls confessed to eating pudding five times! Charles much mortified for we had no roast beef, and cold mince pies for dinner.

Contrast this with the Dickensian Christmas in Victorian times.

Saturday 26th Still a frost, very cold. Messrs Turton and Sutcliffe called. Called at the Court, where we almost made them faint by declaring that Charles had thoughts of not going to the Newcastle Ball. I am painfully interested in reading over again Franklin's 'Journey to the Polar Sea' *(1823)*. I have such a love for those dear sweet men, particularly Tom Richardson*, (the doctor)* and Hood *(the midshipman)*. How it does raise one's ideas of the powers both of mind and body in men, to read of what these English gentlemen endured with such fortitude! Oh, surely they are greater heroes than many who have conquered countries? It is curious to think that even among our every day acquaintances there are some who appear perhaps stressed and uninteresting now, who might, had their profession called them into such scenes, have shown the same patient, noble-hearted endurance. Many luxurious, venison-eating, musketed Franklins, many flute-playing, fireside Richardsons, many dawdling long, lazy bucks - these may be within our own circle.

Sunday 27th Mr Turton preached on the shortness of life. I grieve to say I was not that much interested. A very good sermon in the afternoon on 'The secret of the Lord is with them that fear him.' *(Probably Mr Sutcliffe was the preacher, if she approved.)* Read a delightful paper in Sheppard on the influence to be acquired by our thoughts. I do indeed believe that when the Holy Spirit really influences our minds, that though our thoughts are involuntary, yet the channels they naturally flow in will be more pure.

Monday 28th Drew for Mary. Had the great delight of welcoming home dear little Mary Gater who was very amusing and had had a great success at Manchester.[41]

Georgina's parallel diary from 28th December 1835 to 19th June 1836

At the back of Ellen's first journal there are approximately forty loose sheets of paper, comprising Georgina's journal. It is unusual to find diaries of two sisters living mostly in the same house, having a different slant on the same events. Georgina's journal is added, under the same date in square brackets with the letter **G**. *Her notes usually give some idea of the English obsession – the weather.*

[**G.** Rainy day. Eliza poorly.]

Tuesday 29th Mr Butt, Tom and two Edwards arrived and Jos Wedgwood. The Tayleurs who were expected sent excuse. Rather a dullish evening.

[**G.** Eliza still worse and we were uncomfortable. Mr Butt and his two daughters and Tom came, also Jos Wedgwood. Catherine and Jane were less 'parisienne' than we expected in their dress, save in the article of pocket handkerchiefs. I was quite ashamed of blowing my nose on what by comparison was a dish cloth. Wet evening.]

Wednesday 30th Dr Brady came and gave an unfavourable account of dearest Eliza, who has certainly been less well lately and is low about herself. This is a renewal of anxiety I had not expected, and it is very grievous to hear, but I hope and trust still that God in his mercy will not remove it, as he has done before. Wet day.

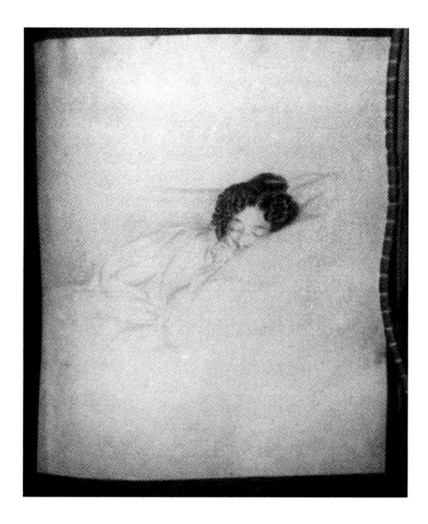

23. Georgina.

Acted a charade in the evening to amuse our friends. Catherine *(Wedgwood)* is a most amiable, excellent, sensible person but, alas, there is a want of nature in her which I constantly feel comes between her and me, and represses the feelings of respect I should otherwise have for her.

[**G**. Dr Brady came to see E. and thought her very low, so ordered her wine and water. Same party as yesterday with the addition of Devereux Hill.]

Thursday 31st We had a sort of discussion or agreement with the colloquial oppressor *(Mr Butt)*, good clever man, on the doctrine of transubstantiation, which he denounced as tending to scepticism, because it commanded belief in what was contrary to the evidence of our senses. I argued that according to the explanation they gave therefore of their own doctrine, it was however contrary to our understandings and beliefs – not opposed to the evidence of our senses, because they grant that the elements still partake of all the external properties and appearances of bread and wine. He was, of course, much too powerful an antagonist for me to have any chance.

All the company went and we were left to hear our own reflections. Mine were very sorrowful. The increased uneasiness about our precious Eliza added to the solemn thoughts, always produced by the end of the year, pressed heavily upon us. On looking back upon this year, I have indeed much cause for gratitude, for a good deal of joy and happiness have been mine! The year began with anxiety and sorrow at Shrewsbury, and the day I began my journal was one of such agonising feelings as I think I ever experienced, even during Eliza's most imminent danger. Then our Malvern residence was very, very happy - more happy perhaps than this autumn and winter, though they have been more productive of times of excited high spirits. If it should please God to afflict us by Eliza's illness taking a worse turn, I should then look back on the past year as mercifully free from active anxiety than I have suffered disappointment in a quarter *(of Hugh Acland)*, from which I expected nothing but happiness and satisfaction, and I hope I am grateful for it, and this is a wholesome lesson to contemplate; if in another point of view as a year, which has brought me so much nearer my life's end, as another year of opportunities unimproved of vain visions of imaginary happiness, of trifling and vexatious, cares for the things of this world, of broken resolutions and languid devotions, and mixed with these, alas, in how small a proportion, some few moments filled with higher and better feelings, some aspirations after the good, so quickly followed though by a return to the evil. How long shall I continue thus, without feeling more decided improvement? In his own good time, may God perfect the good work, which I have some hope he has begun in me!
Snow

[**G.** Wet day. Company went. Eliza better. Charles went to Dorfold.]

1836

January 1st I am thankful to say Eliza seems rather better and I think this drawback will be a transient one. But still I find the necessity of keeping my mind in a state of preparation for what it may please God to send us! This, I hope, may be done without destroying present happiness by gloomy forebodings, always remembering that 'he by whom our bright hours shine, our darkest *?* may rule.'

The most, perhaps the only, entirely happy person in the house today was Mary Gater, whose ecstasy at being allowed to stay for the servants' dance was beyond expression. It was a most interesting and amusing sight to see her executing all the keystation figures of the country dance, and contriving to tabber *(archaic 'drum')* with her feet as nearly as possible in the same time and style as her partner, J. Southwell, every gesture - all the time expressing such a degree of conscious joy, overpowering joy!

The annual custom of the singers performing at the dining room door was attended in me with overwhelming sensations. It was four years ago since I heard it, having been away from home the last three New Year's Days. Old Betsey told how she had had what they always call a 'comfortable' ball, and we all went to bed in tolerable spirits.

[**G.** 1836 !!! The beginning of another year brings with it many solemn reflections. I only wish I could keep half the resolutions I have made, and I should be a much better and a much happier person, which is one and the same thing. Frost, snow.]

Saturday 2nd Cold, bad day – snow on the ground. Set Charles to read 'Mansfield Park'. How I delight in that book! I fancy all the people so well. I confess I think Edmund and Fanny too much alike to marry. I think he is something like W. Egerton though, of course, taller or more like a hero rather.

[**G.** Nothing.]

Sunday 3rd Staid at home this morning with Eliza - no occasion, though Mr Short chatted for an hour. *(Does Eliza now have two doctors, the local Mr Short as well as Dr Brady in attendance?)*

Church in the afternoon. Mr Turton preached on 'The ivory head is a crown of glory.' This he hardly could have done two or three years ago, when his own stained locks were obscured by a black dye, which of all head drapes was the least glorious, I think.

Read an excellent chapter in Sheppard *(probably Sheppard's Bible)* - find the greatest comfort in my dear 'Sacra *?*' which I have now read many months and mean to continue in preference to any other book of the Lord.

[**G.** *(Morning service)* – 'The shepherds returned, glorifying and praising God,' and 'The ivory head is a crown of glory'.

Monday 4th January The usual routine of drawing, pony driving, reading, working and no wish for any thing else. Mr Turton called or not – really can't say - but most likely he did.

[**G.** I have nothing. Fine.]

Tuesday 5th Woke with a most decided aversion to Charles' ball at Newcastle, but with no good excuse. Walked poor M.A. Meek, who is almost blind.

Grieved to hear Mrs Tollemache has lost her last baby. Her trials this way have been terrible at least, and I think with still-born, or living some little time live.

Went to the ball anticipating little or no pleasure and was agreeably surprised at finding it a very good ball. Hugh Acland and young Woodhouse were there, and I was quite astonished at the flow of animal spirits I felt as I pranced down the country dance. I do hope this was an innocent amusement. I am sure it was quite distinct from any vanity or flirtatiousness. Heard my admired hero, Mr Prior, was a third wrangler at Cambridge, *(implying that he gained the third highest mark in mathematics,)* which did not diminish my admiration of him, nor my opinion of my own inner conviction. Came home at three o'clock and went to bed.

Is Hugh Acland now the penitent suitor?

[**G.** Ellen and Carry went to the Newcastle Ball, which was a very good one. Fine.]

Wednesday 6th Set off to Chester. Found the Humberstons all alone and spent a quiet evening. They were all very nice and Philip H. is as nice a pleasant, gentleman-like youth as can be.

[**G.** Ellen and Carry went to Chester. Hugh Acland and W. Wodehouse arrived. The two cousins never lost an opportunity of contradicting each other. Mr W.'s family pride would have ensured him much respect at Whitmore, but it failed to do anything here but afford much amusement. I was extra democratic on the occasion.]

Thursday 7th Sat and worked, went and shopped, saw the world in Brown's shop.⁴² Three officers, one a Mr Dixon, a nice man and cousin to Mr Hodgson, and a most impudent, self-satisfied Chester beau who sat and begged and held a wine glass to his eye. We went to the ball. It was a brilliant one: Miss Brooke was the belle and most lovely she looked. I danced with Hugh Acland and W. Woodhouse, who came from Betley on purpose for it. Mr Wilkinson, who presented me in a most amusing way to Mr Dixon etc. I did all I could in introducing our two young men to some partners.

[**G.** The two youths set off for Chester immediately after breakfast, Hugh bearing a note from me to Ellen, containing the account of the preceding evening's conversation - which Ellen unguardedly began to read aloud before the young aristocrats, whose temper being touchy in a high degree - I must forever be in his bad books. Fine.]

Friday 8th Took a walk on the walls. A few more men came to dinner and we went to a dancing party at Mr Potts's - rather stupid to us from not knowing many people. Carry and I got innumerable compliments from Mrs Twemlow on our looks in consequence of our wearing braided hair.

[**G.** The cousins came back to breakfast much pleased with the ball. Mr W. went away. Charles and Mary arrived at seven o'clock, after we had given them up - Mary looking well. Now, I thought, as she appeared, we are really in for it! *(Georgina is not as reticent as Ellen in revealing her true feelings about Mary.)*

It was an odd evening for we had Mr Locke, who loses nothing on farther acquaintance; his mind is a very cultivated one, and I never saw a man of talent so entirely free from conceit. I wish such men stood thicker on the ground. Wet evening.]

Saturday 9th Left the Humberstons and drove home, where we found Mary and Caroline Wigley arrived in high preservation, and Hugh still here too. The young Twemlows came to dinner and in the evening they were all amused and shocked by Mr Oakes' electrifying machine.

[**G.** Ellen and Carry home. Mary Ann Twemlow and her two brothers dined here to meet Hugh Acland, and also for the purpose of being present at Mr Oakes's lecture on Electricity, which for a village school was really a wonderful performance. The explosions, however, drove me away before its conclusion. Frost.] ⁴³

Sunday 10ᵗʰ January Went to church as usual.

[**G.** *(Morning sermon)* – 'Martha and Mary' *(Evening)* – 'Forsake the foolish and live.']

Monday 11ᵗʰ Drew as usual and in the evening acted charades with Hugh Acland. *The words were:* 'mission' and 'corporation'.

[**G.** Hugh Acland, Ellen and Carry acted charades. He is a clever monkey. Thaw.]

Throughout Georgina's comments about Hugh Acland, there is a feeling of her disapproval of him, as a suitor for Ellen.

24. The bride, Miss Fanny Crewe, afterwards Mrs R Wedgwood.

Tuesday 12ᵗʰ Bad day, kept to the house. Robert Wedgwood and Miss Crewe, as his wife, came for the first time to dinner. After this can anything in this world deserve to be called astonishing? It really distressed me to find how much our old friendship feelings were altered with him – a sort of constraint came over both him and ourselves. Hugh was very much disgusted and could hardly help showing it. Let him take care, for who would have been so outrageous against it as Robert himself!

Hugh has been let into family secrets. Later we learn from Georgina that there was a match expected between Penelope and Robert Wedgwood.

[**G.** Mr and Mrs R. Wedgwood dined. I cannot like her; she is too deep. I hope he does not already regret his folly, but he looks altered, and twice where I accidentally heard him speak to her in the passage, I was struck by his cold way of speaking. Frost.]

Wednesday 13th We walked with Hugh. Anne, Mary and Philip Humberston arrived and the evening was spent most jollily in acting charades. Our words were: 'courtesy', 'knight errant' and 'listless'. The last was a capital scene with a set of questions and answers composed by Hugh, as full of ludicrous blunders as possible.

[**G.** The R. Wedgwoods went, and Anne, Mary and Philip Humberston came. Character acting. Thaw.]

Thursday 14th Hugh departed - a great loss- the dear little fellow is so full of life and spirit. Emma Wedgwood came and we had a merry game of 'bouts rimés'.

[**G.** Emma Wedgwood came and Hugh Acland went away. Snow.]

Friday 15th **January 1836** This day was the anniversary of one of the most distressing of my life, but yet it passed cheerfully enough, thanks to dear Emma, who is the delightful companion possible. *(The year before Marianne's child was still-born.)* We amused ourselves by acting charades, comedy, opera, and critic. Very glad that Caroline Wigley met Emma. She was pleased with her playing.

[**G.** Same party. Frost.]

Saturday 16th Caroline W. went – very sorry to lose her. Met with one of those trials, which, alas, have become frequent of late. Took pains to analyse my own feelings and I really believe I was actuated only by tender sympathy. I hope I may receive these mortifications as sent or, rather permitted, for some good purpose and that I may be enabled entirely to separate my natural feelings of sorrow from any of resentment or morbid sensibility, or to put the very most favourable construction possible on conduct, I am quite unable to understand. Quiet evening.

[**G.** *On this occasion Georgina does not tell us what had upset Ellen.* Emma Wedgwood went, also C. Wigley. Frost.]

Sunday 17th Church twice and school once. An excellent sermon on godly sorrow.

[**G.** Morning - Mr T: 'Rejoice in the Lord always.' Evening - Mr S: 'The sorrow of the world works through death.' Thaw.]

Monday 18th The Humberstons left us and we were very sorry to lose them - Mary is such a nice, uncommon sort of little girl. Henry and Robert Clive *(from Styche),* Mr Clewes and Harriet and Emma Tayleur arrived. Won 5d – a bet on the whist table. Music and chatted.

[**G.** Hannah and Lucy Tayleur, Robert and Henry Clive, (and Mr Clewes is a tolerably nice youth) – not a well chosen party. Wet.]

Tuesday 19th Those mean Clives shrank off this morning, though they were expected to stay. Not very well nor spirited today. Played chess with Lucy and beat her - to my great surprise.

[**G.** R. and H. Clive sneeked off, unknown to Charles. Walked to Balterley Heath with the two Tayleurs. Nice chat. Fine.]

Wednesday 20th January Found out this morning that the Tayleurs' cousin, Miss Warner, is intimately acquainted with our hero, Mr Robert Marlborough Prior *(also spelt as Pryor, born in 1807),* as his name proves to be.

Carry and I went to Rease Heath, expecting to meet a large party and found only two clergymen besides themselves. Mr Hordern was an amenable sort of man, who has been a great ladykiller in his day and is now married with three children, has money - £1000 a year. His success among the damsels surprises me for he is very conceited evidently - there's the rub. Found Mrs Henry still stiff and sententious in manner. The children - very nice.

[**G**. Tayleurs went. Ellen and Carry went to Reaseheath. Fine.]

Thursday 21st Walked to Dorfold *(about 2 miles)*. Saw the T.s and Corbetts of Darnhall. Lady Robert invisible. Major and Mrs Pollock dined. Never more inclined to murder than when Mrs Hordern began to tell a long dull tale to Major Pollock, just as I had succeeded in quietly encouraging the modest veteran into talking about the Peninsular War *(1808-1814)*, and don't like Mrs Hordern any better, which is odd.

25. Dorfold Hall, the home of the main branch of the Tomkinsons.

[**G**. Nothing. Fine.]

Friday 22nd Called at Pool on the way home. Saw Mrs Massie and her niece, Mrs Jones and her son, Owen Jones, an ugly, vulgar, 'noble, fine' child, of a year and a half, with great eyes and a snub nose, not quite dry, and an upper lip half a yard long, in a smart braided frock, under which I ill-naturedly spied a pretty, yellow flannel petticoat.

A hieroglyphic letter from Harriet Lister. Little Harry is four years old and amused us by saying, "Is Mr Hordern married? Yes, I know he is, for I saw the ring on his finger!" The majority of rings are, I think, on the single men's fingers.

[**G.** A letter from Harriet Lister insisting on our writing again, though she declared she will not and cannot write letters. Fine.]

Saturday 23rd One of the highest winds in the night I ever remember. Wrote to Jane Lawrence. Read Tom Moore's very wicked 'The Fudges of England' *(1835)* and began Southey's 'Colloquies' *(Sir Thomas More Colloquies 1829)*. Began reading 'The Gipsy' aloud, which promises well. *(The latter was a play by Caroline Norton 1830.)*

[**G.** Nothing.]

Sunday 24th Wet. Church twice.

[**G.** Mr T.: 'How the God of all grace etc, after that ye have suffered a while.' Evening: 'God is a spirit.']

Monday 25th January Called on M.A. Northen at the parsonage. Found her in a very happy state, apparently as happy as if she were going to marry the most delightful man in the world. Oh, how surprisingly differently are human beings constructed! Thus thought I when at dinner I sat next *[to]* her hero - the man of her heart!

When I see the men that girls of our acquaintance do marry, many of them with higher attractions and better charms than ourselves, (though, of course, in this case it is but an evaluing) it makes me think how very unlikely it is that any thing better should fall to one's own share, and this produces a conviction and determination that an old maid I must and will be. I had rather be married in imagination to some imaginary being, than in flesh and blood reality to some commonplace person.

This was quite a spring day and I sat in an armchair with the window open, in such a pleasant, fanciful reverie state, reading that pretty dreamy romantic first volume of Lamartine's 'Voyage en Orient'*(1835)*. Amused at his talking of his 'frissons sterils d'Agleterre.' He says, 'Bien, amour et poésie sont les trois mots que je voudrais seules graves sur ma pierre' – and very comprehensive words they are indeed, expressing all that makes our present existence deliciously happy. Read the other day Sharp's essays. 'It is to our understanding we must trust for our amusement, but to our affections for happiness.' And yet not to earthly affections only, for they, alas, may fail us!

Dr Wilson, Captain Mc Dermott, Messrs Short and Sutcliffe dined. Beat Mr S. at chess. Wrote to Harriet Lister and told her that I was so bitten with a fancy for London lawyers that I intended to try to persuade Papa and Mamma to remove house to a house in Lincoln Inn Fields.

[**G.** Called on the bride elect. Found her in a great state of happiness. In the evening we had her beloved, Dr Wilson, together with Capt Mc Dermott and Messrs Short and Sutcliffe. Dr Wilson not pleasing in manners or appearance, but on the whole a decent man.]

Tuesday 26th Charles, Georgina and I dined at the Court and met Lord and Lady Buller and the Twemlows of Peatswood - pleasant chat with Mrs T.

[**G.** Dined at the Court. Lord and Lady Buller and Mr and Mrs E.B. Mr and Mrs Twemlow. Dullish.]

Wednesday 27th Mrs B.'s baby and the Turton babies came up here. Called at the Court and they called here and Lady Buller was here all day, so that really the day passed in perfect idleness. Comfortable evening enough and detachment, on duty at the Court.

[**G.** A lare party of callers from the Court. Papa, Mama, Penelope and Carry dined at the Court. Fine.]

Thursday 28th Drew, and thought, and wrote to Marianne, and read Lamartine. He says so well old true thoughts so often – 'La solitude et la mort,......'*(this quotation continues in French for seven lines. Lamartine was a major French Romantic poet, noted for his autobiographical poem, 'Le Lac'.)*

Friday 29th Dreary looking day - rain and cold, sleet and rain. Dined at the parsonage where we found Dr Wilson, a brother and two sisters, the latter seemed nice, good sort of people but had a strong Scottish or North Country accent.

[**G.** Snow and rain all day.]

Saturday 30th Read 'The Gipsy' and 'The Latherstone', and Mrs Trollope's 'Paris' *(a novelist and travel writer, 1779-1863)* an entertaining book, though I do dislike the woman. She cannot resist lugging in her political opinions neck and shoulders in long pages, and this to me is offensive in any writer, in a woman doubly so. Then she appears to me irreligious and aristocratically vulgar. Her abusing Victor Hugo and his immoral, indecent plays, and then giving one the plot of one of them by way of openness, is most infamous taste.

Mr Locke, the clever engineer, came to tea. Received a letter from dear Annabel, directed under cover to Mr Wedgwood, who has been out of Parliament a year.

[**G.** Mr Locke spent the evening here; very pleasant, but not so talkative as his last visit. Wet.]

Sunday 31st Church twice. Read Erskine on 'The Internal Evidence for the Truth of Revealed Religion' *(1820)*. It is a delightful book.

[**G.** Mr T. - Morning: 'Looking diligently lest any man fall from the grace of God.' Evening - Mr S.: 'Labour not for the meat which perisheth.']

A birth

Mary Wicksted has decided to be confined in Betley, where the future heir to the estate will be born. At this time Marianne, her sister-in-law in Welshpool, has not had any live births.

February 1st 1836 This long talked of lying in month has set in. May we see its close with happy thankful hearts!

Called on M.A. Northen and found a hypocritical burst of enquiry after poor Mrs Wettenhall, and Georgina, resisting the entreaty to enter with a sentimentality, whispering, "We had better not, thank you."

A grand scene in the evening - Hickory, Dickory Dock, the mouse ran up, not the clock, but poor Carry's petticoats, who screaming like one possessed, repulsed the intruder. Her nerves were all much shaken and we returned with our workboxes in our hands, huddling like scared wild-fowl, into the library, where the rest of the evening was spent in peace.

A letter from M.A. Egerton from Naples. She seems low, but amused us by her strictures on Susan Torleton's marriage. She says she has beauty and talents and withal a religious mind, which I am sure she will need to prevent her growing vicious, forever tacked on to the hum drum major. Oh, Women, ye are severe on the very deeds, ye daily commit !

[**G**. *(In contrast to Ellen's amusing description -)* In the evening a mouse ran up Carry's gown, causing a great disturbance.]

Tuesday 2nd Woke up in the morning, ate breakfast and tea. Read Trollope till I was completely cloyed, then betook me to Arnott's Physics (1827)[44] and Villiers' Tragedies *(1672)*, finished up with knitting a blanket or reading a novel aloud.

[**G**. Nothing. Fine.]

A side of Georgina's diary has been roughly torn out, covering the period from Wednesday and most of Thursday.

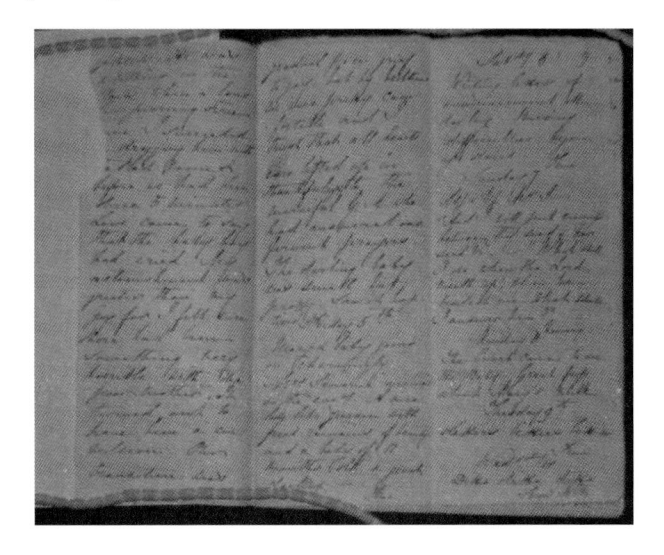

26. Georgina's diary, with the torn page.

Wednesday 3rd February Got up again. How very odd! Did exactly the same things:

Receipt for making a comfortable, inoffensive quiet day:
  of drawing a good deal,
  of eating rather less,
  of walking some,
  of talking a vast quantity,
  mix all up with a good deal of lolling, yawning,
  add plenty of good jokes as salt, and a little crossness as pepper and et voilà ! *(She has omitted 'reading'.)*

Thursday 4th Heard as soon as I woke that Mary had been taken ill at two o'clock, and that Belisse and Short were in attendance. Here was a pretty thing – Mrs Severne *(Mary's sister)* not here yet. M. Southwell out of the way. However, hearing that all was going well, we ate our breakfasts in good spirits.

M.A. Northern called directly after and hooked me in to go to her wedding, which I shall particularly dislike, but it is an ill wind etc. Emma Wedgwood by this means secures a clean bed-fellow.

About luncheon time we began to get impatient for the birth. Poor Charles was very nervous and kept coming in and out to see, and mourning over poor Mary's sufferings, but I was never frightened or uncomfortable, till after three o'clock when a dreadful alarm spread all over the house. She had been suddenly seized with a frightful convulsive fit. They were obliged to bleed her largely, immediately, and they were going to bring the child into the world artificially.

Our agony was intense: Mamma looked like a corpse. Eliza was seized with difficulty in breathing, and poor Charles writhed on the stone stairs, embracing the banisters, while Georgy embraced him. Soon to the infinite relief of everyone, the cry of a child was heard, and wonderful to tell, a boy was born alive and well. Great was our thankfulness. It was an hour before we could feel at all comfortable about poor dear Mary, who was insensible and then fell into a comfortable sleep.

We sent off the express to her mother, and the evening was spent in mutual congratulations, and hearing from the doctors the particulars of the merciful and narrow escape. Thank God for it!

[**G**. *After the torn page, the diary continues mid sentence:* he was writhing on the stairs when a long, long piercing scream *(word torn out)*. I succeeded in dragging him into a back room, and before we had been there five minutes, Lowe came to say that a baby boy had cried. My astonishment was greater than my joy, for I felt sure there had been something very horrible with the poor mother. It turned out to have been a convulsion. Our transition was gradual from grief to joy, but by bed-time, we were pretty comfortable and I trust that all hearts were lifted up in thankfulness to the merciful God who had answered our fervent prayers. The darling baby was small but pretty, soon to be baptised.]

Friday 5th February Mr Turton came up to baptize the precious baby and we all knelt round and fervently with thankful hearts implored the blessings of God's grace for our darling. Oh, may he be spiritually blessed and may his dear parents be enabled really to feel the overpowering importance of his eternal interests. His name is George Edmund and a very pretty creature it is - I think like Charles in the upper part of the face.

All going well. Wrote ten letters and boasted and nursed the baby. Mrs Severne *(Mary's sister, Anna)* arrived in the evening, and we all rejoiced together. She brought her baby with her – a sweet creature. Went to see Mrs Pollard and heard all the amusing details of how Mr Robinson ran in and out like a hen wanting to lay and called, "I say Becca, I say Bessy. Have ye heard of Mrs Wicksted and her astrologising husband? Last 8th September I told her that if she replied in sincerity he would draw a figure for her, and now it proved a boy etc!"

[**G**. Mary and the baby going on charmingly. Mrs Severne arrived in the evening – a nice lady-like person with fresh remains of beauty, and a baby of eleven months old, a great darling. Fine.]

Saturday 6th Dearest little Mary Gater, who had been sent away twice by cruel servants, came with Penelope to see the baby and looked so pleased. Her spirits had been quite oppressed with her disappointment.

[**G.** Writing letters of announcement all day long. Nursing difficulties began upstairs. Fine.]

Sunday 7th Such an applicable lesson 'In sorrow shalt thou bring forth children.' A merry peal as we came out. Mrs Wareham's child came up to see. Went to church with thankful hearts.

[**G.** *(Sermons):* 'And I will put enmity between thy seed and her seed,' and 'What shall I do when the Lord riseth up, when he visiteth me, what shall I answer him?' Showery.]

Monday 8th Nothing but writing and receiving letters and having nursery details.

[**G.** The Court came to see the baby. Great fuss about Mary's milk.]

Tuesday 9th A rather bothering day. Mrs Rea is a sensible old woman, not fussy but cross: Mrs Severne is desperately fussy but not cross at all. They don't agree well at all indeed. Mrs S. in her anxiety interferes too much. Poor Mary has a good deal of difficulty with her nursing.

[**G.** Letters, letters, letters. Fine.]

Wednesday 10th **February** We were amused this evening by a formal address from Charles on the subject of matrimony, advising us all in the strongest way never to commit such folly. He thinks much of the pains and perils of childbirth.

We call our babe and the nurse - George and the dragon.

[**G.** Ditto, ditto, ditto. Snow, wet.]

Thursday 11th George is a week old today. He really, I think, promises to be a beauty when he fills out.

I can't think what makes it so impossible for me to write my journal. It can't be monotony of our days for that I have often had to struggle with.

[**G.** Saw Mary for the first time - very happy she looked.]

It seems incredible that in the same large household Mary has not seen rest of the family since she gave birth.

Friday 12th [G. Called on Miss Wettenhall out of Christian charity.]

Saturday 13th Lapsed in reading and drawing and amused with random recollections of the House of Commons.

[G. One of poor Marianne's low letters came; she talks of her grief as it was a year ago, and with loss of hope. Fine.]

Sunday 14th Rather poorly. Went to church twice.

[G. Morning - Mr T.: 'Be careful for nothing be, etc'. Evening - Mr S. :'O woman, great is thy faith, etc.' Fine.]

Monday 15th February Most lovely warm day. Saw George washed and dressed. He has a sweet, pretty face and well formed limbs, but is surprisingly small, I think, in the limbs. He surely will be very slender.

[G. A spring day. Baby, baby -]

Tuesday 16th Great amusement from hearing Mary Humberston in a note to Carry, deploring poor Major and Mrs Tomkinson arriving at Wellington by broad daylight with nothing to do but wait for dinner. We say if we had been Miss Susan we would have travelled somewhere. The very rattling of the wheels would have been a diversion to paying post boys, and ordering out horses is the major's forte - the very thing he thrives in.

Highly delighted at an invitation to Maer to meet - Baugh !

I hope for happy results, but we are all determined on secrecy, for the rustling of a leaf might scare away the timid nymph from the snare, which I do hope her Darwin has laid for her – a most nice suitable Darwin he is. Heartily wished him success two or three years ago and now more than ever.

[G. Nothing but babies. Fine.]

Wednesday 17th Enjoyed the society of dear little Eddy Severne exceedingly. He is getting quite attached to us and hugs our necks with his dear soft arms.

[**G.** Nothing but the usual amusements that the charming baby, Edmund Severne, affords us, and a peep at George W. High wind.]

Thursday 18th A great reverse of fortune awaited us today in the form of a note from Maer saying that owing etc - they could not receive the party next Tuesday. Thus all our hopes were blasted, all our future visits to Dulwich destroyed. We bore all with patience and fortitude and calm conviction that what is to be will be, and what is not to be, won't be.

It should be explained that Mr Baugh Allen was master of Dulwich College, and brother of Jessie Sismondi. He had expressed his liking for Penelope.

[**G.** Drove out with the new pony; not at all frightened. Frost. *(This would have been a major achievement for a person with one arm.)*]

Friday 19th Jessie and Harry called. Then came Mr and Mrs Blackburn, and then Miss Mainwaring and Mary Russell. I went to see Eddy, such a sweet sight, and had a long chat with Mrs Severne. She is a dear, sweet woman, but certainly contrasted by living entirely out of an association with her species, strange ups and downs.

Again the stars shine not brightly but with a Dulwich light – another note – the party on again and a visit here promised. Oh, working Destiny, thou spinnest thy thread thy own way!

[**G.** Troops of morning callers: Harry and Jessie, Mr and Mrs Blackburn, Miss J. Mainwaring and Mary Russell. Frost.]

Saturday 20th February Mrs Severne and her dear baby departed. We were very sorry to lose them, though Mrs S. is far too formal and also too sensitive to allow of one's feeling very much at one's ease with her in the midel *(sic)* of a large family. Though by oneself one feels one could be quite comfortable by being on one's guard - though to be sure 'on one's guard' is never so very comfortable.

[**G.** Dear Edmund, the delight of our hearts, and his good mother went away. Frost.]

Return to normality after the birth

Again suitors for her sisters are the topics high on Ellen's agenda.

Sunday 21st Church and sacrament. 'Create in me a clean and humble servant.' Sad wanderings of thought. A good deal of each day is passed in watching the baby and going to visit Mary. This is very pleasant, but I think I am being littered in shawls.

[**G.** Mr T.: 'Create in me a clean and humble servant.']

Monday 22nd Did a good deal of work in all ways. Still reading Lamartine. I like what he says of travelling so much. I wonder whether I ever shall travel, or do any of those exciting, pleasant things, or whether I shall live hum drum, yet happy, all my life. Sometimes I think I should be capable of engaging any active, stirring scenes so much more, while youth and its imaginations last, and before any great deep sorrow has produced that certain something in our feelings which, however, as time may heal, they still must prevent our ever having again the same sort of light-heartedness. There again, I think I am capable now of being happy in the hum drum state. And perhaps the stirring in my life may come when age and sorrow have taken the edge of my enjoying powers, and the undergrowth of little pleasures have no longer the power to delight or amuse.

[**G.** Nothing. Wet.]

Tuesday 23rd A sad disappointment met me at breakfast – an annoying draught of vexation. Mamma had thought it right to tell Penelope that Baugh was to be at Maer and she refused to go. Alas, for castle building ! Mamma, Georgy and Carry went to Maer and left me to mourn. Quiet evening, watching the suckling etc.

[**G.** Obliged to go to Maer unexpectedly, owing to Penelope refusing to meet her old admirer *(Mr Baugh Allen)*. Only Mr B. Allen and Mr Tomlinson. A bet with the former as to the relative situation of Liverpool and Edinburgh. To my utter astonishment the latter proved to be more to the west. Wet *(for the last two days.)*]

Wednesday 24th They returned from Maer, having had a pleasant evening. Mr *(Baugh)*Allen reminded them of our argument he and I had about proposals, in which I took the part of women who 'gave' their admirers 'to understand', instead of letting their offer be refused. I am (sure *omitted*) this is often done from principle, but I begin to change my mind to think the other plan the best, for all the thanks they get is that the reason creatures make out there was no occasion, and so I shall tell Mr Allen tomorrow.

We were all enraged at being told that Edinburgh was west of Liverpool, but so it is.

[**G.** Came home. Frost and snow.]

Thursday 25th February Began to read 'Pride and Prejudice' *(1813)* to Mary. A very good book for the purpose, but I don't like it so well as 'Mansfield Park' *(1814)* or 'Persuasion' *(1817)*. It is a broad farce and the humour less delicate, and the story not so feeling or pretty.

[**G.** Nothing Frost.]

Friday 26th Lord Crewe called and staid three hours, but would not dine because dining here would serve to kill another day, viz Monday. *(This was Hungerford Crewe, who was the same age as Ellen.)*

This is pure economy. Elizabeth Wedgwood and Mr *(Baugh)* Allen arrived. Nothing could appear more prosperous than the 'affaires de coeur'. He was ?willing: she was killing: my spirits are at boiling heat. E.W. seemed very sympathising when we talked of the obloquy and contempt, which being seven sisters brought on us. Mr A. told Georgina the story of a man, who was driven off marrying an apothecary's daughter by his brother pounding with a pestle and mortar on his ears.

Oh, Charles had a letter from Joe *(Sykes)*, saying he is coming here next month. How perverse is fate, which said of an occasional and fleeting vision only to make, if possible, these uninteresting, ugly men who do not spare their visits, less acceptable than ever! *(Ellen again was very harsh on Psyche who seemed to like her.)*

27. Charles Wicksted.

[**G.** Mr B. Allen and Elizabeth Wedgwood dined. Renewal of symptoms. Kindly received. Frost, snow. *Was Georgina showing the signs of the family weakness, depression?*]

Saturday 27th The departure was marked by a little scuffle of an extra double shaking of hands and an inaudible whisper. Sure this will come to something! *(We discovered later that Ellen was referring to the proposed liaison between Penelope and Mr Baugh Allen, to whom the Wedgwoods were related.)*

We were amused in the evening by a report in the 'Staffordshire Mercury' of a dinner given to Charles on Thursday by his hunting adorers, at which Papa's, Mary's, and the baby's healths were drunk, or so, I suppose, were half the company. Papa was given as 'A fine old English gentleman', and the song was given with additional verses for the occasion.

[**G**. My 28th birthday. Perturbation of spirit. Much dissatisfied with my state of mind. This is a troublesome world, but I dare not wish myself out of it. Mr B. Allen went and said something to Penelope at parting. We are much puzzled. Frost and snow.]

Sunday 28th Staid at home with Eliza who had a painful attack of oppression in her breathing. It happily lasts a very short time but it is very distressing.

Read Chalmer's sermon on the expulsive power of a new affection - *(Thomas Chalmers - theologian 1780-1847)*. It is that the love of God can alone expel the love of the world. Unless this new affection is felt and most powerfully too, the world will and must have our love in some way or another. It is not necessary for this that our hearts should be set on those pleasures and vanities, which even a shallow observer can pronounce to be frivolous and worthless. We may despise these and have the world in our hearts. It is another and more deceitful form, but the evil is still the same. Our affections are still upon the earth if they are not in heaven. Either heaven or earth is our first consideration. They cannot both occupy the same space in our hearts. Oh! surely those who by nature are most capable of loving earth and its blessings and its beauties too well are those who should most endeavour to give all their best to God. Of those to whom much is given in any way, of them will much be required. The feelings of the heart, as well as the powers of the mind, are talents committed to our charge, and if many of those best and sweetest feelings bring their own disappointments and sufferings here, yet still if, as I believe, they may all, by grace, be made sources of undying joy hereafter. They are precious blessings to be grateful for.

[**G** . *(Sermon)* 'Watch and pray till you enter not into temptation.' I am sure I cannot watch nor pray as I ought. Snow and rain.]

Monday 29th I had to write a diplomatic note to Mrs Buller about the baby's robe, which arrived yesterday, and did not look worth five guineas, though very elegant.

Hungerford or rather Lord Crewe dined here. We think we observe already an improvement in appearance and manner from his new situation. He told us he had found the Wedgwoods so uncomfortable with John Crewe, packing up all the furniture, that he had asked them to Crewe, very kindly.

March 1st 1836 Hungerford Crewe told me that Lady Anglesey had told Brooke Greville that Mrs Cunliffe wished Anne to marry Lord Clarence Paget! That would have been a match to be sure! Nothing happened.

[**G**. Drove in the pony chair. Wet evening *(and wet on Monday.)*]

Wednesday 2nd Read Jeanne Baillet's Tragedies *(now forgotten)*. Really, she gives one a subject of jealous husbands – no less than four in a sorry play. I do think tragedy writing is for women of all things most hopeless. I know she is much admired but I cannot. How inferior to 'Philip van Artevelde' *(by Sir Henry Taylor 1790-1837)*.

The Court called and in the midst of their sit, it was discovered that Mary Gater was concealed under the table. They were suddenly shocked, but I thought seemed pacified when I reminded them that she could not hear our discourse. The poor little thing was frightened to death, and when dragged from her lair, buried herself in my cloak and then was conveyed out of the room.

[**G**. Eliza very poorly and low. Miss Fletcher and Mrs T. came to see the baby. Fine.]

Thursday 3rd Walked to Wrine Hill. Coming home stopped at the Southwell's door, and while chattering, suddenly turned round and beheld Mr Willoughby Crewe *(the rector of Mucklestone)* just arrived from Paris, looking as sickly and sore as need be, but very civil and bland as usual. We talked full gallop for ten minutes when he resumed his post chaise and I my walk.

Friday 4th Nothing happened that I can recollect. Oh, a letter from Jane Lawrence. M. Gavillyan better.

Saturday 5th March Henry Tomkinson called and made himself very agreeable. He ate cold pig with us and looked as handsome as Adonis. Heard that young Glegg had ingeniously tormented his father by marrying his mistress and incurring a debt of £9,000. A letter from Harriet Tayleur giving information concerning our hero, that his name is Robert, not Marlborough, a second not an oldest son and that he is as amiable as clever! This we did not venture to pronounce on. He has two sisters – Ellen and Caroline, but more extraordinary than all is – only twenty-four! *(Ellen must have been making more enquiries about the Pryors.)*

A long call from the Twemlows.

[**G.** *For the past three days Georgina has written, 'Nothing' and not even commented on the weather.*]

Sunday 6th Church and school. Rather in a lazy dull-minded way.

[**G.** Mr T.: 'Behold I lay in iron and stone.' Mr S.: 'And they took knowledge from them etc.' –an old sermon.]

Monday 7th Didn't do anything except the usual – eating, work, reading, varied by looking at the young squaller upstairs.

[**G.** H. Tomkinson called - much improved. Heard of Mrs John Gleig's infamous marriage, such are parents' trials. It makes me tremble for George *(the baby)*. Fine. Four or five wet, black days.]

Tuesday 8th Carry and I set off in the phaeton to call on the Butts, and found Lady Elde and her husband there. She was bearable though very affected and 'posée.' He is in appearance like Lord Talbot in figure with a handsome coarse face. He was very agreeable and perfectly easy, but I could imagine him very coarse on the slightest provocation - clever, very good tempered, and coarse without being vulgar. That is his character according to my remarks. The baby was divine – so fat and chubby. C. E. laughed very much about, what she calls, my philanthropy in declaring that I should go to M.A. Northen's wedding, ready to do her every kindness except envying her, which, of course, one's knowledge of human nature tells one would be by far this the most gratifying compliment I could pay her.

Read for the tenth time the third volume of 'Pride and Prejudice'. How excellent it is! Mr Bennet is enchanting, but Lydia's disgrace far too bad. Great want of taste and delicacy towards her heroines.

Wednesday 9th Working all morning; wasting time it would be, only I do think Lord Crewe called, and had intended us a two hours' sit, had not Mr Robinson also called and spoilt his fun and thus drove him off.

A most comfortable letter from Marianne, the best we have had for months. She wants me to go to her.

Thursday 10th March and **Friday 11th** Nothing, I believe. Indeed the only wonder is I have been able to journalise at all this week.

[**G.** Nothing. Four or five wet, black days.]

Saturday 12th Walked out and Lord Crewe called to take leave and frank some letters. I was obliged to assist.[45] This made Mary and Caroline laugh, and I am laughing at Carry about Joe *(Sykes)* very severely, her having stolen him from me in London and

> On Malvern's Height I was his delight,
> To make this matter worse
> And as I live
> She did contrive
> To take him with her to Worcester.

It seems obvious that Lord Crewe had been paying Ellen a considerable amount of attention in the past few weeks, and it even appears that she had changed her mind about him since the discussion with Emma Wedgwood on May 22nd 1835.

Much chagrined by the news that Mr Childe has not come. We shall have only a sort of abortion of a hunting party next week, but we are to make a bold stroke and send over to Peatswood on Monday.

Sunday 13th A very pretty sermon on Joseph and his brethren. Much afraid Mary is rather more alarmed about her mother by today's letter.

[**G.** Morning sermon Mr T. :'God hath found out the iniquity of thy servant.' Evening Mr T...*illegible* Fine.]

Monday 14th Emma and Catherine *(Wedgwood)* came to call and see the baby. They admire him much.

Arrived - Messrs Beech and Sykes. Found the latter in rather low spirits. I worked like a post horse all evening to make talk.

[G. Catherine Darwin and Emma Wedgwood called – both in great form. Mr Beech and Joe Sykes arrived. The former is indefatigable with his very small talk. The two friends amused us by their constant exchanges of knowing glances. Wind and rain.]

Tuesday 15th March Such a snowy, horrid day. They hunted at Crewe and had no sport. We are very much amused by the youthfulness of our two men. They are so like lads, all so green yet not very pretty adolescents either. They have a telegraph constantly between themselves, which makes one quite nervous. (Wondered how anything so superior as Mr Prior could be Lord of his Bench, though I do think he is not silly, and certainly amiable.)

[G, Carry and I walked to Wrine Hill with Joe – such *?think* the rank and fashion of the village, who doubtless speculated much on such a marvellous occurrence! Cold wind.]

Wednesday 16th Mr Beech went to hunt with the Cheshires and returned in the highest glee, having seen the Misses Gleggs, Miss Brooke and besides, all the fine riding of Cheshire. Poor Mr Sykes obliged to stay at home and walk with the ladies here. Again I laboured in the good cause of conversation.

The Court dined. M.A. Twemlow had a good fly at Mr Beech at dinner, but we think his value for her is diminished by discovering she is not much in Cheshire Society. He must consider that this house is the key to that paradise.

[G. The Court dined here. We cherish in hope of establishing M.A. Twemlow at the Shaws, which there are state reasons for wishing. *(Match-making?)* Cold and rainy.]

Thursday 17th The gents went to breakfast at Dorfold. The Twemlows of Peatswood came here. She as usual is very pleasant and entertaining. Lord Crewe and Mr Ludworth called *(in the morning)*. Went to see Emma Biddulph, husband and child.... Major Tomkinson called and seemed obviously happy - new married people are not pleasant company at least if they are ?tired and ?proud. The evening not very brilliant. *(The entry for this day is in miniscule handwriting with additional lines superimposed; it is almost illegible.)*

Friday 18th Walked and talked with Mrs Twemlow. In the evening we acted charades. She was capital as a boy and an old man. Her forte is the broadest farce. Her wit is not of an elegant nature, but she does it all with so much spirit and is, in her own natural character, so feminine and so nice, that she is always eminently successful.

[**G.** Mrs Twemlow acted with Mr Sykes, Ellen and Carry a capital charade; 'courtship.' Mr Beech and Psyche were quite dazzled by the brilliancy of Mrs Twemlow's talents. They are not however the best part of her. Rain and snow.]

Saturday 19th They, that is the Twemlows, departed, having engaged Georgy to go to them next week *(a couple of words are illegible.)* I have promised to go to Maer in the gig. The evening passed off well. Mr Sykes was amusing.

Sunday 20th March Mr Turton had a cough which caused us to have two very good sermons from Mr Sutcliffe. Charles made an epigram on the subject, which I must put down:

> Says Turton, "I have got a cough
> Indeed I can't endure it.
> My brethren, I must put you off.
> To Buxton Baths I must be off
> And leave you all to cure it."   (Curate

[**G.** Mr Sutcliffe's second sermon on 'Take away thy folly from the Sabbath.' A subject which always shows one how defective we are in this duty. Fine and warm]

A feeling of guilt overcame Georgina that, on the Sabbath, only religious thoughts should dominate. It seems most unusual that Ellen should be so light-hearted on Sunday. Normally she reads theological works exclusively. Perhaps her brother's mocking of the vicar had raised her spirits.

Monday 21st Went hunting on foot at the kennels. Saw the fox swim across the Pool. Mr Beech departed. Quiet, chatty evening.

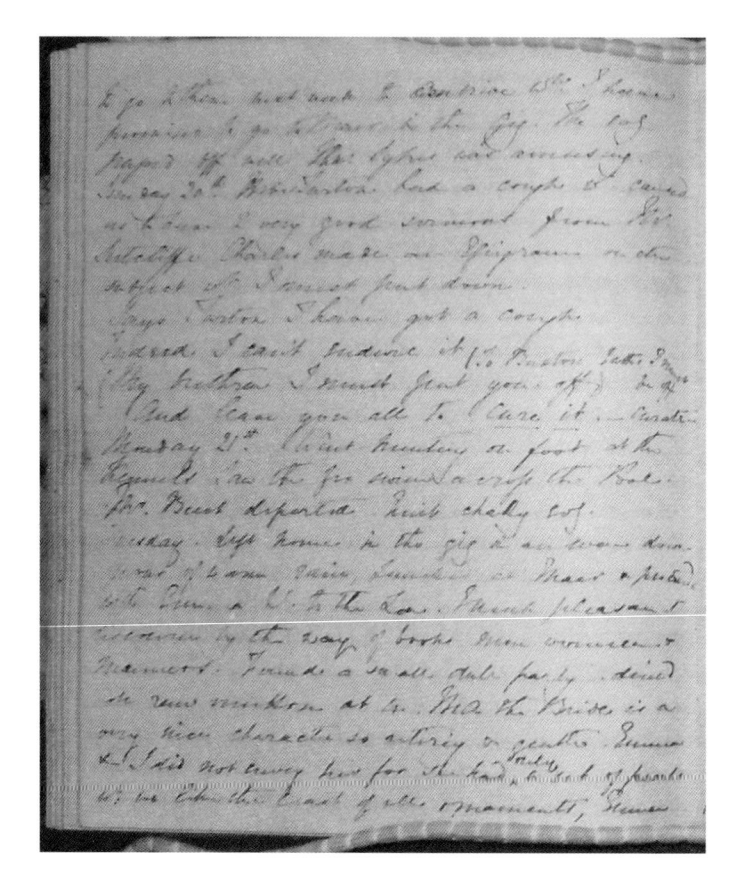

28. Page 134 from Ellen's journal, which is 7 x 8 inches.

The wedding of Dr Wilson of Newcastle and M.A. Northen of Lea House in the parish of Adbaston, near Eccleshall now takes place. The Rev Henry Turton officiated. Earlier Ellen had said that by going to the marriage, Emma Wedgwood was ensuring 'a clean bedfellow'. The custom of sharing beds for the upper classes seems unusual to the modern reader. Ellen and her sister now write their diaries from different venues.

Tuesday 22ⁿᵈ Left home in the gig in an even downpour of warm rain. Lunched at Maer and proceeded with Emma Wedgwood to the Lea. Much pleasant discourse by way of books, men, women, and manners. Found a small, dull party, dined on raw mutton at four. M.A., the bride, is a very nice character, so retiring and gentle. Emma and I did not envy her, for she had only a set of pearls, which we like least as ornaments. Emma gave her a lecture on 'Married Lady Airs', telling her to ring the bell and to say, "Coals - Tea," in an authoritative voice and to be very solemn and 'posée' in her manners.

Emma and I agreed in bed that it is quite shocking how such a solemn, holy thing as a marriage is profaned by the extraordinary promises and importance given to the matter of dress. It is made the principal ingredient. Delighted today by a passage in Bulwer *(a politician)* in which, speaking of the state of a person whose earthly happiness is centred in one object, he describes it as a state of fear and constant dread of change - of ruin, like a miser travelling along a road beset with dangers of carrying all his treasure with him.

Wednesday 23rd A bitter, cold morning. All the ladies so smart. Mr Moore of Eccleshall - so pleasant: old father Turton - so gay. Driving to the church received a splash of mud on my fair face, arriving always beautiful. I feel sure they'll be happy and perhaps they love each other as well, as more refined people do, but I could not feel any sentiment about them.

They drove off to Buxton at two o'clock and then Emma and I took leave and came to Maer, I cursing cocoa and wedding cake in my stomach all the way. Found the dear old lady *(Elizabeth Wedgwood 1764-1846)* very brisk and had a quiet, cosy evening.

Meanwhile Georgina was left at home and found it 'dullish' without Ellen, and she had the responsibility of entertaining Psyche. The following days she spent at Peatswood.

[G. 23rd Carry and I and Mama went to Peatswood. The party in the house were: Col and Mrs Glegg, a very nice happy pair, Misses Selina and Georgina Cotes and two lively pleasant guests – Mr Baugh (Alllen), my aversion, and William Egerton, my delight. Diners were W. and H. Tayleur and William Dod. I sat by the latter, who is a specimen of inanimate, agreeable and a rare article certainly. A charade - 'bar-sack'. Mr Baugh to do him justice was a capital coadjutor for Mrs Twemlow, though I should not, however, have liked acting with him. The soldier was quite novel. Peals, squeals and roars of laughter. Wet.

24th Oceans of talk. I and Mrs Glegg had two hours without ceasing, while the others were out. She told me she had always wished to marry a man older than herself. Sat with W. Egerton at dinner. Exceedingly pleasant - Geology, Theology and Physiognomy. Charade encore – 'patri-mony'. Mr Baugh as Pat's Judy was perfect to look at, but we thought him a little too loving. Snow and hail.

25th Sorry to leave the party, which seldom happens. Charles and Psyche went to Shawe.[42] Snow and rain.]

Both the diarists are now writing from Betley.

Thursday 24th Came home, told the news and entertained Psyche in the evening. Found Mary in rather a fuss about her child, for whom every living creature advises something different.

Friday 25th March Bazarred all the morning. Georgy and Carry came home and amused us much by their histories of their very pleasant visit. They met two Miss Cotes, and Col and Mrs Glegg and they all fell in love with each other. They acted charades: 'bar-sack', and capitally they must have done it. Carry had a little Pryor conversation with H. Tayleur, who gave her the description of Miss Warner's letter, in which she says she evidently, in spite of all her praise, thinks him not equal to Mr Marlborough Pryor who, I am sure, must have stolen her heart, poor soul. It was indeed useful to travel abroad with such a creature.

Mr Sykes and Charles went to dine and sleep at Shawe.[46] The former is corrupting our minds by lending us French novels to read. He also lent me C. Lamb's 'Elia' 1st series *(1823)*. Charmed with the papers on modern gallantry and the manners of married people. It is very a exaggerated style of writing, but very amusing, always and often, very true. Speaking of feelings which may be borne if only implied, they are most offensive if declared. He says drolly that were a man to walk up to a young lady and tell her she was neither handsome nor rich enough for him and he would not marry her, he would deserve kicking for his impertinence. Yet the same thought is constantly implied by his having frequent opportunities of seeking her in marriage, yet never as though ..*words illegible* not reasonable if women would ever make this the ground of a quarrel!

We heard that the terrible death of poor Miss Machin had stopped the party at Mrs Shakerley's, and sent Mr Beech to the Gleggs. Surely this was a stroke of fate to prosper his suit? I think he's not to be checked, like the lining of his coats.

29. Charles Wickstead.

Saturday 26th A wretched, stormy, sleety day. They returned from Shawe very late. They met various old women there (Mr Beech has slipped his hooks) and don't *(sic)* go to Willington. He is calmly determined not to fall in love, but to walk into it when matrimony will be quite convenient. He will 'love wisely' but not 'too well'. *('Othello')*

Charles is horrified with Miss Ledwich; she is a mixture of a French governess and a Medusa.

[**G**. The two gents came home, full of the gorgeous Miss Ledwich, and Mr Beech's not humble companion. Snow and rain.]

Sunday 27th A beautiful sermon on Hebrews 4 v.15. The line is a most difficult one to draw between the Saviour's having experienced our infirmities and frailties without having felt the temptation to sin in our nature of guilt.

Weakness and suffering are so internally connected that we cannot separate our ideas of each.

This day had its trials. The now almost consistency of seeing dearest Eliza more languid than formerly, (and others of a minor, yet less wholesome nature – I don't mean by this less intended for our good, but more of the nature of temptation to sin). Oh, how I wish that witnessing the faults of others might only have the effect of making me more than ever disgusted with my own. I do think nobody ever sins in this house without my making it the occasion of doing so too, either ostensibly or seemingly.

Monday 28th Cold but wet day spent entirely in the house, reading, working for the bazaar, and talking. Psyche was our companion - he has lent us some French novels, which are well written, but give one such a notion of the want of moral feeling in Paris, as making one quite sick. I believe M de Balzac is as moral a novelist as any of them.

[**G.** went to church. Wet, snowy.]

The deteriorating illness of Eliza

It has become obvious that the Tollet family have become more and more worried about Eliza, and their social life becomes rather more limited. They have tried to keep up the pretence that she was improving.

Tuesday 29th Dr Brady came. He evidently thinks Eliza worse indeed. It is impossible not to perceive that her breathing becomes more oppressed. She is ever more cheerful than usual. I feel miserable, but it is an absolute duty to keep up; she perceives the least lowness and nothing can distress her so much. She questions us today about Dr Brady's opinion. I told her he thought her pulse weaker. She is thoroughly aware of her own precarious state, that to go into more particulars appears to me useless misery to myself and agitation to her. In the last fortnight I have been brought from tolerable comfort about the precious creature to a state of wretched apprehension.

[**G.** Church. Dr Brady came. Thought Eliza worse - her breathing certainly is, but her strength is not so much less as I supposed it would be, if what he has said for many months were quite correct - partially, alas, no doubt it is.]

Wednesday 30th March A day of anxiety and sorrow, yet of a peaceful kind. Eliza very poorly, suffering from breath, yet so full of sweet, sweet cheerfulness, which seems to increase with her complaint. I begin to think I shan't go to Welshpool, though unless she is decidedly worse, I must from duty, but the presence of each one she loves is comfort and support to dearest Eliza. I am sure it is a blessed privilege to feel this. I cannot help yet, hoping that strength may be gained in finer weather, which may enable her to struggle with this sad oppression.

[**G.** Too wet to go to church.]

Thursday 31st Up till one o'clock ?staying with Darling E. who was suffering most of the night, not a good one. Afterwards was very bad but she came downstairs, dined with us as usual and was cheerful in the evening and herself prepared our playing at an intellectual game to amuse Mr Sykes. Mamma and Mary went to Brand. Mrs H. Tomkinson and Miss Fanny called.

[**G.** Church. Dear E. very poorly – her breathing getting worse and worse. Wet evening.]

Good Friday April 1st 1836 Up till one o'clock this morning with darling E., who was suffering much with her breath and afterwards her night was very bad, but she came downstairs, and I sat with her while the rest went to church. She said, "I have for some days looked forward to suffering much today, but on no day could I bear it so well." I read a great deal to her – Keble *(1792-1866, a religious writer)*, the Psalms and lessons and 'Farewell to Time'. Talked a good deal and found that she, blessed soul that she is, felt only the dread of bodily pains which she thinks await her! Oh, this day of agony! When can I forget it? Every breath she drew was torture to me. I felt as if it was more than I could bear. Oh, thou who didst suffer for us all take the sorrows of thy servant and support us under our own. Wrote to Marianne about E., dear soul.

[**G.** Church. Mr T.: 'He suffered for us, leaving an example.' A wretched day. Dearest E. suffering sadly with her breath all day and almost sleepless nights. Her strength is diminishing daily. Oh, when will this end? Wet evening.]

Saturday 2nd If any change - an easier night, but sad suffering all the morning, and one bad attack in the afternoon. Dr Brady here many hours - his opinion plainly is that a blessed end is near, but we have seen her strength. This is so much more that we can hardly believe, though an accidental thing might end all soon. I felt a sort of apathetic, languid misery all day, but at night all the bitterness of our trial came so strongly before me, that I felt as if it was too much to bear, yet thank heaven I do not murmur, but to witness this suffering of one so loved, and to know it must sooner or later end - my advisor, my friend, my more than sister, whose boundless love was never diminished by all my faults, though always faithful in pointing them out to me. Thank God, she has not the misery of seeing any of us laid low by sickness. How it should have torn her tender heart.

[**G.** Rather better. Dr B. came. He thinks her weaker than she really is, but we cannot doubt that his opinion in the main is correct viz that any rallying can be only temporary. Snow, rain.]

Easter Sunday April 3rd This blessed day has been one of consolation. She is more easy in body and more alive in mind, I think, and has countenance more placid. More patient, more heavenly, she could not be. In her worst attacks of rattling and oppression, not an impatient look or movement ever escapes her and she speaks with cheerfulness of health. Went to church and received the sacrament.

[**G.** Still E. improves. Sat up two or three hours – more sleep at night. Church in the morning, no service. Sacrament. Many conflicting and agitating thoughts. Such reasons as these make one feel as if prayers in prosperity were no prayers at all. Snowing.]

Monday 4th A better night than we expected, for I had been tortured by hearing her say she should try not to sleep. Waking brought such oppression but was mercifully otherwise, and today has been one of comparative ease. Dr Brady came and he says what we all can see, that she is temporarily relieved.

How long it may last we know not, but for every moment of freedom from suffering, God be thanked.

She was moved into the next bedroom and was able to bear reading a good while.

[**G.** Our dear invalid continues better. Dr Brady thinks her much relieved than he expected to find her. We must try to be thankful for every reprieve, instead of dwelling on sad anticipation. Fine.]

Tuesday 5th April A tolerable night, much the same. A letter from Marianne, which had comfort as well as sorrow in it. A delightful one from dear William, who is the greatest blessing in the shape of a mother-in-law that any people ever had. *(This is difficult to interpret. Does Ellen mean 'son-in-law'?)* If it were possible how glad we should be to have him here, but it cannot be.

[**G.** A pretty good day with dear E., but a sad night of restlessness and oppression. Poor Mary Wicksted heard for the first time that her mother's case is hopeless.]

Wednesday 6th Last night - a very restless one. I was delighted to find Eliza had asked for me several times, but Mary Southwell did not come to me till five in the morning. She soon became more composed and easier, and continued tolerable all day. Another letter. Poor dear Marianne made me very low. I fear her health is not so good as when in London. Carry and I sat with Eliza till twelve o'clock when she fell asleep, after scraping her throat for an hour in a trying way.

[**G.** Dear E. had a great deal of fatiguing expectoration, but it procured the blessing of a good night. Raining.]

Thursday 7th Had the infinite comfort of hearing that dearest Eliza slept from the time we left her till half past four. This was not a very good day. She had four very slight attacks of palpitations. She talked a great deal of her own state and seemed more excited than usual. I am very much against the idea of immediate danger being constantly presented to her dear mind. The much earlier preparation for death and constant expectation are two different things, and I am sure that our human nature is more capable of bearing the blessed parts of the change, when it is supposed to be at a little distance, than when all our natural repugnancies are excited by the idea that the actual bodily struggle is near at hand. She is very cheerful and seems very happy - a lengthened state of suffering is her chief, almost one fear. Carry and I sat up with her till half past one. She suffered much from phlegm; she talked sweetly to us, thanking and wishing us tender nurses in our own sickness - rather let me pray for patience and holiness like hers.

30. Unnamed lady, possibly Eliza.

[G. A day much to be remembered. Mr Turton came to read to our dear E. and I suppose he said something which showed her that her case was more utterly hopeless than she fancied. A great change was perceptible, for she talked a great deal about herself. She asked me how long I thought it would be till she was released. "I wish I knew a little more about the change. Perhaps I shall know nothing till I find myself somewhere with you." I told her that I had an idea that long protracted sufferings, borne patiently from a desire of conformity to the Will of God, might be the preparation for a higher station in the kingdom of heaven. She replied, "I shall be satisfied with the very lowest place."]

Friday 8th Last night was a very bad one. This morning she asked for a book in which she used to write extracts and, after saying, she hesitated to whom she should give it, cried, "You shall have it, Ellen." Dear treasure it will be, but she leaves behind her a valuable legacy - the remembrance of all her holy life, her example, her admonitions - to what we owe her!

This evening came a letter to Mary, giving such a bad account of her mother that they are to set off tomorrow early. This is what we have long expected.

W. Egerton came, not having received his putting off letter. He was so nice and good that he was quite a comfort.

[**G.** After a very bad night I went to E. and she seemed rather hurried. She exclaimed, "Oh, my darling!" and then went down to holding my face between her hands several minutes. I was grievously overcome, but soon recovered myself and read the Psalms to her.

She was not really worse and in the evening she and Ellen, Carry and I had some delightful conversation.

A letter came to summon Mary W. to Ludlow to see her dying mother.]

Saturday 9th A most excellent night. How ?attrac*tive* they are! Poor dear Mary and Charles and the baby set off, a sad parting. Charles will soon return but Mary will very likely never see darling Eliza again.

We had a great deal of very interesting conversation today. We were saying to Eliza how much we rejoiced that she never had the pain of seeing any one of us in such an illness anymore. Her extreme sensibility would have made her suffer so intensely. "Oh," she said, "I never could have been to you of the comfort you have been to me." Surely there never was anything equal to her love for us? She says that she often feels alarmed at feeling herself so dependent on our sympathy, thinking she ought to lean more entirely on God. But surely these afflictions are God's own precious gift, bestowed to sweeten long sorrow and pain, and if every alleviation they give is received from him, it must be all right? Surely this love of heaven, rather than of earth for its pleasures, last in full force after every other earthly blessing has lost its charm?

Dr Brady came. He is surprised at Eliza's rallying powers, and great indeed they are, but if they are only to lead to hopes which are never to be realised they are only a source of greater trial - but all is well. I feel that she may continue a very long time, and surely every day, though one of persistence to herself, is one of advantage and example to us?

[**G. E.** better. Dr Brady was surprised at her improvement, but happily for us all, he retains unswervingly his bad opinion – otherwise the sanguine ones would again be indulging hopes. Showery.]

Sunday 10th April Another very comfortable night. I stayed with her in the morning. Afternoon - went to church. I was sadly overcome on my return by hearing that Mr Turton, who came to Eliza between services, had quite disturbed her by saying over and over again that he wished he could feel that she was patient and submissive to the will of God. Heaven only knows what he meant or whether he meant nothing! Dear soul, she was too meek to say anything to him about it herself, but I was most anxious to go and talk to him quietly about its being right. I gave it up. Far be it upon me to ?hurt or feel my wounded pride on such a subject. I hope I do not, but sure I am, that as far as any weak, sinful human being can show entire patience and submission, nay even acquiescence in the divine will, she does.

I am sure it is the duty of every clergyman to abstain from flattering the sick on their virtues, but to such a person as Eliza, whose whole life has been spent in preparation for the present state, and she is meek and humble and as free from any idea of her *?sin* as one, who had been the most open sinner, could be.

As Mr Turton goes to London tomorrow, we have determined on asking Mr Leigh of Newcastle to come in his absence, and hope and trust he may be a comfort to sweetest Eliza.

This is probably the same clergyman who visited the Egertons, in Madeley when Lady Eglantine was dying. Only in the past few weeks has it been made clear that Mr Turton has been persona non grata to the family as a whole, and not just to Ellen.

[**G**. Dear E, very well. Morning Mr T.: 'The paths of the lord are mercy and truth,' Evening: 'If by any means I could attain to the resurrection of the dead.' Mr Turton came to see dear E. and he said to her, "I wish I could feel that you were resigned," (to die, I suppose he meant.) Our astonishment at dear E. telling us this, knew no bounds, but he being likely, did not understand what he said himself. Ellen wished <u>me</u> to go with her to meet him, as he as on the point of setting off for London, but I thought this would be a hasty proceeding.

Dear E. talked a good deal about God's designs in her long and peculiar illness and probable death. She said she thought the various changes had been sent to teach her humility. She dwelt upon her thankfulness in being spared the sight of any of us in a morbid illness. She said the texts warning against loving our relations too well were more awful to her than any others. She may indeed have some cause to guard against this species of idolatry, but these we have good reason to know that her self-denial and many other Christian graces could not have so abounded without the grace of God. Fine.]

Monday 11th Another good night. Such a beautiful spring day. I feel that if I had not such a weight to put me down, I should be happy to skip and jump like a child.

Mr Sykes and I have great battles about the modern French novel for which he has a fervour just now - and a very corrupting fervour I should be afraid it might be. He advises the writing of H. de Bergerac that, no doubt it is polished writing, but I like not the tone of immorality that pervades every line. It is so disgusting to me that I cannot sit quiet as I read it. It is like listening to a person who is relating as facts what you know all the time to be false. Mr Sykes evidently considers M de Balzac a (?)professed metaphysical : I call him a universal, contemptible sophist.

[**G**. A good day. Charles returned from Ludlow. Fine.]

Tuesday 12th The men went hunting and my dear little agreeable, deaf friend, Mr Saunderson arrived. Carry and I walked him about the grounds. He is the greatest admirer of this place of what he calls its sylvan beauties. He was very agreeable at dinner. Indeed he is a man of delightful mind. *(Mr Saunderson was one of a group of four men who drove up to the hall to look at Charles' hounds on 10th April, 1835.)*

Oh, I am condemned to candour to confess myself perfectly charmed with the first part of Balzac's 'Père Goriot', *(first published in its entirety in 1835. This is a sudden contradiction of her earlier criticism!)* If his sense of right did but bear a small proportion to the talent shown in this book, what a delightful writer he would have been. It is quite of a different stamp to any of the others I have read in a much purer taste, but I'm told it goes off.

Played chess with Mr Saunderson, who beat me twice.

This is Charles' last day of hunting. He actually gives up the hounds. I am sorry for the facing of parting, but do, in my heart believe, that he, dear soul, will be a better and healthier and happier man, when he has given up this irritating and laborious pursuit.

At this point Ellen's first journal ends and the second follows immediately.

[**G.** Dear E. continues to sleep well and to be comfortable in all respects, much more so than when she was exerting herself to come downstairs.

Mr Saunderson, our dear little, new old friend came self-asked. The most agreeable, deaf man in the world, I should think - refinement of mind, that greatest of charm's way conspicuous. He has been, alas deplorably blind on religious subjects, but I hope his eyes are gradually opening. Wet.]

Journal Two: April 1836 – October 1836

April 13th 1836 Mr Sykes departed after having been here a month. He seemed sorry to go as was natural. He left behind him a legacy, which has given rise to much entertainment and discussion. It is a book whereof he is author called essays on a few subjects of general interest. Mr Saunderson has been reading and criticising. He is pleased much with the one on 'The Position of the English Aristocracy'. He makes a remark which I dare say, from what I know of the character is true, viz, that he writes much better on a steady, solemn subject like politics than on any light topics like fox hunting or coaching etc. In spite of all his passion for sporting of this kind, his nature is not calculated for it. It would be well if he could get rid of all the stage coach part of his character. He wants refinement, he does not want strength of thought, but he is deficient in elevation of mind and in delicacy of feeling and taste - which after all, though it may seem a feminine quality is, to my mind, almost as indispensable in a man as in a woman.

Ellen seemed very hard on poor Mr Sykes, again.

We had a pleasant day with our little friend, *(Mr Saunderson).* The only objection I have to his society is that he would make us too conceited. This pleasure in our society is so very flattering, and I think Mamma must have been surprised when he began vaunting her daughters to her.

A letter from Marianne - she is confined to the sofa and sadly wants a sister, but for the present I cannot think of leaving Eliza, though I confess, as far as the nursing goes, one might be very well spared.

[**G.** Joe Sykes went with much appearance of regret on his part, and some feeling of like, though no appearance, on ours. He is certainly wanting in something besides the greatest want of religion, but what the 'something' is, I know not, and never shall, unless he should marry Caroline, which he will not do at present, at all events. I played chess with Mr Saunderson, and had the satisfaction of making a very good defence. We gave him a cipher to find out, which, I think, he seems likely not to do. It is just the thing for women to do better than men.

A good day with dear E. Read two of Mr Dodsworth's new sermons to her. I had hard work to read the one on the Resurrection with a steady voice. Wet.]

Thursday 14th Our dear little Mr Saunderson departed He amused me last night by admiring the 'Johnsonian' style of secret directions I wrote for him. I hope he does not consider it a rare merit in a woman to write English.

Today we moved from the drawing room to the breakfast room – a change to me and never an agreeable one. I think a large bow window has always a good effect on one's spirits, just at a time when Eliza was at the worst. I felt the presence of anyone besides ourselves a great distress, but since then I have thought of a great advantage. She is very comforted today, and goes on having good nights.

[**G.** Dear little Mr Saunderson went. The night before Mama gave him a message from Eliza in reference to a conversation she and I and he had had in the autumn, on the subject of consolation in affliction. He received it silently but with an expression of intense feeling in his countenance, and I hope it will make him consider the subject. Dear E. very well. Showery.]

Friday 15th April Poor Mrs Wigley continues just in the same state, happily not suffering acute pain, but taking but little notice.

I finished 'Le Père Goriot'. It is certainly a most striking story. The description of the 'Maison Vauquer' and the 'pensionnaire' is wonderful. You see all so distinctly, you breathe the very atmosphere of the 'salle à manger'. Then this character of the Père Goriot - his entire devotion to his daughters for whose sake he reduces himself to poverty without feeling any of its privations - their ingratitude, which increases as they become more and more immersed in their follies of 'la vie parisienne' - the occasional out-breakings of better feelings in the younger, who is less heartless - the dreadful truth of the picture of women's vanity when her lover is describing to her on her way to the ball - the deplorable state of her father –

Delphine pleurait, 'Je vais être laide,' pensa-t-elle. Ses larmes séchèrent. 'J'irai garder mon père. Je ne quitterai pas son chevet,' reprit-elle.

'Ah, te voilà comme je te voulais,' s'écria *(Rastignac)*.

- this easily satisfied lover. Eugène's character too – the young man purely brought up, gradually ensnared by the world - his scruples and remorse when he impoverishes his kind mother and doting sisters, whose little savings are all given with joy. The remark,

'Le coeur d'une soeur est une diamant de pureté, un abîme de tendresse.'[1]

- all this is beautiful, very superior indeed to any of those I have read before of M de Balzac.

Modern critical opinion would agree with Ellen that 'Le Père Goriot' is the most influential work of Balzac up to 1836, when Ellen was reading the newly published novel. At the time his writing was controversial. We must remember also that she was not reading it in translation.

[**G**. A good day. Called at the Court. Miss Fletcher very severe on the match between Miss Cotes and Mr Corfield. I am grown wonderfully lenient to my own sex, and that from the charity found by experience. We know so little of each other's feelings. Fine.]

Saturday 16th Charles had another last day with his hounds. It is painful to do anything for the last time, but he brought up his spirits wonderfully and I do think now the thing is settled *(he)* is happier for it. Dearest Eliza was particularly well today.

31. Betley Court.

[**G**. Much as usual.]

Sunday 17th Mamma very poorly and Eliza not quite as well. Staid at home in the morning and lived on the stairs between their rooms. Some officers came to see Charles *(presumably from the Yeomanry)*. Did not stay. Walked with Carry first time this season. Talked of our childhood.

[G. Mr Sutcliffe: 'Lot's escape out of Sodom.' Stayed at home with E. in the evening Mama very poorly but, thank God, at present only bilious, not nervous. Fine.]

Monday 18th Mamma surprisingly well and Eliza pretty well. Wrote to Marianne, promising to go to her. Read some very pretty letters from Dorothy Osborne to Sir William Temple *(1628-1699)*. I think the well educated women of those days were more sophisticated and original than any of us, and when they had educations at all, they were of a more solid kind than ours. I am so frightened when I glance the unfathomable abyss of my own ignorance that I really dare not venture on a further examination, and the task of beginning to enlighten this deep obscurity is so formidable that I feel a shudder, and retire from the contemplation. Thus I go acquiring knowledge, certainly of passing events, dipping into the shallow stream of modern light literature, and I hope picking up some useful grains of experience etc, but still with this yawning gulph *(arhaic)* of darkness and emptiness occasioned by idleness and a bad memory for everything green.

If we consider just how knowledgeable Ellen is, and how much she reads of a serious nature, we realise she is making many disparaging remarks about herself. There is no way her reading could be considered 'light'.

[G. Wrote to Mrs Dodsworth : told her I had compared her husband's sermon on the Eucharist with Bishop Baines' *(1786-1843)* and found they only differed as to the moment, not the nature of the change; the RC supposing it to be effected by the consecration, and Mr D. by the receiving of the bread and wine.

Mama better: Eliza very comfortable. Cold.]

Tuesday 19th Eliza is very much interested in the correspondence between Bishop Jebb [2] and Alexander Knox. She says she feels often that the latter expresses in clear, manly language many of the thoughts and opinions that she has entertained herself on many subjects. How I wish that these reflections of her clear and powerful, though still feminine, mind were preserved – not that I think anyone can commit the inmost thoughts of heart to paper, but still if this dear sister had been in the habit of writing a journal, I am sure there will have been in it much to inherit and delight those who have loved her virtues and admired her talents.[2]

[**G**. Mama worse: Eliza tolerably well. Cold.]

Wednesday 20th April Charles left us for Ludlow where poor Mrs Wigley is dying.

A curious thing happened today which proves the inexpediency of any but straightforward conduct in the affairs of the heart. All indirect enquiries and confidential consultations of indifferent persons are, I do believe, most pernicious and dangerous. This hint I shall give to my nephews or sons *(NB)*. Making a confidant of a sister, I don't think, bad, provided that sister be both sensible and affectionate and discreet, but I think either friends or less near relations quite ineligible for the office. (A letter from poor Mary.)

The 'curious happening' is now explained in Georgina's diary. Ellen was too embarrassed or reluctant to admit what she did accidentally.

[**G**. Charles went to Ludlow expecting to find Mrs Wigley dead. Mama rather better but looking like a lemon: Eliza just the same as usual.

Ellen opened by mistake a letter from Caroline Wigley to Penelope telling her that Mr Baugh Allen had prevailed on her to find out through Mary Wicksted, whether Penelope was favourable to him, and that accordingly she had told him Mary thought Penelope was not. What geese men are, not to risk a refusal by trusting to their own perceptions, rather than employ confidantes who are sure to make some blunder. I cannot think how Mary and Caroline could take so much on them, though they were probably right in their information. Showery.]

The Closing Family Scene

The family is now beset by problems: Marianne, pregnant again, wants Ellen to keep her company, Mrs Tollet is physically unwell, and Eliza's condition is rapidly growing worse. From this point the Tollets have few visitors, and the sole topic understandably is illness.

Thursday 21st Mamma had another bad night. I fear she will be some time getting rid of this painful complaint. Eliza pretty well.

[**G**. Mama worse. Great pain and sickness every night. Mr Short supposes gall stones to be trying to pass. E. pretty well. Fine]

Friday 22nd Mamma again ill in the night, pretty well all day but very yellow. Letters from Charles and William, the latter anxious for me to come to Marianne. I am equally anxious not to disappoint her, but Mamma's continued attacks really make one feel doubtful. I am made very conceited by the commendations which my three, dear sisters make over my intended departure. I am sure it is no pleasure to me to leave them, but I am really sorry for William and Marianne. A sick wife and a sick curate are too much for any one vicar, I was thinking today. Now very happy it is that when by family members one is entirely shut out from all the enjoyments of society, one at the same time loses one's taste and wish for them, and the feeling of dullness does not torment one. Every little improvement in the aspect of affairs, a good night to the invalid, a fine day, a pleasant letter - all these little events assume an importance they would not possess and these are mercifully enabled to support our spirits in seasons, not of active sorrow, but of long continuing uneasiness.

[**G**. Mama still unwell. E. as usual. A letter from William Clive urging Ellen to come to them. Marianne being confined to the sofa, with 'prospects' that I dare not call hopes. She is happier for the present than without them, and so both with respect to her state and Eliza's, we must shut our eyes to the future, except when we pray for help in time of need. Showery.]

Saturday 23rd Mamma had another bad night, so we determined to send for Dr Brady. Before he came Mr Leigh of Newcastle came to see Eliza and he suddenly mentioned to us that our beloved friend Mrs John Wedgwood was dead.[3] The shock was dreadful, though we had been for some time uneasy about her. Surely there never was a woman so formed to be so respected and missed by everyone connected with her. She was more highly gifted by nature than anyone I ever saw, possessing extreme beauty, on which years seemed to have little effect. Talents of a very high order and a charm and manner that is perfectly indescribable, but I believe no-one who ever conversed with her failed to feel her influence, and natural tenderness of heart and susceptibility of impressions, which made her full of expressing sympathy with people. She united a lively cheerfulness of mind and sunshiny temperament, which enabled her to enjoy every flower in her own path to strew them in the way of others too. Added to all these was what was alone lasting and truly valuable, that hearty and genuine piety, that true seeking after holiness which was by God's creed the means of her obtaining, in later years of her life, much clearer views of religious subjects than formerly, and which made her watch the gradual onset of her fatal complaint with such composure and humble hope as true Christians only can feel. We each feel this a personal loss. For myself, there was scarcely a person of my own age, and certainly no-one so much older whose society gave me the real pleasure and satisfaction than hers did, and I feel that hardly anyone remains who loved all those that I love so well as she. This loss, just at the time when, from her coming to live near us again, I had hoped to see more of her, is indeed irreparable and has given me a feeling of gloom I can't express.

When Dr Brady came he ordered Mamma leeches and blisters and said she had an inflammation of the liver.

We heard that poor, dear Mrs Wigley was released from her sufferings.

Ellen has written one and a half sides in her journal as an obituary for Mrs Wedgwood and only one line about Mary's mother who had recently stayed with them in 1835.

[**G**. Mama so ill that we sent for Dr Brady, who immediately pronounced her complaint inflammation of the liver, and ordered leeches and blisters.

Mr Leigh, *(clergyman)*, of Newcastle came to see Eliza, and he told us of the death of our dear delightful friend, Mrs Wedgwood. Such external and internal beauties united I never can expect to see again. The former instead of being a snare only seemed to be the means of increasing the influence of a strong mind, and she never used that influence improperly. She is quite one of those, whose death makes one cling to the idea of recognition in heaven. Wet morning.]

Sunday 24th Mamma much better, surprisingly so. Staid with Eliza who had a bad night but was pretty well. Church in the evening. The sermon on 'The lost sheep' did not interest me as much as usual.

Read a passage in a letter from ?V Kease to Bishop Jebb *(of Limerick)* which pleased me so much because it contains my own humble feelings, expressed so well and by men whose whole heart and soul were devoted to what was good. He says, 'Something lately said leads me to think he may have possibly doubts about me that are very suspect to me to be too much a compromise with the world.' I have thought a little about this, and on the whole I do not think it wonderful. There are some people whose senses must be impressed with a thing before they can conceive it to exist and who can then measure all its energies by the sounds it emits or the appearances it exhibits. To such persons an inward separation from the world is merely unintelligible; it must be palpable and tangible or they cannot take consequence of it. The positive marks of piety too may be ostensible and striking. If they are confined to the closet into the retired walk, they are held problematical. It will probably be said, 'How can a person be so religious when he acts and speaks so like other people and so little resists the actions and practices of the world?' It is not consciousness to want of charity, but that in combination of an animal and spirit, the material part has got a kind of ascendancy which disposes to a grosser, and indisposes to a more abstract mode of apprehending things. To such persons of a decidedly opposite construction will be necessarily unintelligible. I feel I am so to all that class, and I might feel sometimes disheartened by it. *(Ellen's tortuous ramblings continue in the next six lines in such miniscule writing, that it was difficult to understand, or make any sense of the sentences.)*

[G. Mama much better for the remedies, and contrary to our expectations her nerves seem at present uninjured. Morning - Mr Sutcliffe on 'Sickness of Abijah, son of Jeroboam. If any may have a hundred things' etc. We told Eliza of Mrs Wedgwood's death; she was much affected. Wet.]

Monday 25th April Good nights to our invalids. What a blessing!

I am reading or rather glancing over what I have read before: Mrs Jameson's 'Sketches of Literature, Art'[4] etc. How I do long to see Munich and Dresden – indeed, I cannot bear to think of living my life without seeing the Madonna del Sisto.[5] I dream over her descriptions of pictures and imagine them before me, till I gradually get into a sort of fanciful reverie, in which I imagine myself enjoying in turns all the intoxicating delights that fine paintings and sculptures and music and above all glorious scenery can give etc. This is the romance of my life. I awake from my dream and see its realities before me – a sick room, a beloved sister weak and often therefore suffering. I come down from my high imaginations to begin to make gruel, and such is happily the pliability of the human mind and interest in that too.

Dr Brady came and gave a very good report of our invalids. Indeed it was a very good day with them.

[**G.** Mama still improving. Dr Brady quite astonished. Eliza pretty well. Fine.]

Tuesday 26th Georgy and Carry went to call on Mrs Wilson. I staid with Eliza, who was not so well as usual all day and at evening grew very poorly. This is most unfortunate as it will make me more uncomfortable at leaving her. However I do hope and believe it is only temporary.

Read again what I had read before and could not forget viz that book of all others that enchanted me as a child – 'Mrs Leycester's School' *(1808)* was written by Charles Lamb and his sister, who in the period he describes in his essays as Bridget Elia.

[**G.** Mama getting better. Carry and I went to call on the bride, Mrs (Dr) Wilson, whom we found overflowing with happiness, which however great is more or less transient and therefore not to be envied. Called also on Mrs (Dr) Davidson whose husband has not been successful in his treatment of her complaint.

On our return we found poor Eliza very weak and suffering from oppression. Wet evening.]

Wednesday 27th This is dearest Carry's birthday. She is really twenty-one and yet how very young she still appears to me! The whole family is now past its first youth: the last in the procession has immerged *(archaic)* from the bright fields and shady woods, and begins her path along the dusty road.

[**G.** E. rather better and able to sit up in the evening. Mama better. Wet evening.]

It seems very strange to us that there has been no family recognition of Carry's special birthday.

Ellen goes to Welshpool

It is possible that Mrs Tollet, as well as Carry and Georgina, saw how distraught Ellen was becoming in trying to nurse Eliza. Despite her conscience Ellen is persuaded to go to her sister, Marianne.

Thursday 28th This morning with a heavy heart I left my darling Eliza. She had, happily for me, had a good night, but it was a great trial leaving her and Georgy and Carry too, who will, of course, have additional weight on their hands from my absence, and who, I know, will miss me - as I am happy to think I have sometimes been enabled, by the good animal spirits I am blest with, to be a cheering companion to my beloved wife and child.

My lovely drive was passed in deep reflection. Just as I entered Shrewsbury, I was completely overcome by meeting Robert Wedgwood returning from his dear mother's funeral. His look of deep sorrow struck me so much that I would have given the world to indulge my bitter feelings, but as the carriage stopped at the inn, I saw dear William waiting for me, so I was obliged to spare myself.

On reaching Welshpool I found Marianne looking tolerably, and in good spirits, but I sadly fear she will not go on with the child. *(This will be at least her fourth pregnancy.)*

[**G.** Ellen went to Welshpool and to our dismay that very night Eliza was worse than she had been for a month. From six o'clock till two she was struggling with the phlegm, and about half past twelve she had one of those frightful spasms which we know must one day prove fatal. Carry and I were the only ones with her, but I called Penelope in an agony of terror. When the dear creature recovered, she exclaimed, "Oh, what a mercy it would be if God would take me!" - except at that moment I was wonderfully calm externally, and read many psalms and prayers. This night gave me an awful foretaste of the future. May God in his mercy increase our strength!]

Friday 29th Wrote to Mary and Jessie Wedgwood. Felt low and uncomfortable for having lain awake all night. Miss Corbett called and was very pleasant.

[**G**. Eliza better than could have been expected! Wrote to poor Ellen.]

Saturday 30th Walked with William to the castle *(Powis)*. Lucy and Charlotte came here and staid a good while – nice unaffected girls as can be. After they were gone I read a letter from Georgy, giving me an account of a dreadful night darling Eliza had had on Thursday. It is a misery to me to think of her suffering, and I myself am not there to try to comfort her and them! How extraordinary that this attack should come the very day I left her! Blessed darling, I feel every hour I am away from her an hour lost, and sometimes I repent having come here. I hope I did it for the right motives.

[**G**. Eliza tolerably well. Received a delightful letter from dear Jessie Wedgwood, containing some account of her mother's last sacraments, which, though full of intense suffering, were permitted to be most consolatory to her poor husband and children. She repeated, "My dear loves," constantly in her insensibility, a most affecting anecdote for us to hear, who knew what an extraordinary capacity of loving she showed through life. Now her love is expressed in a way that alone could satisfy it.]

May 1st 1836 A day of great sorrow - my anxiety for the post was intense. It brought rather a better account. Church twice - sacrament. Wrote to my dear Georgy.

[**G**. Our sufferer easy and calm. Morning - Mr Sutcliffe: 'The ambassadors sent to Hezikiah after his sickness.' The lord left him to try him.' Evening: 'Lazarus and Dives....']

Monday 2nd Read German. William dined at the castle, so I dined alone. Late at night I had the comfort of a letter from Carry, giving another comfortable account of dearest Eliza, and enclosing a letter from Jessie Wedgwood, which was a most delightful one on the subject of her incomparable mother, also one from Mary Humberston announcing the intended marriage of Sophy to Captain Eccles. I am very glad of it.

Tuesday 3rd Read the new edition of Boswell. It has Croker's notes[6] and a great many besides, and though they may add very much to the accuracy of one's impressions from the book, I am sure they very much destroy their vividness and prevent one from going along with one's author in a way it is pleasant to do. It is like having a person constantly corrected on little points while they are telling a good story.

Had a conversation with Marianne on the subject of some of those feelings and expressions of herself, which have pained us so much. As long as she does not see them to be wrong, they cannot be corrected - they are only smothered or softened by circumstances and are liable to return. Much do I believe was owing to weakened frame and nerves, but how important it is to regulate our minds while we are in health.

A line was drawn across the journal at this point. Ellen does not continue writing her journal now until the 29th May 1836. Georgina, however, expresses her thoughts of grief in her daily account.

Georgina's Journal only

It seems fortuitous now that information is given about Eliza for the next few days. Ellen must have treasured her sister's journal all her life.

[**G. Monday 2nd** Not a good day with dearest Eliza. Much trial by Mr Short talking to her in his usual strain of doing this and that to regain strength.]

[**G. Tuesday 3rd** Oh, my beloved sister, how can I record, as I could wish, the events of this last day of thy suffering existence, so dreadful, yet delightful. In spite of the keen anguish I endured, I could almost for my own sake, wish that it could come over again, that I might dwell with, if possible, more intensity of devotion on thy last looks and words!

When I went to our dear creature on my way down stairs, she had had a great deal of oppression in the night, but added, "It is much better now." I went down to breakfast and returned again to her room as usual. Betsey left it when I came in, but Anne was cleaning the grate. I scarcely opened my book, when quite suddenly a most frightful rattling of phlegm came on. I flew to her bedside but alas! I could not support her for she lay on the wrong side of the bed for me. The symptoms grew more and more awful and she had kissed her hand to me and with the most angelic smile, pointed upwards, before the others could come. God forgive me, but my self control quite forsook me. We all thought every moment would be her last, for the hue of death was on her face, which was nevertheless enlivened with such smiles as might have convinced an infidel that there was within an immortal soul! She continually pointed upwards saying, "There, there," and when she could articulate more she said, "I shall be with Christ," and "Pray for me to go."

I then saw that she was not going at that time, and in a few moments she herself perceived that she was reviving and this seemed a great trial, and indeed it was so to us.

In about an hour from the beginning of the attack her breathing returned to the usual state, and she seemed much less exhausted. Indeed she was in rather an excited state. She was able to bear a great deal of reality. We sent to Mr Sutcliffe to give her the last Sacrament but he was out and dear E. said, "O, if Mr Leigh could but come today." These words had not been uttered an hour when he actually came, by accident, as it might be called, but it was one of those events that one can acknowledge more particularly as a merciful arrangement by the hand of God. I never saw our loved one's face so animated to health as when she said, "Thank God," on hearing of the arrival of Mr Leigh.

He first administered the Sacrament to all of us, and Eliza repeated the responses louder than any of us could do. I shall never forget listening to her saying, "Therefore with the angels etc," knowing how soon she herself be one of that glorious company. I hope it is not wrong to feel that this ceremony, always so solemn and affecting, will hence forward be rendered still more so.

She talked a great deal afterwards to Mr Leigh. She told him that her only fear was that her dying agonies might tempt her to distrust the mercy of God. He told her not to be afraid but to keep the eye of faith readily fixed on Christ. She then added, "But I was very happy in that attack this morning, was not I, Georgy, love?" turning to me with one of those sweet, beaming looks so peculiar to herself. She said after some more conversation with Mr L., "I believe I am a member of Christ's church, and as such that I shall be united to Him for ever."

After Mr L. went away, I had some more conversation with Eliza. I referred again to the peculiar support she had received in what she had supposed to be her dying moments. She said, "O, I am so afraid of acting a part. Do you think I should have smiled in that way if I had been in a room by myself?" I hope I was right in answering that probably she might not, but that the desire to glorify God in death, and to impart comfort to others was doubtless given by God. I then reminded her that many of God's most faithful servants had been tried with the harsh painful deaths, and instanced the late one of dear Mrs Wedgwood; she instantly said, "How I wish Eliza *(Wedgwood)* and Jessie would come tomorrow," but that 'tomorrow' for her *(meant)* in heaven. She called at intervals all the evening; she said to Charles, "You must come to this, remember, before long."

"Yes, I know I must."

She added with most impressive solemnity, "O, remember it; remember it."

At eleven o'clock I asked her if I should read her a prayer, which it had been my privilege to do every night. She said yes. And took the book herself to find the one she wished. Sometime after this, as she seemed quiet and we hoped she would go to sleep, we left her to go and lie down in our rooms, with strict conjurations to be called if she were worse. We had not been away half an hour when we were summoned, but the struggle had come on so suddenly and violently as to deprive her of consciousness. We, at least Carry and I, were spared hearing one awful noise, and those two we did hear were of a kind to make us thankful we had been spared that one, though of course if we had any idea that the end of our beloved one was so near, we would not for the worlds have left her for a moment. The whole scene was closed in ten minutes, so compared with some, our darling was gently dealt with at the last.

There is something so impressively solemn in the knowledge that a soul is passing out of time with eternity, that it seems for a time to check the expressions of grief. And nothing but the lowest sobs disturbed the stillness. Though I do believe no earthly sound could during the last two or three minutes have reached our dying sister.

We were so fearful of any mistake that we continued kneeling in silence some time after the spirit had fled, and then came the first dreadful pang of separation. O, who can imagine it! I kissed her dear face and examined its fearful expression, and how I longed to be with her; she had crossed the narrow stream which divided the heavenly land to ours, and which makes poor timorous mortals starved and thirsty. Let us make ourselves more sure that <u>nothing</u> else may come between us and heaven, and that like our blessed sister the spirit may be willing to go, though the flesh be weak.]

[**G. Wednesday 4**[th] A day of dreadful sorrow, aggravated by the idea of Ellen's sufferings on the morrow. One cannot wish to keep the freshness of grief, but how earnestly I pray that some of our feelings may never pass away, and then indeed we have cause to bless God for this affliction!]

[**G. Thursday 5**[th] **May** Poor dear Ellen came. It was a dreadful meeting! She behaved very well in refraining from much expression of self reproach. When she is called upon hereafter really to see a beloved sister dying, she will know what she was spared in this instance.]

[**G.Friday 6**[th] A calmer day.]

[**G.Saturday 7**[th] Ellen went to look at the lifeless form of dearest Eliza, but I did not. I wished to avoid a second parting and I feared to weaken the idea that she was not there.

I had a kind note from Mr Leigh with some good advice, which I pray that I may be enabled to follow. I think what I have witnessed will make me more anxious, not only to obtain good hope through grace myself, but that others should do the same – for who can sufficiently pity those who not only have the passage through death, but the change to which it leads?]

[**G. Sunday 8**[th] A new day to us. Letters from A Vaughan and Mrs Alington - they have lost almost a sister and so they express themselves.]

[**G. Monday 9**[th] Dear William Clive came and brought a somewhat improved account of poor Marianne. She is anxious to have some of us with her, but we cannot separate yet.]

[**G. Tuesday 10th May** The day of my sister's funeral, and my feelings were less harrowed up than I had expected, for though that tabernacle, so long inhabited by that blessed spirit, one must feel to love in a certain degree. I had taken such pains to cultivate a sort of communion with her real self above, that I was able to think with composure of what might be so dreadful. The words, 'in sure and certain hope,' I constantly repeated, and when poor Papa came in afterwards that was all he could say. May we all through grace obtain that good hope. William Clive went away, to our sorrow.]

At this time it was not usual for ladies to attend funerals.

[**G. Wednesday 11th** Our dear fellow mourners, Mr Wedgwood, Eliza and Jessie, came to see us. It was an agitating meeting, but we had a great deal of comfort in talking to them of our dear departed one and theirs.]

32. Betley Church 1838

[**G. Thursday 12th** Charlotte Langton and Elizabeth Wedgwood came to see us.]

[**G. Friday 13th** Miss Fletcher and Mrs F. Twemlow called. A charming poem from sweet Georgina Bloomfield, full of sympathy and love.]

[**G. Saturday 14th** Nothing.]

[**G. Sunday 15th May** A most trying day. The sorrow produced in church is however of a soothing, holy sort, which has something in it allied to pleasure. I felt strongly the mercy of being spared to pray more than I have ever done, I trust, by the ordinances of God's house.

Mr Sutcliffe with much kind intention preached on 'Blessed are the dead' etc. If it had been a more powerful service it would have been too much for us. Evening: 'Father, I will that they whom thou hast given me, may be with me when I die.]

[**G. Monday 16th** Much relieved by a better account of poor Marianne from her dear, good husband.]

[**G. Tuesday 17th** Nothing. Fine and hot.]

[**G. Wednesday 18th** Mr and Mrs Oldershaw called. Fine.]

[**G. Thursday 19th May** Dr Brady called and we had a long talk with him about Marianne and her prospects. He thinks, I plainly see, there is more risk than Mr Bickerstall does in an artificially produced labour. Fine.]

[**G. Friday 20th** Received a kind, affectionate letter from dear Mrs Kingscote, who is one of the few happily married women who have hearts enough for everybody. She felt her own sister's death so keenly that she knows how to pity others. Fine.]

[**G. Saturday 21st** Jos Allen and Robert Wedgwood called. The scarlet fever prevents our going out among the poor people, which would be a nice employment for us.]

[**G. Sunday 22nd** Morning - Mr Sutcliffe: 'And they were all filled with the Holy Ghost.' Evening - Mr Turton 'As many were led by the spirit of God, they were the sons of God *?(words illegible)*]

[**G. Monday 23rd** and **Tuesday 24th** Nothing *and* Fine *for both*.]

[**G.Wednesday 25th** Poor dear Charles left this house as his home for ever, as long as it is ours - that is to say a melancholy consideration, but this is not at a time we can lament as we might once have done, an event which will make our lives more monotonous. Fine.]

Charles moved temporarily to Brand Hall near Norton-in-Hales, the house they had viewed earlier. Thereafter they lived at Shakenhurst, inherited by Mary, where he and Mary spent very happy lives. He was kind, gentle and a popular local squire and Mary enjoyed entertaining her guests, gossiping and cultivating her garden.

[**G. Thursday 26th** A sad account of dear Marianne from William Clive, an inflammation brought on by excessive sickness. Fine.]

[**G. Friday 27th** A better account of Marianne. Fine.]

[**G. Saturday 28th** Went to Brand, their baby looking *(word illegible)* grown. Fine.]

Ellen resumes her pen

May 29th 1836 The painful task of writing my journal has been long neglected - at first from feeling too much shaken both in body and mind, and latterly partly from our occupation in writing and from a dread in undertaking it. On the very day I last wrote in the book, my precious Eliza died. Oh, what a world of sorrow is contained in these words! The tender dutiful daughter, the devoted sister, the most agreeable companion - all these we lost in her!

On Wednesday 4th I first heard of her increased illness, at least of their idea of imminent danger, and on Thursday morning I set out. Oh, that terrible journey! When I got to Tern Hill and saw Charles come to meet me, I knew all, and notwithstanding all the months of preparation for the blow, it seemed to strike as suddenly as if it was certainly unexpected. Such moments as those are what must ever be remembered, and they must have an influence on all one's future feelings, and the heart that has once known deep sorrow may again feel happiness and joy, but the same it never can be.

I found all my dear fellow sufferers as well as one could expect. I felt sadly selfish at first in adding so much to their grief by my own - but now had bitterness about it that - thank God, they were spared. They had been permitted to soothe the last hours of our beloved one; they had heard her last precious words and seen her dear smiles - but I had been absent from her. Oh, to reflect on her having had the pain of parting from me, to think that she had wished for me and was not gratified - this is most bitter, but God's will be done! I know I was spared much in not witnessing the sufferings of the last day, and I humbly trust I did not act from evil motives therefore - that I was guided and overruled by an almighty and all merciful Father.

On Tuesday 3rd in the morning when Georgy was alone with her, dearest Eliza was seized with a violent attack of suffocating difficulty of breathing. Her countenance was overspread by the hue of death, and Georgy thought the moment was come. In the midst of the suffering her face was lifted up with the most heavenly smiles and pointing upward she exclaimed, "There, there," and afterwards, "I shall soon be with God!"

To the surprise of all, this attack after lasting an hour went off, and she lay all day looking much as usual talking in a strong voice. Charles happily came home and she talked to him and gave him advice most providentially. Mr Leigh came from Newcastle, and gave her the sacrament. She said to him with the greatest animation that I know, "I am a member of Christ's mystical church and as such I shall be united to him forever."

"You will, you will," he replied.

When Georgy alluded to the happiness she had shown and seeing her sufferings in the morning, she said,

"Oh, I am so afraid of acting a part, I am afraid I should not have done the same if no-one had been in the room."

They told her truly that it was God's will that she should glorify him by showing the comfort he gave her. I believe all he ever said of me that day was, 'Poor Ellen,' but I know how much these words expressed of love and pity. She had sent me a message before, that she counted the hours till my return - a return she was never to witness here. But, oh, how great the joy if she should ever receive me where she is! God grant it is in his own good time.

Soon after twelve at night, all was over of her earthly sufferings, and her eternal peace and joy began. Almost her last words were to desire the good kind Mary Southwell, "Not to sit on that hard seat," – the careful regard for others, strong in death. Happy, blessed, angelic sister, may we ever remember thy holy example, to have grace and strength to follow it!

For the first ten days after this event, I felt quite overpowered, both in mind and body. I had no power of exertion and passed the whole day doing nothing, or reading her journal or religious book, but I felt as though I was in a dream of misery.

On Monday 9th May, dearest William came and the next day he followed the remains of the sister he loved and admired to the grave.

The first people we saw afterwards were the dear Wedgwoods, who in the midst of their own grief could feel for ours.

I have had the most melancholy, though interesting, occupation in looking over all our loved one's papers etc. The changes in the characters and feelings of some of her friends. which these old memorials display, are to me so heart-sickening - some of them, whose earthly friendship was so warm, now chilled either by time or circumstances - though, alone of her early friends, is the same that she ever was - the true, the faithful, the beloved Eliza Alington. That friendship was one of them so rarely found, that no separation of distance and occupations could change. When I think how formed she was to be loved and valued and admired, and how entirely was unchanged and unchangeable her feelings of affection were, it grieves me to think that me alone out of her own family can be said to have really and thoroughly enjoyed and returned her peculiar friendship in this life. Truly if this were all I had to hope for, all we had to enjoy, all we had to occupy our hearts, there would be a vast disproportion between our capacities and the demand for them. This must be more and more felt as one grows older, and the brilliant colours in which our young imaginations have clothed the distant prospect fade away as appearances, and give way to more sombre and less inviting appearances.

Far away was this earth, if earth were all,
Though brightened oft by dear affection's kiss.

and yet it is a most beautiful, beautiful world and we all love it too well. I am sure I do. I acknowledge with gratitude, though with trembling, the many, many earthly blessings and enjoyments I have, but those who can so much enjoy, must suffer much too.

Sunday 29th May I was twenty four. First youth nearly passed, allowing it to blast into twenty-five. Mine has been hitherto a very uneventful life, and sometimes I put a wish for more stirring scenes, more active employments, but know not, I think, real important occupation on my hands the mortals can be employed on – in the case of my immortal soul with this I need never be idle - for my own endeavours are necessary, indispensable, though of themselves, useless.

[**G.** No sermon. Receiving the sacrament for the first time since that never to be forgotten day, and kneeling as we now did immediately over the earthly remains of our dear blessed being with whom we last partook. It was a great trial, but there was much comfort with it. Evening - Mr Turton: 'Though fellowship is with the father 'etc. Fine.]

33. The view to the church where Eliza is buried

Monday 30th Mr Foljambe and dear Mr Hodgson came to buy Charles' hounds. Felt very low, but interested in Charles' friends. Poor Mr F. is interesting because he knows what a mourner he has been and, I do believe, still is. Mr H. is an old acquaintance of ours and a firm favourite.

[**G.** Charles' friends, Messrs. Foljambe, Hodgson and Sir T. Boughey came to settle about his hounds. Mr Foljambe must be always interesting as a rare example of a long, mourning widower, though I fear his sorrow has not quite done all it was intended to do for him. His friend, Mr Hodgson, is a man universally and deservedly loved and respected. That such a man should be as he is, is a mystery. Fine.]

June 1st 1836 Dearest Carry went to Welshpool. Marianne has been very ill. I went with her as far as Brand, and found the dear baby quite astonishing grown and Mary very well.

Thursday 2nd The Wedgwoods called and a great event appeared - the rain coming after a month's drought. We are reading the history of *The most Striking Events of* a Twelfth months' Campaign with Zumalacarregui [7] *(1836)*. It is the bloodiest book I ever read, but very clearly written and gives one a great idea of the talents of the guerrilla chief – but how any English officer can be forced to go and fight in that barbarous civil war for the mere love of excitement, I cannot imagine.

[**G.** *commented that Thursday was* fine, *and Friday had* a wet evening.]

(Ellen has no entry for Tuesday and Friday.)

Saturday 4th Dear Eliza Wedgwood came. She can feel for us, and we for her, so well that her company is very delightful to us. We had a letter from Carry, giving us a very poor account of Marianne, who suffers sadly from pains in the head.

[**G.** A letter from Carry with a very indifferent account of Marianne. Eliza Wedgwood came. Her society is always a pleasure and enjoyment. She is quite such a Christian, as one expects to see her removed to a better world - her work in this appearing to us to be done. Showery.]

Sunday 5th June Rather a wet day. A good deal of conversation with Eliza W. on religious subjects, which I hope is improving to me. It is rare to see a person so devotedly religious, yet so totally free from any of those phrases and technicalities and also from the bigotry of a party, as she is.

[**G**. No school. Morning - Mr Sutcliffe: 'The lord hath pleasure in his people.' Evening - Mr S: 'These shall depart with everlasting punishment.' Wet.]

Monday 6th Robert Wedgwood came to dine and take Eliza *(his sister)* before going on a tour with his wife. It is most distressing to see how deeply the happiness of his family is affected by his horrid marriage.

[**G**. A rather better account of Poor M. Showery.]

Tuesday 7th In spite of the rain, Mr and Mrs Tayleur came.

[**G**. Dear Eliza Wedgwood went, Mr and Mrs Tayleur came. Showery.]

Wednesday 8th Gained some gardening knowledge from Mrs Tayleur. Half killed myself with moving the geraniums into the house.

I am quite low when I think of so soon losing the company of dear little Mary Gater, but we ought to be most thankful to have got her into the school with one trial - 365 votes! It is really a great victory for Penelope.

[**G**. Tayleurs.]

The Manchester School for the Deaf and Dumb educated children from the age of eight to thirteen. The regulations stipulated that 'each child must bring the security of two respected housekeepers, to provide him or her with sufficient and proper clothing, during his or her continuance in the school, and in the case of sickness, death or being deficient in intellect, to remove the child from the school.' Mary Gater had been sponsored by the Tollets. Fourteen girls had been listed for election in May 1836 with a complicated system of voting, dependent on the amount of donations to the school each supporter had given. Mary was fortunate because there were seven places for fourteen applicants. Every year £20 had to be raised to support each child.[8]

MANCHESTER SCHOOL FOR THE DEAF AND DUMB.

34. A drawing from the brochure of the School

Thursday 9th The Tayleurs went. Mamma and Georgy went to Keel and agreed for Jessie to go with us to Woodside *(in Birkenhead)*, which I am very glad of. A letter from dearest Carry – an improved account of Marianne, and thank heaven, she writes in good spirits.

[**G**. Mr and Mrs Tayleur went. Mama and I went to the shop at Newcastle, called at Keel, settled to take Jessie W. to Woodside with us. *She had commented that it was* raining *on Wednesday,* showery *on Thursday and Friday and* fine *on Saturday.*]

Friday 10th June We go every day to see poor Betsey Yoxall, who is nearly dying. It is a most melancholy spectacle, a woman who has led a most hardened, careless life, suffering in body and restless in mind, with an expression of discontent, almost of anger in her face, and without any of that deep sense of her sin, which alone could give some comfort in her state.

[**G.** Better account of Marianne. Fine.]

(Ellen does not make an entry on Saturday.)

Sunday 12th I am reading again 'The Young Christian' and I like it extremely. It is clear and plain.

[**G**. Morning - Mr S.: 'Parable of the wedding feast. 'Evening - Mr T.:'The two builders. Fine.]

Monday 13th Charles, Mary and the dear child came, the latter looking fat and lovely, and very good. We had a very pleasant evening, and I felt how happy I should have been, if it were not that one beloved one and precious one is gone, but this thought 'Where is she gone?' comes to silence selfish musing and to make one feel it sacrilege to wish her here again.

[**G**. Charles, Mary and the darling boy came. A grand display at washing time. Lovely sight. Fine.]

Tuesday 14th Beautiful day. Drove Mary and Georgy out. Watered the flowers and passed a happy day – happiness though that was embittered by sad thoughts and remembrances, which my happiness will always be in the future.

[**G**. Mrs Wilbraham and her daughter, Harriet, called. Baby much admired. *(She was the wife of the vicar from Audley.)*]

Wednesday 15th June The Wicksted family departed, Mary preparing for leaving home. I read Bulwer's 'Rienzi', *(The Last of the Tribunes' 1835)* in a great hurry but was delighted with it. I like it far better than 'Pompeii' *(1834)*. It quite laid hold of my imagination.

[**G**.Charles and Mary went.]

Liverpool or Venice of the North

In the 1830s Liverpool was a bustling, fast developing town of the very wealthy and the very poor. For a number of years the Liverpool coast had been regarded as a holiday destination where the waters of the Mersey were thought to be salubrious. After the amputation of Georgina's arm she was recommended to go to Crosby to bathe in the sea water. The hotel where the Tollets were staying in Woodside was probably chosen because of its proximity to the steamer ferry to Liverpool. This was the shortest crossing of the Mersey, known for its treacherous currents. The Wirral was rapidly growing as a commuter belt for Liverpool, now a major sea-port.

On one occasion Ellen visited The Institute for the Deaf and Dumb which was in Wood Street. It had been designed to give free instruction to mute children of poor parents': wealthy parents were expected to pay. At the side of the school was a commodious house for those pupils who lived some distance away.[9]

35. Painting from the album.

Thursday 16th Mamma, Georgy and I set off and were joined at Nantwich by Jessie Wedgwood, and proceeded to Woodside, where we found a clean hotel. The sight of the Mersey made me feel very low.

[**G.** Mama, Ellen and I, with Jessie Wedgwood, set off for Woodside. Dined at Chester and I went to a chattering dentist. Woodside Hotel we found very comfortable. Fine.]

Friday 17th Went shopping. Read Mrs Marsh's new book.[10] It is very poor and commonplace as far as we have read. Bought the new tragedy, 'Ion' *(by Thomas Noon Talfourd 1835).*

[**G.** We twice walked to the shops in the evening.]

Saturday 18th Letters from Carry, Annabel and Emma Wedgwood. Good accounts of Marianne, and glorious news of Augusta Vaughan's happiness and Halford's triumphs.

[**G.** Another shopping expedition. Fine.]

Sunday 19th Went to hear Mr Knox, who both morning and evening preached funeral sermons, which to me are always very painful. He has too much the manner of a popular preacher to satisfy one, but he is evidently very earnest.

[**G.** Went to Birkenhead church. Mr Knox wants simplicity, but is otherwise an excellent preacher. We went in the evening; the sermons were funeral ones: 'The one thing that is needful ....' and 'but Mary' etc. Windy.]

This was the last entry of Georgina's diary.

Monday 20th June Georgy and I set out to shop and see Jane Lawrence, *(the friend Ellen has been corresponding with during past year)*. We met her at *(word illegible)*, and passed the whole morning with her. She was attentive and pleasant as usual. Finished the first 'Tale of the Woods and Fields'. There is so much exaggerated expression in it and little new or original, that I cannot think it will add one grain to her reputation. The last scenes are most harrowing, too pathetic and too agonising to be introduced in a novel, I think.

Tuesday 21st Today Jane was to have come, but alas, it is a day of severe downpour, such a drizzling, dirty spectacle from the windows! I am solacing myself with Willis' 'Pencillings by the Way' *(1835)*, which is a pleasant book.

Wednesday 22nd Again very wet, showery day.

Thursday 23rd Went to meet Jane in Bold Street, and she took us to the Deaf and Dumb school. Most of the children were gone home, but five boys remained, and were so interesting and charming. They quite took to me from seeing I understood them, and began telling me all their news. When I fall into poverty, I think I must take to teaching the deaf and dumb. I had much rather teach them than talking children.[11]

Friday 24th Read 'Ion'. It is a beautiful tragedy, and very touching, and such pure taste. Disappointed at Papa's non appearance. Took a pleasant walk on the little sands.

Began Captain Back's 'Narrative of the Arctic Land Expedition *(to the mouth of the Great Fish River' 1836)*, which would, I think, be interesting. I should have been rather disappointed if I had been he at Ross' getting home without any assistance. *(Ross was his brother.)*

Saturday 25th June Papa came – all well and safe. Jane spent the day with us and told us all the tale of Mlle D'Albini and the Duke of ..? Let me remember apropos of this folly and sin of mine.

Sunday 26th Went with Papa, Georgina and Jessie to J. Lawrence's who then joined our party to go to hear Mr Mc Neil. And now what shall I say? How express about the astonishment and delight I feel of hearing, without exception, the most powerful, the most argumentative, the most eloquent sermon I have ever heard. I feel as if it were the first, the only real sermon I ever heard. The text was Hebrews 3 -5th verse. The argument was in favour of the actual rein of Christ on earth as a king and judge - Christ as deduced from the time of Moses, in his judicial character, and being incomplete without this. He quoted many passages, particularly in the Psalms, put the subject in as clear a light, that it was impossible not to be convinced of the truth of the applications. Then he was obliged to leave the subject only just opened. No written sermon was ever more highly systematic and regular in its construction, nor more unhesitatingly and perspicuously delivered than this extempore one. Of course, no written discourse was ever given with such brilliant, overflowing, feeling eloquence - set aside all religious interest in the subject, all conviction of the importance to oneself and to consider such a sermon surely as the height of human talent. I defy any person of intellect not to be delighted with it. I cannot but be aware that Mr Mc Neil's eternal advantage give him additional effect. He is extremely handsome with a most intellectual and expressive face, and a voice such as I never heard before - clear, deep, sweet and apparently inexhaustible.

Monday 27th Set off to Liverpool, joined J. Lawrence. She took us to see a beautiful monument in bas relief by Gibson[12] to the wife of a Mr Byrom, who died in childbirth. The husband was there to show it. He is extremely handsome, though not a refined man with an expression of melancholy. It is now near four years since she died and he has suffered dreadfully. We also saw his magnificent child, who seemed sadly spoilt, which made one sadder, even more than the eyes of his mother's monument.

Tuesday 28th We steamed away at eleven o'clock to go and hear Mr McNeil again. It was a selection of the prayers from the liturgy and afterwards a most interesting explanation of a passage of scripture, the first chapter Colossians and the twenty fourth verse. He did it most clearly and forcibly, but of course it did not afford an opportunity for the eloquence of Sunday.

Wednesday 29th This day was my blessed Eliza's birthday. Oh, how happily passed by her glorified spirit in heaven!

Thursday 30th Went to Jane's and Mrs Bickerton. The former took me to Cunningham's nursery, when I was delighted and bought five beautiful geraniums for 10/5d *(about 52 pence)*.

July 1st **1836** We went to spend the day at New Brighton, which is a fine open sea place, but the loose sand hills between the houses and the sea are terribly fatiguing, and we were hotter than ever we were before. We got to the hotel then exhausted, and for the dinner, which proved to be one of high and raw lamb.

Saturday 2nd A day of rest. I called however on Mrs Stewart and saw her baby, the ditto of herself. Mr David Hodgson called; he is a strong McNeilite, and will not even allow that he is too violent against the Catholics. General Lawrence also called.

Sunday 3rd Went to Birkenhead church. Papa and ?Mrs Wedgwood went to St Jude's and were as much delighted with Mr McNeil as we were last Sunday. He preached the communion service.

Monday 4th A very hot day, and I hardly stirred at all.

Tuesday 5th Went with Georgina to the W. Earles. Found Mrs E. and Jane in distress, having heard of ?R Gently's dangerous illness, and a better account came while we were there.

36. Mrs Earle, related to the Tollets.

Wednesday 6th July Preparations for departure. The dear Bickerstalls came and drank tea. We were in a sad hurry.

Thursday 7th We set off early to breakfast with Mrs Swan at Chorlton. We did not arrive there till after ten and saw no signs of immediate breakfast, and soon found she knew nothing of our intended meal. Our poor stomachs were much distressed at this, but by eleven o'clock a good breakfast was ready. Meanwhile I had fleeced my cousin of all sorts of flowers. Got home to dinner. Mrs Earle arrived to tea.

A fortnight in Betley

Friday 8th Returning home gives rise to many painful feelings. I could barely say I am more reminded of her I have lost, because wherever I am, her image is ever present with me. No hour ever passes without my thinking of her, but here, perhaps, the associations and reflections assume a more affecting character, and also appear more as a sad reality than the melancholy, yet sometimes soothing dream of past trials and blessings.

(Saturday – no entry)

Sunday 10th July Two most excellent sermons from Mr Sutcliffe, one on 'The Feeding of the Multitude' and the other on the 'Banco Fig Tree'.

37. Mr Tayleur and Miss E. Tayleur of Buntingsdale

Monday 11th Mrs Earle left us, but I did not see the dear old lady depart, as I set off at eight o'clock to go to breakfast at the Brand *(Hall)*, and I arrived just in time, and gave Mary all the purchases I had made for her in Liverpool, which I hope gave satisfaction. Dear baby George was looking much improved both in size and beauty.

Charles drove me to Buntingsdale in the afternoon and soon after my arrival, dear Carry drove up. We dined, walked in the garden and chattered till bed time, and I finished a very rachetting but pleasant enough day.

Tuesday 12th After coaxing Mrs Tayleur out of cuttings of all her best geraniums, came home.

Wednesday 13th Gardened etc. The last day with darling Mary Gater. She was less gay than usual and very tender in her manner, but all grief is swallowed up in the joy and importance of possessing a box full of clothes with a lock and key.

It was Penelope, in particular, who had taken such a keen interest in the education of Mary Gater. Penelope worked for the local branch of the Deaf and Dumb Society in the Potteries, and continued for many years to collect the names of needy children in the area, so that they could be educated in Manchester in the special school.

From the information supplied to those entering to the Manchester School for the Deaf and Dumb we discover that Mary Gater would have had a medical examination to see whether she would be a suitable pupil. Details about her health, (such as having good eyesight, having received the cow pox inoculation and information about whether she had suffered whooping cough and measles) would have been supplied before she could be admitted. It was also a requirement for her to have been baptised. The box which she took would contain the regulatory items of clothing, which 'must be repaired and kept by her friends during her continuance there': for girls in 1836 the list was:

Six shifts
Six pair of black and dark stockings
Six pocket handkerchiefs
Four night-caps
Four dark coloured gowns or frocks
Two flannel and two stuff petticoats
Two pockets
Four pincloths, or bibs and aprons
Two tippets or shawls
Two pair of gloves
One black cloak or spencer
One hat or bonnet
Two pair shoes
Two combs and a comb brush
Two towels [13]

Thursday 14th Our little, poor lamb departed after being kissed by every maid in the house, not excepting Black. When I began to give some solemn admonitions at parting, she spelt out, "Mary come. Mary come," very vehemently, and put up six or seven fingers to show she should be back in a week. Poor little soul, I fear she will be unhappy at first.

Mamma, Penelope, Georgy and I went to Maer and Keel and had pleasant calls.

Perhaps, as before Mamma has taken her daughters out to take their minds from the plight of Mary Gater on leaving her adopted home.

38. Keele Hall 1810.

Friday 15th July The long expected rain came in the morning, and Charles, Mary and the baby in the afternoon. In the evening came sitting on thorns *(half-rhyming for 'thunderstorms')*, one of which ran in deep, and though I was reading and nobody thought I had heard, I had a good ten minutes of heart bumping, face flushing etc. Carry, I suppose, feels youth is even more troubled at those things than I am. I feel great danger of seeking consolation for disappointments in our earthly concerns, in others equally earthly, instead of seeking it from the only true source, and making every moment of suffering such an occasion of changing more than ever to perishable objects of affection, instead of its urging one to fix those affections more and more above this earth and all it contains. I must also learn to guard against an excess of sensibility, or rather let me call it irritability, which makes trifles affect my happiness so much more than I ought.

Saturday 16th Carry and I had a hard morning's work potting geraniums. Emma Wedgwood came to tea.

Sunday 17th Two excellent sermons – one on the knowledge of our own characters and of the truth to be gained from the scriptures and the importance of remembering this; the other on the instances of God's favour of the widow of Sarepta and Naaman, the Assyrian.

Monday 18th The Wicksteds went. We went to the workhouse to see dear old S. Hawkins who is near eighty and suffering from a cancer. Her whole existence for the last ten years has been one of suffering, yet she is cheerful and inspiring, an example indeed. It is really beautiful to see poor old George Wilding ministering to his poor companion's mind and body. They are the only two beings in the workhouse blessed with intellects and not being mad, idiotic or in dotage.

Welshpool again and the law

Perhaps Ellen and her mother and father are now visiting Marianne and William more on a social visit than trying to keep up her spirits. As yet there has been no announcement of 'a little expectation'. William's vicarage was just above the main street, next to St Mary's Church. He also was in charge of two other parishes in Shropshire. The house had a sizeable garden stretching down to the road and the town centre, with pasture land extending to the canal. There were views across the valley to the Long Mountain.

Tuesday 19th Packed up and performed many melancholy duties

Wednesday 20th July Took leave of home, and as I kissed the fresh soft cheeks of my sweet, sweet Georgy and Carry, I felt how hard it was to part even for a short time, and the recollection of the long parting that had taken place between us and our equally dear Carry and me. Oh, what a lesson that is between near relations, when sympathy in tastes and characters and feelings is joined to the natural love of kindred! I feel that one can never be thankful enough for being allowed to enjoy such a blessed connection.

Arrived at Welshpool. We found Marianne well and in good spirits.

Thursday 21st In the afternoon Miss Corbet and her brother called and we went in a hard shower of rain to look over the garden wall at the entrée of the Judge. Alone in his father's carriage, the far famed and much admired Halford came first. Soon followed the procession, and dripping wet we starers came in. Papa and William walked down to meet them, and then the Judge and his son came up to dinner. In the evening the Judge and I had a good deal of conversation with dear, good, clever Halford. Oh, how intensely proud I should be if I were Augusta! *(his mother)*

He brought us his essay, which I saw, at the first glance, was above my comprehension. What a humiliating contemplation that is, that of one's own ignorance, when it is brought before one, by being in the presence either bodily or spiritually, either in person or through a book, of a really manly understanding. Weak minds and strong hearts are our women's portion, and circumstances seen all to concur to increase the natural tendency, but never let us regret it. If we feel as I do that, though worse our fate on earth in many respects, yet heaven is nearer of access to us. If from our natural susceptibility of impressions, liveliness of imagination, we are in the slightest degree more inclined to receive religious truth, and thus to be led to raise those large, boundless affections of ours to those objects which are worthy of all, and more than all, and which can never fail or disappoint us - then let us rather rejoice that a woman's mind, a woman's power, a woman's heart is ours.

Friday 22nd At one o'clock the marshal came for us and took us into the court, where I had never been before. There Mamma and I sat on each side of the judge and heard a rather good case of salmon stealing. The prisoner was a bad looking man, and I could hardly feel sorry for him. The study of faces was very amusing to me. I wonder lawyers are such pleasant men in private as they, I think, generally are. It is to me such a heartless, soulless occupation. *(We must remember that George Tollet was a lawyer, as was Mr Pryor.)*

A quiet evening, for Papa and William dined with the judge, so Mamma, Captain Justice and I ate here.

Saturday 23rd We went to the court again and heard the opening of a case about a few yards of land, which is made as much fuss about as if it were a large estate. The counsel who spoke was a wretched performer full of terrible bad emphasis and bad grammar, but in spite of this, all thought justice was on his side, whether the law was, remained to be proved. I was amused on the whole with the scene.

Lady Lucy and the ?Pughs etc. called.

Sunday 24th A most excellent sermon from dearest William. The morning - on 'The spirit beareth *(a couple of illegible words)* with our spirit that we are the sons of God'. He remarked how much we should be found wanting if we were only hedged by our own consciences etc. After church Lady Lucy and the girls came.

In the afternoon Halford came in to wish us goodbye, as he was going to walk to Dolgelly, *(a distance of about twenty-five miles)*. We thought him not looking well. How can he ever make a lawyer? He lives in a world of his own and his mind seems constantly going on high matters. Surely it can never come down to all the little work necessary for a lawyer. There is something about him that inspires me almost with almost a feeling of awe - whether it is only my own extreme admiration of goodness and talent or whether it is anything in him more awful than in anyone else, I don't know. But I suspect he is a little shy and this is always infectious.

Monday 25th July Went into court at nine – stayed till three and in again from four to half past six, and at half past I went to the castle *(Powis)* to dinner.[14] About eight, the judge arrived and dinner was commenced upon. Oh, it was a very weary dinner! The judge and Lord Clive buttered each other and then the judge ladyshipped Lady Lucy and so strong was the courteous infection that Papa began to lordship the judge. The conversation was learned and gené and that, in a party of seven is positively unbearable.

Tuesday 26th Drew for Lady Lucy this morning. I am not eating toads, but I was glad of the employment. I had a long talk on the trial with Mr Griffiths, the attorney.

39. Wallop near Welshpool, the home of the Severnes.

Wednesday 27th Papa and Mamma left for Wallop, and just after luncheon, Charles and Mary arrived. We had hardly expected them, but were very glad to see them. They had a most lovely drive. Pleasant evening. Mary much mused with our tame Captain *(Captain Justice)* whom she thinks a most desirable piece of property.

Have the Tollet parents brought Ellen on this visit to introduce her to eligible suitors? So far she has seen lawyers, and now Captain Justice, who visited Betley with Robert Clive earlier in the year.

Thursday 28th We went with Charles and Mary to the top of the park *(at Powis Castle)*. Rather a hazy view.

Friday 29th Charles and Mary went.

Saturday 30th July Lady Lucy and five of her children came to see Marianne. They are a nice set of unaffected, sociable creatures as I ever saw.

Sunday 31st The same party with the addition of a long Adonian youth as tutor, and a short old lady as governess. Mr, Mrs and Miss Corbet came to take leave.

Summer in London

Travelling in great comfort in the britzka, the group set out on a journey of about 180 miles to London. The route had been well planned for them to see some of the most splendid recent architectural sights, especially in Birmingham.

August 1st 1836 After much bustle and fuss, which began at eight o'clock in the morning, we were at ten o'clock safely stowed in Lord Clive's britzka, in which we lay very comfortably and off we drove. We got to Birmingham that night and saw for the second time that beautiful Town Hall, [15] which pleases me more than any modern building I ever saw. We also saw the new school, a very fine gothic building by Barry.[16] The carving of the stone is the best I have seen, so very soft and round - one can hardly believe the material is stone. Saw the bronze model of the Warwick Vase.[17] How indescribably graceful the handles and wreaths are!

Tuesday 2nd Got to Oxford to dinner. More impressed with the sight of this city than I had ever expected. I longed to have been a man to have been educated here, and wondered how anyone could be frivolous or vicious among such venerable buildings. We walked down to the river from Christ Church and I thought of Charles and of the generations past who had succeeded one another in the enjoyments and labours, the follies and vices of a college life.

The same thoughts had been expressed more forcibly by her ancestor, Elizabeth Tollet (1694-1754), in the poem 'To my brother in St John's College in Cambridge'; her brothers also had enjoyed the education that she coveted.[18]

Wednesday 3rd We arrived in Grosvenor St, and very melancholy my feelings were on entering the house in which happy days had been spent with one now lost forever. Henry Clive dropped in this evening.

Thursday 4th I had the great delight of seeing my dear, dear friend Annabel Crewe. She is not at all altered in any respect, but grown taller. She is just as simple, as pure minded, as sweet tempered as ever, and Marianne and I both agreed that it was a truly delightful feeling, that of being so completely satisfied with anyone. William and I, and Annie and Henry did a little shopping, and saw Mrs Cunniliffe for one moment. In the evening went to see Mrs Sykes at the Warren Hotel. *(Was she the mother of Psyche? She seems to be appearing in another holiday destination of Ellen.)*

Friday 5th August Went to see the Diorama,[19] a very sea-sickly sight. Not very wonderful. A beautiful. Lady de Bache called, looking very elegant. Dear William went back with Lord Clive today to our great sorrow.

Saturday 6th Miss Bagot and Mrs Danille called, and Lady John Russell, who looked very pretty but very languid, and I thought not so very pleasing as when I last saw her as Lady Ribblesdale. Then came the Duchess of Montrose who was very silent but seemed to like our talking to her. Mary dined here in the evening. As we were sitting who should drop in but Miss Coape. She was sadly puzzled, I'm sure. *(She had visited Betley Hall on October 9th when Ellen imitated her before she arrived.)*

Sunday 7th Went to hear Mr Scobell in Vere St. A good sermon but too 'malapropistic' for my taste. After luncheon I half killed myself walking to Knightsbridge to see Mrs Lister, who was not at home. As we were dining, in came dear Annie and we spent a pleasant evening together.

Monday 8th Went to see the British Gallery. Was rather disappointed by the two Murillos bought by the Duke of Sutherland from Soult's collection. Delighted with the exhibition altogether, and also with the National Gallery.[20] Caroline Bury came – she is little altered by the ten years absence and is very sensible and excellent creature, and I think myself very fortunate that my choice of a school friend has proved so judicious.

This is the first time that Ellen has mentioned that she actually went to school. Earlier Penelope recommended that the Wedgwoods, who took one of the Tollet's houses in Betley, should employ a governess to educate their children whilst they were young, just as the granddaughters of George Tollet were taught.[21]

Tuesday 9th Walked with Caroline to some shops in Regent Street. Lady de Bache called and brought her little girl, one of the most pleasing children I ever saw. The boy is gloriously handsome with very nice manners. Caroline lost a £5 note, which after a great search was at last found in my pocket, when I had had it with her handkerchief in mistake for my own.

Wednesday 10th August Charles and Mary went, and Mrs Sykes took me to see pictures. The Duchess of Montrose and Lady Emily Montague called and many others. After dinner walked with the Captain *(Justice)* to Park St, Westminster, and drank tea with Miss Williams and Miss Bagot. Came home by street lamp light - lovely evening lights for Betley Pool.

Thursday 11th Lady de Bache took me in her britzka first to see Henry's picture at Woods', where I saw a most touching portrait of a grandson of Lord Egremont, who is dying of consumption. It is not too painful but so affecting that I longed to be alone and cry. Then she took me over to the Zoological Gardens, [22] where I saw the giraffes, and she and I chatted while the children skipped about like young lambs.

Friday 12th The morning of this day of carnage was spent in walking to Covent Garden Market. I was disappointed. It is not near so striking a sight as the Liverpool one, though, of course, the collection of fruit is much finer. *(No explanation of the carnage is given.)*

Poor dear Captain went. *(We should perhaps assume that Captain Justice came with them from Welshpool.)* Such a loss to us. I don't reason what we shall do – no-one to ring the bell, or walk out or do anything useful.

Saturday 13th Lady Plummer came and staid nearly all day. *(Was she the sister of the Rev Turton?)* Then came Mrs Verne and Mrs Browne and Mrs Nickill. At nearly six a thundering knock and a strange figure entered by the name, Miss Ikey. This acquaintance of our morning visit has produced much fruit certainly. With her was Miss Blount, Mary's friend too, and they both made themselves pleasant, though Miss I. is only demi-sane, I believe, and her old face peeping from out a gipsy hat and showers of ringlets looked like anything but what a discreet woman's face of a certain age ought to look.

Caroline Wigley had met Miss Ikey too. Apparently she was notorious as an old maid who was desperate to trap a husband. It was rumoured that she had proposed to at least twelve men and 'been refused by all.' She was described as 'the maddest woman that goes loose. She chose to dine and sit all day in a straw bonnet and long veil.' [23]

Sunday 14th was such a wet day that I could not go to church in the morning. Mrs Nickill came and went to hear Mr Dodsworth. Mr and Mrs N. dined here and we went in the evening to ? Mary's Chapel, but heard a very uninteresting sermon from Mr Mayors.

Monday 15th August Lady de Bache was to have taken me to the Nickills, but was prevented by her friend's being in labour, and the poor thing had a dead child.

Tuesday 16th I went in a fly [24] with R[25]... to Richmond. It was rather a happy day. But I did not see the view to advantage and was rather disappointed. However I admired the park exceedingly. We had a delightful drive, and my gossiping driver, and a tea party in the evening - Mr, Mrs and Greville Moines, Mr and Mrs Master and Miss Carlton and Lord and Lady James Stuart. I was much amused with hearing Mrs Cuniliffe and Mrs Moines talk. I like Mr M. exceedingly and wish he had had the luck to choose a less tormenting wife.

Wednesday 17th The sun shone bright through the trees and upon my latticed windows. I opened my eyes and they woke upon the forms of two huge bugs, bugs! I had never seen them before and after purifying myself with cold water, dressed and sat reading.

Took a delightful saunter with Annie and then drove home that is to Grosvenor St, where I found Marianne very well, and having had Miss Bagot, Mr B. Allen and the Duchess of Northumberland in my absence.

Thursday 18th The little Nickills spent the day and were very good and pleasant. I went with Lady de B. to the Millbank gaol, and found dear Mrs Nickill very comfortable. *(What was she doing there?)*

Friday 19th Went after breakfast to the Holme, where I found Hester Hawkins ill in bed, so I was obliged to go to York Terrace, where I spent the morning, and then Elizabeth Dodsworth took me to Westminster Abbey, where we heard the service, and the glorious organ delighted me beyond measure - besides it was my first sight of the interior.

Saturday 20th August I forget what happened but on **Sunday 21st** I went to *?(word illegible)* Chapel with Lady de Bache after having breakfasted with her in a beautiful furnished house, and having heard darling Rosie repeat seven of eight hymns and a parable, walked home to luncheon.

40. Mrs Dodsworth and Mrs Haden.

Monday 22nd Went to Waterloo House. Shopping with Miss Coape. I don't think I had a signal success – not much, as I saw prettier gowns in the windows than those I bought.

Tuesday 23rd A very wet afternoon. Mr R. Justice called. The carriage came to fetch me to go to Richmond. A tolerable night. At least saw no bugs.

Wednesday 24th After drawing the view from the window and dining early, we set off (and we were: Mr M., Annabel and myself) to Hampton Court. Passed Strawberry Hill (which disappointed me terribly), and the fine chestnuts in Bushy Park and then arrived at the palace. I was quite delighted with the cartoons. I think my favourites are 'The Healing in the Temple' and 'Paul Preaching at Athens'[26]. We came home and drank tea, and then went to the play and saw Mrs Nesbitt in the 'Belle's Stratagem'[27] and a very good farce called 'The Wedding Day'. She is a very pretty actress - except one of her coadjutors were *(sic)* the most obscene, vulgar, horrid set without a single H.

Thursday 25th August Mrs C.*(Lady Crewe?)* brought me back and sat a good while here. Found that the Duchess of Northumberland had been and had seen my drawings, and been as lively and nice as ever. Miss Bagot came and W. Hawkins and Hector in the evening.

Friday 26th Wet morning. Captain Justice arrived. Walked and talked. The Nickills came to tea.

(Time gap.)

Monday 12th September 1836 My journal has been entirely neglected the last fortnight. There is a sort of idle business in London even at this time of year which makes time pass without ever doing anything useful. We have had the usual routine of callers etc. The new people I have seen have been Mrs Blount and a young daughter, the Duchess of Northumberland, who is a woman quite to my heart's liking, as far as I could see and the Miss Walpoles, who were very pleasant.

The chief event was our going (William, Marianne and myself) to visit Mr Selwyn at his father's house at Richmond. We had a very pleasant time. The only fault we could find was with the over cleanliness and white glare of the house, and our only fear was lest its clean mistress should unexpectedly return and be shocked at us, dirty Londoners.

I walked round Kew Gardens, where there are many fine and uncommon trees and the most beautiful cedars I ever saw. In the morning Mr Selwyn and Henry rowed me from Kew to Twickenham. I never enjoyed anything more in my life. It was a lovely morning and one of those days when there is a sort of fine blue, atmospheric look about the distance, and yet no haziness – the river was so bright and clear and the reflections of the fine trees so picturesque. There is a group of abials *(sic)* near Twickenham which are the most graceful trees I ever saw. We came home on Thursday 8th.

The following are retrospective entries:

Mr and Mrs Nickill dined with us, and **Friday 9th** Poor dear old William went away *(to his parishioners in Welshpool).*

Saturday 10th September Captain Justice arrived, having heard of his brother's illness, and Penelope also came up in the evening. We heard from Mamma, who gave a very interesting account of an interview that a neighbour has had with darling Mary Gater, who is improving in her accomplishments. She has not forgotten home and us, for she burst into tears on seeing Holding.

Sunday 11th I went with Penelope to hear Mr Dodsworth - a very good sermon, but I do not quite understand his opinions about baptism. In the evening Lord Powis called, and as he is nearly blind we had a great scene of confusions.

Betley in conclusion

October 17th 1836 I don't know exactly why, but I found it quite impossible to keep my journal regularly in London, so I gave it up until the usual routine of home life should be renewed. It certainly was not gaiety in London which dissipated my mind, but there was a something which, I suppose, belongs to the atmosphere of a great city which is at least a part of the effect it produces on country constitutions, both of the body and mind.

41. Mr Alington.

One of the most interesting treats in my sojourn in Grosvenor St was seeing dearest Eliza Alington, the beloved, the faithful and the worthy friend of our darling Eliza. We meet in sorrow, for both our hearts were full of tender recollections of the one we have lost, and added to this, the dear soul is called upon to bear the heavy, heavy trial of being the eldest daughter in a state of health for which there is more to fear than to hope for dear little Lizzie! It is more painful to see one so young and so sweet called upon to endure suffering, which it requires, as we well know, so much faith and so much habitual discipline to enable a person to bear well. But strength can be given even to the weakest.

Papa came to town for a few days, which he enjoyed very much. He found great changes and improvements and delighted us by showing his strength and activity in walking many miles every day.

I took my leave of dearest Marianne, mother-to-be. We shall not meet again till she has gone through her great trial - an event which will either make her the happiest of the happy, or plunge her a third time into deep distress. It is fearful to contemplate, and I hardly care think of it; God grant we may be full of gratitude or of submission when the time comes.

42. The Roebuck Inn, Newcastle about 1800: Ellen has now become free to travel, unaccompanied.

I accomplished my very first journey in a coach since I was a child with very great ease and safety, but without any of those amusing adventures which attend Penelope's voyages.

The period from 1836 - 1841

The day by day journal ends with a time gap of five years before the final one begins. During that time the age of Victoria was celebrated with great pomp in the village of Betley. It was also a time of change, because with the advent of the railway, people could move about more freely. Main lines had reached Crewe by July 1837, when the Grand Junction Railway, designed by George Stephenson and Joseph Locke, was opened between Liverpool, Manchester and Birmingham.

However a few facts about the Tollet household are known.

Francis Twemlow and George Tollet were vice-presidents of the local Branch of the Deaf and Dumb society in 1836, and then after two years, the latter became the chairman. From the correspondence between George Tollet and Mr E. Wood, the secretary, we can see that he was most concerned in helping to improve the lot of the poor. He suggested that the names of the subscribers to the association should be published, in order to raise more money for the school in Manchester. Both he and Penelope were major subscribers. In 1836 the Branch of the Association was in its infancy and rules were being formulated. George Tollet sent a letter to E. Wood stating that he had read the proposals for the new report and discussed the ideas with his daughter who was unable to take a positive role, because of her sex. This was to build an institution for the blind, deaf and dumb in the area.[1]

The story of Mary Gater in Manchester continued. An occasion which must have created a considerable subject for discussion was the return of the local children from the railway station in June 1839. Parents or guardians were always advised by the school when the children were to be collected for the vacation. Their transport was by train from Manchester to this area. Penelope Tollet wrote, 'Miss Tollet will be much obliged to Mr Powell to inform her when the day is fixed for the return of the deaf and dumb children. If they return by second class train, Mary Gater will meet them at Basford, if by a first class at Crewe.' Another boy from Newcastle would have the same travel arrangements as those of Mary.

However their plans were not successful, because the other children from this area did not leave the train at Whitmore, the junction for Newcastle. There was panic and a hasty exchange of letters sent immediately by train.

> Mr Bingham and Mr Patterson to Mr J. Powell Secretary to the Branch Association for the Deaf and Dumb, Burslem.
>
> June 24th 1839
> Dear Sir,
> I am very much surprised that the children have not arrived, as they were sent on Saturday by the 4 o'clock pm second class train, particular instructions given to the conductor, both by Mr Patterson and the manager at the station here to leave Gater and Lawton at Basford and the rest at Whitmore, their bags were also directed, so that I cannot understand their non arrival. I will send Mr Patterson immediately to the office to make some enquiry and if he can ascertain anything respecting their non-appearance at Whitmore. He will send word in this letter.
> Yours obediently,
> N. B. Bingham
>
> Secondary message:
> The director will write by the next train to the Basford and Whitmore stations to make an enquiry respecting the children - where they have arrived. The Guard by whom they were sent has not arrived from Birmingham.
>
> Underneath I have just seen the guards who stated they were taken on to Stafford station, but would be forwarded by the train the next morning. I shall be down at Whitmore by the 4 o'clock train to know whether they have been met with and forwarded properly.
> Yours truly
> A Patterson.   Railway Office

Again Penelope wrote a formal note to Mr Powell, Burslem, saying that she was happy 'to inform Mr Powell that Lawton and Gater arrived safe at Basford station on Saturday. Miss Tollet is sorry to hear of the mistake respecting the other children.' The letter was stamped 'Ju 26 stle- under'.

The letters from other parents of the children were more enlightening. On 27th June James Carter wrote,

> Sir, my dauter eli came safe home on Sunday the 23 day of june a woman brought them from N/C. Sir, I Will pay the fair When She goes back. Sir, please to send a Note a few Days before they go back. Your humble servent,/ James Carter.

Another parent sent a letter to Mr Powell explaining the missing hours. His son arrived on

> Sunday morning by Mr Green's Omnibus from Whitmore. All that I can learn is that they slept at the inn at Stafford, returned by the railway to Whitmore. I took one part of the children and my sister the other to their own homes - except the father of the little boy from Stone - he fetched him.[2]

After completing her education in Manchester, Mary Gater was employed by the Tollets. She was reported to be a good farmhouse servant, successfully making cheese and earning her livelihood.

One of the recurring themes in Ellen's journals was of marriage. In a conversation with Emma Wedgwood, she commented that she would rather marry for love and money, but rejected the possibility of an uncultured suitor like Lord Hungerford Crewe. Marriages between people of differing ages were scorned, as with the third marriage of Mrs Acland to the ageing Mr Hinckley, nor did she wish to marry 'some commonplace man.' In this context she mentioned the ordinary marriage of her friend, M.A. Northen, to Dr Wilson of Newcastle. Had she wished to be totally independent, it would have been difficult, unless she were a writer, governess or teacher. The thought of teaching had not escaped her; she stated that she would rather teach deaf and dumb children than 'speaking' children. This was not for her a serious option.

From 1835-6 there were possibly a few opportunities for her to marry. She could have encouraged Hugh Acland, Psyche or Lord Crewe, who showed some interest. Her relatives were trying to produce eligible bachelors for her at Christmas 1835 and in London 1836, but despite her 'animal spirits' she remained single. As a consolation to herself, she said, 'Everyone seems to marry sooner or later,' perhaps hoping the perfect man would appear. The prospect of having children was mentioned on 4th April 1835 when she commented she could not understand why Marianne and Mary Wicksted wanted to produce children: 'the trouble of being a mother is too great for one to desire it very vehemently, I think.' Yet she loved children herself. Her obsessive devotion to another person was revealed in her third journal, when she may be thought to have the best of both worlds. She was fortunate as an upper class lady to have an income large enough to employ servants, with the freedom to do as she wished. Her maternal grandmother had left legacies to all the Tollet girls.

At the back of her first journal there was an essay written on celibacy for women, which seems to us very old fashioned. (The writing was very difficult to transcribe.)

> It is this same false and vulgar state of opinion with regard to celibacy in women, to which I attribute the very great want of real gallantry of feeling among the men of the present day. Those who live in good society preserve the appearance of it towards each individual respectable woman, but hear their general remarks, their conversations with each other, and you will discover that there is little besides the outward show which every gentleman knows is becoming to him. It is true that the immediate cause of this is the degradation which has brought on itself by the disgusting designs of mothers and the scarcely less evident, though far more palatable attacks of their daughters, which every man with any competence has had experience of - but all this eagerness, this capacity for matrimony in itself, whence does it proceed? - not entirely from a wise assurance of its advantages as a state, but from a dread of the ignominy of celibacy which almost every mother feels for her daughters, which to every daughter is taught from earliest growth to being a severe misfortune, if not a public disgrace.[3]

She was deploring the fact that girls were conditioned to expect marriage as the only option in life.

On December 21st 1835 during the discussion with Mr Butt on loyalty in marriage, he argued that men may be allowed to make mistakes. Ellen disagreed. She thought there should be equality. Was she an early feminist? In the 1830s she was too early to embrace the idea of the equality of the sexes in life generally - her religion taught female submission, and she would not question it.

The social life of the Tollets resumed its normal pattern in 1837. So far we have seen their life from the point of view of the daughters. In the following letter, when George Tollet was trying to arrange a meeting with Mr E. Wood, we see how busy he was, when he wrote in April, saying that his wife and daughters were going to London and he had to see them off on Wednesday. On Thursday he had a turnpike meeting, which he had had to abandon, for a more urgent engagement upon one of his Foxley Farms.

> On Friday I go to my son's and don't return until Monday when I expect Lord Bloomfield and his son on their way from Ireland, and they may come any day that week, and I expect my son and Mrs Wicksted on Wednesday or Thursday in that week and then return from Mr Shirley's Hunt. *(Charles Wicksted had earlier announced that he had renounced fox hunting.)* They leave their little boy here and, in the absence of Mrs Tollet and my daughters, I must be the sole nurse ....

He leaves himself open for a meeting on 24th, 25th, 26th, but prefers the 28th. He comments that he was so pleased to hear a good report of Mary Gater, and was happy that such institutions, as that in Manchester, were having such a good effect. On the 3rd or 4th May he was going to London himself, 'so that I shall be there in the midst of all the great rail-road battles as a quiet looker-on.'[4]

In 1837 George Tollet declined the highest offer given to him - of a baronetcy by Lord Melbourne for his service to the Whigs. How his family reacted to this we do not know.

As always Mary, who now has a second son, Charles, took a keen interest in the courtships of her sisters-in-law. We know that Mr Baugh Allen had made enquiries about Penelope, and we now learn through a letter to her sister Caroline Wigley that he was very interested in Georgina. Once again the two Wigley sisters have been match-making. On 11th July 1837 Mary wrote:

> What do you think of the aged Baugh *(from Dulwich College)* again appearing on the tapis and calling upon them just after breakfast one day last week, not to reproach his old love, not to sigh and say nothing, but to thrust a real live letter with a real live offer into Georgina's hand, saying he had long admired her, hoping if she did not approve his suit she would continue to treat him with her former 'innocent confidence', but if 'he nestled in a corner of her heart' he begged she would express the feeling and make him the happiest of men. I find he told them that same memorable day that he is in regular correspondence with you about the offers and is now bringing about a compromise. There's a noddy for you.[5]

We can imagine the anger if Ellen had discovered that Mary was up to her old tricks of trying to marry off her sisters. Penelope, we learn, had rejected another suitor, Major Tomkinson.

Ellen was reputed to write a very good Collins. On one occasion, when she and Georgy had been staying with Caroline Archer Clive (née Wigley), she wrote to thank her saying, 'I should wish for three or four weeks of fun during the winter and two dinners a week for the London season. Let me know your lowest price.' Then she went on to say that Marianne had told them of a marriage of an old woman of eighty two and a man of twenty.

> It makes me think seriously of Hugh Acland and Psyche. Oh! Our Psyche has sent us another of his books, a precious composition containing translations from Béranger, in which such helps to versification as 'Thoul't, T'would, T'will' etc are used freely. Criticisms on de Balzac full of low morality and bad English. He hopes, in the preface, that those who admired the sporting style of his former writings will discover something of the same vein etc, etc, etc. I wish you had heard your cousin *(Marianne's husband, William Clive),* on Sunday. He began by leaving out the 'not' in the seventh commandment and then turned over two leaves in his sermon, in consequence of which he informed us that the happiness which would succeed the Second Advent was a 'state in which all, from the least to the greatest, shall enjoy – the patronage of the Roman Emperor.' I gave all your messages to Papa but he turned pale when I said the fowl was

boiled, so remember, it is not etiquette to boil very large fowls – they expect to be roasted etc. [6]

Ellen was obviously still concerned about a marital life she could have had with either of her former suitors, Hugh Acland or Joseph Sykes.

The friendship of the Tolletts and the Maer Wedgwoods continued. George Tollet was answering questions from Charles Darwin about the cross-breeding of animals, as was Charles Wicksted about inherent traits in fox hounds, later published.[7] Emma Wedgwood and the Tollet sisters were communicating as before.

Returning to the topic of marriage, we learn from Emma Wedgwood in 1838 that Carry's wedding had been delayed because 'some fathers are not as generous as other fathers ... the upshot is that he *(Thomas Stevens)* must be ordained and get a curacy before they can be married.'[8]

Great was the joy in November 1838 when the engagement of Emma Wedgwood to Charles Darwin was announced. Emma wrote that she was sorry to think of the contrast between the smoothness and happiness of her courtship and that of Carry and Thomas Stevens. Three sisters - Georgina, Caroline and Ellen sent a letter, on the same piece of paper, to congratulate her. Georgina wrote:

> I hope I am as glad as I ought to be at the thing happening that I have been longing for, but you ought to be gratified at my selfish sorrow when I think of losing my earliest friend. It is seldom one thinks of <u>two</u> people so enviable as we think you and Charles; we think you are as lucky as you could possibly wish, but we must allow that ...he is indeed a blessed man. I certainly was surprised at it coming so soon; it was very handsome in him to fancy he doubted. It is very like a marriage of Miss Austen's. Can I say more! Those greedy girls, Ellen and Carry are crying out to write. You must come any day before Friday in next week. I don't give Catherine Darwin any credit for what you call her good nature. I shall write to her soon and tell her what I think of her luck.
> Heaven bless you
> Your loving friend/ G. Tollet

> Penelope says you are guilty ....right in supposing her peculiarly struck with the delight of marrying a man who is so much in print.

Georgina was referring to Charles Darwin's *The Zoology of the Voyage of the HMS Beagle*, published in 1838.

Carry wrote:

> I feel as if it was almost too good news to be true – Marianne and I were praying for it only the other day – I grieve for poor Georgy and Ellen their misfortunes, since to come all at once, but I think if you can provide geologists for one I can engage to a poor ?Lt Com., or good clergyman for the other - you will be most especially missed at my wedding. I have always thought it such a comfort to leave E. and G. in your care, but by good luck you may be in a good country and I'm sure the presence of such a happy bride will be lucky. Never mind, soon you're married, but be very thankful not to hang fire – I am one of <u>his</u> warmest admirers. How proud you will be of him!!! I can well understand your feelings at first - we shall have much flow of soul when we meet. Poor Dear Elizabeth!!! Love and condolences to him, but she is so unselfish – Bless you, dearest old soul./ C.O.T.

Ellen wrote:

> Dear old soul, I think it quite unfeeling that Elizabeth was not mentioned by Georgy and Carry till just at the last, so I shall begin with pitying him. I really was not much surprised; I had thought it so very likely – almost sure to be, but not so soon. What a fool he would have been to have married one of these little Jack Horners! You two will have a chimney that smokes or something of that sort to prevent your being quite intoxicated. It will be enchanting to come and see you but you will be an untold loss - you are the only single girl of our own up in this country worth caring much for - but life is short and one ought to be cheerful as long as one is neither cold nor hungry. I am both just now
> With 5000 loves, your loving friend/ E.H.T.[9]

The youngest daughter, Caroline Octavia Tollet, was married to the Rev Thomas Stevens of Bradfield, Berkshire on 5th June, 1839 at Betley. The Tollet family must have been happy that Carry would be living so close to them in the neighbouring village of Keele. There was a happy report of the marriage by Mary Wicksted, writing to her sister Caroline.

We have just married off Carry on a brilliant morning in a brilliant way. We were all well dressed, and though I say it that should not say it, I was the best. My London gown was of a delicate indescribable lilac shot with white and shaded leaves, and I looked so uncommonly lovely that to my surprise and gratification, I received two kisses from Tom in the short space of one hour. This great feat makes me determined to keep the yellow bonnet..... Bunting by particular desire went down to church with us and looked lovely – almost as lovely as his mother.[10]

43. Caroline, the youngest of the Tollet daughters

The following year on 14th May, Carry died in childbirth, aged 25. Ellen informed her friend, Emma Darwin, how deeply distressed she became when 'she was given the comfort of spending the last hours with her, and the whole time Tom was reading the Communion Service, she had my head and kept stroking it.' The loss of a second sister to Ellen was grievous for she 'was all my joy, my hope, my interest in this life'.[11] After the bereavement, Marianne and the others were to go to the Liverpool coast or to Shakenhurst. Their mother was said to be rather weak in health.

Before the beginning of the third journal in 1841 the Tollets knew that Mary Wicksted was expecting a third child, and that Marianne, who had had still-births in 1835, 1837 and 1839, was to be confined again. Ellen had gone to London to be with her and William for the birth.

Journal 3   1841-1846

Unlike the first and second journals, Ellen's writing now is in continuous prose over longer periods of time on one topic only. It is about Minny, who was her niece.

February 1841 Marianne Caroline Clive *(Minny)* was born a quarter past twelve on the night of Monday 8th of February or rather on the morning of the 9th of February 1841. She was rather a small child but very much alive and screaming and kicking, and her eyes very wide open, and this strength of eyes continued - she had never the slightest appearance of redness or weakness about the eyes so common in the first month.

The dreadful affliction, with which it pleased God to visit, in removing the mother from the child just when her fondest earthly wish was at last gratified, the intense anxiety and misery, which in three days after the birth entirely absorbed all my faculties, prevented my making any particular observations on the poor little infant, and it was hardly for a moment the object of any attention until the first days of sorrow were over.

The child then appeared as a little fragile creature, of whom we were bound to take the greatest care for the father's sake, but our hearts, so used to sorrow as ours, could feel little hope as to the probability of preserving even this morsel of comfort, and each morning when I woke, I fully expected evil news of this baby.

The first alarm was caused by the nurse discovering a small lump, about the size of a pea, having just the appearance of a risen vein just over the heart. She declared she found it increase, and showed it to Dr H., who said it certainly looked like a vein but desired Dr Lorock should see it. This was the first moment I knew I cared for the child, but it was chiefly for William's sake. When this horrid idea was put into my mind, the first determination was not to tell him till Lorock had pronounced what the real danger was. He came and I hardly felt strength to ask him what this new horror was, when he smiled and said, "I have removed it. It was a little bit of dirty wool which had adhered closely to the skin and had been daily increased by the nurse, avoiding carefully to touch it, when she washed the child, but administering powder in profusion every time."

A few day's afterwards baby was really languid and could not suck, but four drops of sal volatile *(ammonium carbonate)* in milk revived her. *(This seems to be a drastic remedy.)* At a fortnight old, the child had begun to smile and look into the nurse's face and though we rather discouraged it, it was plain to everyone that it took decided notice. The expression of her eyes was remarkable for its earnestness.

The funeral of Marianne took place in Welshpool on 24th February 1841. It was reported that William, the vicar, was very much loved there. As a sign of respect to him, the townspeople had "every blind drawn down" and gave "the appearance of general mourning - such was the sympathy of the flock towards their good and kind shepherd."[1]

At three weeks and three days old, we were allowed to leave London by railway for Betley. The journey, 156 miles, was performed in safety, but the baby started and screamed at the sudden letting off of steam close to our carriage. When we got home, her stomach was disordered and her sleep not good for some days. After this she grew delightfully, and her intelligence increased rapidly, until at eight weeks old, a remarkable proof of it occurred in her noticing Cupid and Psyche[2] on the ceiling in the library. She fixed her eyes on them and began a sort of earnest cooing conversation, and this she did regularly every day for a week or two, when gradually her attention was divided by various other objects in the rooms and she thought no more of 'the boys'.

We left Betley for Welshpool early in May and before that time she had begun to sit on the nurse's knee and amuse herself with a thimble and reel of cotton, knocking them down with her tiny fists and quite enjoying the fun. She also picked up a very small button from the floor with her finger and thumb. Georgina and I staid with her at Welshpool till July, and in September, she came again to Betley, when the first tooth appeared on the 19th of October.

She began very early to use her legs very actively, and could raise herself on the lap, by pressing her foot against you, but though a light, straight child, formed for walking early, her ankles and feet were so remarkably small that we dare not encourage much walking, and she did not go quite alone till after fourteen months old.

She was not weaned till the end of March *(1842)* when I went to Welshpool, having left her in January, and was quite surprised at the extraordinary reception she gave me. I had begun to take my bonnet and cloak off before I spoke to her, fearing that I might frighten her, when William exclaimed, "Oh, Ellen, she is going to cry because you don't notice her." I looked up and saw her with her arms spread out and her whole countenance expressing the greatest excitement. When I took her she nestled her face against mine and kissed me and made noises, expressions of wonder and pleasure. When I went upstairs she took me to the nurses and pointed to me, smacking her lips to show how she had kissed me. She would hardly leave me for a moment for several days without crying. At this time she was looking rather delicate and I believe if she had been weaned these months before, it would have been better, but she was backward in teething.

The East Front by Paul Sandby Munn, 1817. This watercolour shows the castle shortly before the east tower was raised in height by Sir Robert Smirke

44. Powis Castle.

I took her one day in the carriage to Powis Castle, where she had never been since we left in January. When we got to the last hill going up to the castle, from were you can see the road turning up to the gate, she put forward her hand, pointed upwards and said, "Bow, wow." Then I remembered that the last time she went she was with William, who particularly showed her the great dogs.

We brought her to Betley and she improved fast after she was weaned in flesh and strength. On our way to Betley we stopped at Styche to visit William's brothers. I remember well her delight at playing with billiard balls, and when Robert, *(Lord Clive),* came to Betley a week or two afterwards, the moment she saw him she began knocking her knuckles together to imitate the delightful play he had taught her.

She was now at a rather troublesome age - forever on her feet, yet always requiring a finger. I shall never forget the fatigue of having her entirely on my hands for two days and a night when her nurse went home, and she would go to no creature but me. It was warm, ?*weak* weather in April and it gave me a compassion for nurses.

When once she was quite turned out, it was delightful, and by the time her little words were beginning to converse, she could say Papa and several other words. One day I was standing over her cot waiting for her to wake. She half opened her eyes and before I thought she could have distinguished me, the sweetest smile came over her face, and she said, "Pretty Ar," meaning 'aunt'. She constantly called Georgina, "Pretty Ar," and seemed to admire her excessively, stroking her face, pulling her curls, and when we rejoined her in Welshpool in July *(1842)* she could say "Aunty" quite plain. She said nothing then for the first few days, treating us with the greatest distinction, and now for the first time we have to suffer sharp trouble about her for a little while.

She began to be very cross and poorly and we gave her some castor oil, but this did not do. So feverish and ill she appeared one Sunday morning that we sent for Mr H. Jones - but before he came, it was time to go to church. Though longing to stay with her, we all went. What a wretched two hours I passed, for I had been last in the nursery, and seen how very bad, and a fear and horror were telling on my mind all the time.

When we came back, we found Mr J. who had immediately lanced her gums, which he found much swelled and inflamed with four teeth approaching. He then put her into a warm bath with cold bladders to her head, and if he had stopped here, or only given some gentle aperient she would, I believe, have been well directly. But he sent her a dose of calomel. [3]

She had not taken it quite half an hour when she became violently sick and she kept vomiting continually for seven hours, with nothing but water from the stomach. The bowels acted violently in a most unpleasant manner – not the least symptom of accumulation but an absence of bile, and this never came right for several days. We went to bed in great trouble, for her thirst was intense, and she kept begging for water and bringing it up. We set all the doors open, that we might hear every sound. To our great joy she slept a little, and when I went to the room at three o'clock, I found her skin moister; in short, all was right, except the irritation from the calomel, and this lasted for days. She had a vast uneasiness in the bowels, and got well very slowly, but she cut four teeth very shortly and quite recovered her health, but looked pale and slender, having grown much in height and not in breadth.

We persuaded William to let us bring her home to Betley in September *(1842)*, where Charles and Mary and their children already were. It was most amusing to see our darling's introduction to her cousins, with whom she was quite delighted - only rather inclined to bite and pinch the baby of her own age.[4] This continued for several days and led to sad scenes, but very soon the injured Mab *(Mary)* began to retaliate, and it ended in the tables being completely turned, which I was very glad of, as I had much rather my own pet was bitten than the biter, and it was a good lesson for her.

She was quite a little taller than Mab, but not nearly so broad and fine a child. Her extraordinary spirit showed itself with the boys *(George and Charles)*, for whom she was quite a companion, romping away with them and afraid of nothing. She was by this now become very reasonable, and when she was inclined to be selfish about her playthings was easily persuaded into being good-natured. She always called her grandpa "Diddle- doddle", because he sang "Hey diddle diddle" etc. One day, hearing him scrape his throat, she imitated it so exactly and did so whenever she saw him.

When she left us, she stopped a day at Styche, as we had done on the way to Betley in the spring, and as soon as she went upstairs she began trying to find aunty in the room where I had slept nearly six months before, and was not satisfied till she had felt in the bed. When she got home she had to call us at the door and then go to her nurse with a grave face, saying, "Aunty out."

45. Styche Hall (a recent photograph), the home of Minny's uncle, Lord Robert Clive.

The next of our family to see her was Penelope, who came in November and staid till January *(1843)*. One day Minny met a gentleman out walking, who held out his hand to shake hands, on which she said, "Take off our gloves."

The end of January Georgina and I came and found her walking in the garden. On first seeing us she thought we were visitors, but gradually the truth came upon her. Each moment her face got brighter, till she hugged and kissed us and called us "Aunty Lady", and this she did for several days.

Her expression of countenance is bewitching, so very merry and pretty, and her constant demonstrations of affection are very remarkable. She understands all the plays of imagination, and every evening she amuses herself with pretending to fetch us things from the shop – "a fig, a pear, a bicky - not rhubarb, No! – an egg – bake an egg," and she pretends to whip it up. One day a little girl came to play. She was very good but so silent that Minny thought she had offended her and said, "Minny be good; Minny –very good dirl," stroking the little girl's face and using every means to please her.

We went for four days to Walcot,[5] where the Powis family is now staying, and her behaviour there was very nice, just enough to show modesty, yet never crying and appearing spoilt. She is inexpressibly fond of Harriet and Willy who are very kind to her. She was dancing one day in the drawing room, when Lady

Emily fetched Neil ?Tholey to see her. He came near and looked at her, on which she stopped and without saying a word merely beckoned him away with her hand, over and over again with amusing dignity.

Soon after our return from Walcot, the trial of parting from her nurse came upon her. She bore it better than we expected, but for several days *(she)* appeared to think there was some mystery and very much avoided talking about her. The new nursery governess came the next day. She took to her at first sight and was very friendly till we mentioned taking her to the nursery, when she began to cry and said, "No, no Pitter, pitter." By having her a great deal with us, and with my rocking her to sleep, we got over her troubles very well.

For the last two or three weeks of the nurse's stay, she had become very rebellious in the nursery - very good with us, but crying - passionate about the newest trifles with the nurse. I could not account for this, though I thought it must proceed from the nurse's manner - being gloomy from her vexation of leaving. She was very kind to the child, and she told me when she went that she had no heart to reprove her, and thereupon she tried to be mistress. Whatever it was, the curious fact is that, after having had three or four or more screaming passions every day, we have now never had one for nearly a week.

The other day she took up some paper with writing in red made on it, and I heard her bewailing herself, saying, "Oh dear, look, poor, poor - "
So I said, "Minny, what do you think it is?"
"Oh, poor Nelly's blood."

Her entreaties to me at night, "Aunty Nelly, yock Minny," are very touching, but for two nights she has allowed Miss Sanders to rock her but, "Aunty Nelly, sing 'Bye, bye, Grandpapa.'"

Yesterday, Sunday, I had been playing with her in the morning, but Aunt Charlotte came to see her, and I followed her into the nursery, dressed for church. She kissed Aunty Charlotte, then with the look of *(word illegible)* dropped me a curtsey, held out her hand and said, "Dood morning, Aunty Nelly. Minny go to church when she is a bid girl."

"What shall you take in your hand?" – meaning her to say a prayer book.

She replied, "A parasol." Now she has not seen anyone carrying a parasol since the summer.

Tuesday February 21st *(1843)* She measures two feet, nine and a quarter inches in height.

March 22nd I have not kept my journal daily as I had intended - so many things employ me. I have found the work of education to have really begun in the last few weeks, and I have been quite astonished to find how much the little difficulties we have had to contend with, as to temper, have annoyed me. She has been not quite well in health - the bowels disordered and this has affected her temper, and I feel foolishly discouraged, and thought she must be ill managed. But now she is well again, and though self willed and sometimes passionate, I am quite contented with seeing her sometimes resist a temptation, often really trying to be good, and what is best of all – she really has conquered one or two bad habits. For instance, instead of picking the sealing wax off a letter and putting it into her mouth, she now always brings it to me and asks me to throw it away. Her naughtiness is always very short, and she almost always volunteers to say, "Be dood," but she is so strong and so quiet in all her feelings of pleasure and disappointment, that our little contests are necessarily rather frequent. When she was poorly and naughty I was quite astonished at ?trials of sin which seemed quite spontaneous. For instance, once when we were up in the nursery, without our speaking to her or noticing her, she suddenly screamed out quite vindictively, "I won't kiss Aunty Nelly; I won't kiss Aunty Georgy." Indeed she seemed particularly naughty and spiteful to me, her special favourite and companion at all other times. This made me think I must have mismanaged her, yet now she seems all very satisfactory.

Her horror of the doctor was terrible. She would scream and cry if his name were mentioned, and make use of all sorts of little acts to prevent his coming upstairs. She is of a very caressing nature, so much so that the requests for kisses are almost always made by her, instead of to her - that is with Georgy and me, though darlingly fond of her father, it is not in the same way.

She is perfectly generous in every way, both as to giving away eatables, of lending playthings, and considering that she has a keen enjoyment of good things, is not at all greedy. When not quite well, she has often come to the dessert saying, "Little Minny, not have a fig. No," and she bears the refusal of anything to eat well.

Her love of children is quite remarkable, and it is with difficulty we can prevent her hugging and kissing every child she meets in the road, and if we do but mention a baby she begs to see it.

One of her favourite amusements is writing or rather drawing with a pencil all sort of hieroglyphics, which she explains as cows, dogs etc. Just now she was stroking the pencil across the paper exclaiming, "There's a long tail, Aunty Nelly. There's a long tail." She just looked at her pencil point and said, "It wants a little bit cutting."

Sunday March 26th Tumbled down on the gravel, and hurt her forehead, cried very little. While eating her meat and potatoes, she said, "I want some pudding."
I answered, "You shall have some of my pudding,"
to which she said, "That be fun from Aunty Nelly's pudding."

It was a bright gleaming afternoon with a high wind. She came into the drawing room and from the further end from the window exclaimed, "Look lights." There was a bright gleam across the Long Mountain, then no sooner on the window or even on the foreground.
I said, "Rock me, for I have a headache."
She replied, "Rock me, for I have a headache."
"Let me feel your tooth – there that tooth make egg ache."
She is very odd sometimes in crying for no apparently very slight causes. I was telling her a story of Larry Turton and drawing his sisters' dolls.[6] She began, "I want Larry Turton's wheelbaddow." In spite of my reminding her she had two upstairs, she cried real tears. Yet she is very good and obedient for several days, and has hardly given any trouble.

Wednesday: We took her to Powis Castle. She talked unexpectedly all the way up there, saying alternately these two sentences: "Little Minny like to go to cousin Harriet," and "Like a new bonnet," as she had a new straw bonnet for the first time. But when we got there she was rather shy and inclined to cling to Aunty Nelly, but she was quite good and played with her cousins.

October 1843: I am very silly for not keeping a regular journal of those happy days of innocent childhood. They will soon be passed away, even if I am allowed to watch them all, and yet when I am with her, I never feel inclined to write about her. It is only when I am parted from her that I wish to commit to writing any of her little sayings. Hearing her and seeing her seems enough for me.

These past months have made a great change - in many ways in none more, thank God, than in her increased healthiness of appearance, and except just at cutting two of the last double teeth, just lately nothing has happened to disturb her. Naughtiness has altered its forms. Her passions are neither so frequent nor nearly so lasting. A little self-willedness and cross way of speaking - but never long fussing now show themselves.

One day walking in the garden she entreated myself to let her run up our walk, while she went another. "You must not touch the raspberries."
"No, sure I won't."

After this she runs up the walk and after once passing the temptation, turns back and begins gathering the fruit as fast as possible. Miss S. slapped her hands, but she did not cry violently, till she said she would tell Aunt Nelly. At

46. Welshpool vicarage, with St Mary's church in the background.

bedtime I talked to her and she seemed penitent. Next morning, walking into the garden, she pointed out the scene of her disgrace, and afterwards said, "I want to be a big girl, Miss S. I want to be a big girl," (almost crying.). Why? "Because then I would go up that walk ever so many times and I would never touch a single raspberry." She showed deep feeling on any allusion to this, and once when I was beginning to tell a story of a boy who took some fruit she was quite distressed and said, "No, no, I don't like it."

On this occasion we began to teach her to say her prayers. "Pray God make me a good girl," and her reverence of manner is quite surprising. She also says grace after meals. The first time her papa was in the room; the moment he had done, she exclaimed with such a look of complacency, "What a good Minny." When I told her that God made the flowers, trees and flowers, she said with great emphasis, "Oh what a good one."

One day she came running from her papa's knee to mine at dessert. I said, "What are you come here for?"

"I am come not for apples, not for pears, not for bicky. I'm come for Aunty Nelly," with a rapturous embrace and such a countenance!

One day she had a stomach ache; I took her in my arms and kissed her, saying nothing. She kissed me and said, "What a good Aunt Nelly to make little Minny well. What a good Aunt Nelly to make little Minny a pretty frock, but not this frock. Mrs Nickill made this frock!" Her notion of a little jealousy of her favour is rather amusing.

Playing with Mrs Nickill's ring, Mrs N. said, "That is Mr N.'s ring." A fortnight afterwards, seeing my mother's wedding ring, she said, "There's a gold ring for Georgina's papa.

January 1844: Our last arrival here was rather less bright than usual. Both Minny and I were poorly, with over a month to feel the full pleasure of our first meeting. For ten days afterwards, though her bodily health was soon restored, her temper did not resume its normal equanimity, and we had sundry scenes of naughtiness.

She is now come round to her usual state or nearly so, and is indeed most engaging and companionable. Some faults of earlier days are already corrected, for instance she takes medicine without resistance - some new ones are sprung up, and more constant watching is necessary to correct them. Her affections are warm beyond all description but her will is a very strong one. I believe no character can be great without this strength of will and I hope it may be turned to good in her. It is not only that she is strong in trying to get her own way, but it is remarkable that she has about everything, however less trifling, a way, a wish and a will of her own.

She is very susceptible and we are obliged to be very cautious about all we say. An old lady came, to whom she was not over civil, and she said afterwards she did not like old women. I replied that Georgy and I would soon be old women. "No, no, I don't like you to be old women." We told her that she would be an old woman if she lived. In the middle of the night or rather lying awake in the morning, she was heard crying and screaming by herself. On enquiring why, she cried she would not like to be an old woman, and she would not be!

This morning it was snowing and she ran to the window saying, "Oh, papa, I am afraid this snow will put your flowers out."

We spend many happy minutes - she seated, sewing by my side and during quiet times she is chattering incessantly.

October 1844: I must try to collect the remembrances of our last visit before they fade away. First there was a happy five weeks at Betley with our darling child here. After she had been here a few weeks, Betsey, the under nurse, arrived from Welshpool and the first meeting was pretty: Minny began asking after everything animate and inanimate, beginning with Polly, the cow, proceeding to Papa's pretty flowers, and "my little garden", and ending with, " Where's my little watering pot? – but it can't water now."

Such joy at going home, and everything was shown to us as quite new. "Look at these nice, pretty stairs!" she exclaimed as she went up to the nursery. This was in the month of June. Her studies were rather increased; at least she began to learn little hymns. One had a verse; 'Kind angels guard me every night / As round my bed they stay.'

"What are angels?"
"Beautiful, good creatures that live in heaven and God tells them to take care of us."
"Oh, Aunty Nelly, I dare say God likes them not to let the fleas bite me." This was the only danger she ever knew of, that could approach her bed!

I began to perceive in May and June that the very warm delight of learning to read was passing away. She was apt to find it hot and to be restless at her lesson - we made it very short, but never once missed it. Very soon the pleasure returned and when we left her in September, she was enjoying her reading very much. Indeed, I have never yet seen one tear or ever had any quarrel about it. The chief difficulties are, I hope, conquered and she can read easy stories. I perceived great self-satisfaction in her. She once said to me, when she had been trusted and had behaved, "I can look up at you so nicely. I am so very good sometimes." I had never said anything about being able to look one in the face, and it was quite an original feeling.

Mr ?Gringol says that self-satisfaction in girls is inevitable in a child because it can only compare its successes with its weaknesses, not with its duties. It appears to me to be a great difficulty not to make obedience either too mechanical nor too much a matter of reason. Instant obedience can only be taught to a young child by fear, as it is no doubt a most convenient state for a child to be in. It may save its life in cases where to fail to obey is to be lost. But it appears to me to be doubtful whether that prompt obedience ought to be the beginning or the end of our labours. This argument I had with William Clive, who thought I too often gave Minny a reason. We both wish to arrive at the same end. I think perfect obedience of the best sort is only to be gained further on, but I should think it a sad failure in our system if it were not gained at all.

Arrived at Welshpool on **Friday 5th December** *(1844)*. Had a most warm welcome. After the first moment, Minny asked, "How's Mrs Turton's baby and how's Mrs Turton's leg?" She looked beautifully well, her face as round as an apple with her speaking eyes - bluer and brighter than ever. Amidst all the world's distress, what a blessing this is! When I look at her I dare not be discontented. The first few days are always marked by more shows of affection as she said, "My dear, sweet, Aunty Nelly, I love you so very much because you are only just come." On Sunday she walked up to G. and said, "That's your left hand, Aunty Georgy. I am very glad dear God put me on two hands."

47. William Clive, now made Archdeacon of Montgomery.

To her great delight, I read her some stories out of the Bible itself, and she has often asked for it again. Her lesson cannot be too long in her opinion, and now it is always our affair to shorten it. Her spirits are immense.

This morning she purposely spilt some tea. I said, "I think you had better say you are sorry."
She responded, "I don't like to say that, because I am sorry to myself." But very soon of her own accord *she went* to William and Georgina saying, "I'm sorry."

Miss Saunders says that very often when she is going to bed she begins to lament, "Oh dear, now the day is gone. How soon it is gone. I am so sorry it has ended," and the first thing on waking, "Now the day is beginning - not ending, I am so glad."

Conversation: "Dear Aunty Nelly, I love you, but I love Papa best. I love Papa best because he is gooder. But Miss Saunders and Bessy - they do not speak so nicely as you do."

The governess at Powis Castle has lost her mother, so Minny began when we were alone to say, "Aunty Nelly, I am very sorry to hear about Miss Lee's mother being dead. Do you think Miss Lee has got some of her hair?"

"Why do you ask?"

"Because - you have some of Aunt Eliza's hair in a brooch."

She then began to talk of those who are gone. I said, "Minnie, darling, you are too little to be told about them. You must wait till you are a big girl." She replied, "How many more will be dead before then?"

I have been poorly and she was never tired of being in my room. Seeing me ready for church after being kept at home for five Sundays, she said, "I think you had much better stay at home and learn to be good out of the Bible."

Sunday 27th January 1845: *(Conversation)* E.*(Ellen)*: There was always God; nobody made God. Minny: Then God made himself. How could he make himself when he was not alive? E.: I can't tell you, my dear. Minny: You must when I am bigger. E.: No, I can't tell myself either. Minny: But you will tell me when we are in heaven when you rise up again. E.: No, I shall not teach you there; God himself will teach you all things. Minny: But you do teach me NOW.

Early in May she came to Betley with her father. One day we went over to Audley. Running across the churchyard, very happy with the Wilbrahams,[7] she suddenly stopped and said, "But I am so sorry for all the people in the graves." Fanny W. said that they were perhaps better off where they were. She replied, "Perhaps they are gone to heaven but still they cannot hear us talk."

One day one of the servants gave her a little bird's egg, the first she had ever had, and her delight was great. Soon after I heard a dreadful crying in the nursery, ran up and found her in a state of great distress. There was no comforting her. Everything that I had urged as consolation was rejected with, "But that won't make my egg not broken." At last she exclaimed with such bitterness, "Really I think nothing is happy with me," but then her conscience pricked and she added, "except seeing little girls - that is happy to be sure," alluding to her little cousin, *(Mab)*. I was quite dismayed to see such strong feelings - such headstrong, rebellious grief over a broken toy. What a picture of our own hearts children display to us - some bright hope crushed, 'some idol of this fancy died afore' calls forth in us just such feelings as this broken egg. It frightened me to think what my darling might have to suffer if this strong will of hers were not subdued. How can this be but by suffering? 'Gently may the needful correction fall.'

Georgina and I returned with her to Welshpool early in June. One day, mentioning the word 'father', I had to remind her that 'papa' meant the same thing. I asked her who was her father in heaven. She answered God. Some minutes later she looked up and said, "Aunty Nelly, my father is Papa, but our father is God."

We went to ?W and there we had a dreadful battle about some castor oil. Being afraid of choking her, I was obliged to give it up at night, but would not let her appear the following day till she had taken it. She held out till two o'clock, when being quite exhausted she let me put it to her lips and swallowed it. It was a sad, sad day and I hope there will be few such struggles. She had not been well with a cough and distemper, and it had shown itself in making her naughty. We had some most happy weeks before we went to Hoylake *(on the Wirral)*. Georgy went home and I went alone with Minny. We arrived at the hotel, all day in pouring rain, but M's spirits were never failing - laughing, talking, laying *(teasing, joking)* every inch of the way. The sea did wonders, and her happiness with the Wicksteds was without allay. She and Mab did charmingly together.

Her sorrow at having to part with me was very affecting. When the day was fixed, she began to grieve. I was awoken one morning at six by hearing her crying in the next room, and on enquiry found it was her bewailing my departure. She breakfasted with me early the morning I went back. Her appetite was quite gone and her tender look of uneasiness was touching. I could not help feeling how blest children are for whom a mother's tender care knows no interruption, who rise up and go to rest every day in the year, secure from partings such as these! However it is a short lived sorrow - a parting from a child.

January 1846: Minny, having been rather naughty, I said how sad it would be if she grew up a naughty girl, and how it would distress her papa. "Yes," she said, "he would be just like old Eli[7], but I hope he would not do that. I hope he would leave it to nature."

The day after Christmas day, she said, "I suppose yesterday was our Lord's birthday in heaven." I said it is his birthday on earth that we keep. "Yes, I know that but I think that yesterday God Almighty and Jesus Lord would sit upon two thrones and all the angels would sing. I don't think they would dance - they would be too holy for that." I said there is nothing unholy in dancing. "Well," she said, "but I can tell you a very great reason why they could not dance - they have no petticoats to hold out!"

Her joy at the thought of going to Powis Castle on Twelfth Night was very pretty - almost the first delight she thought of was going in the dark in the carriage, but she said afterwards, "It was very soon over and I knew it would be." She came away in the midst of all the fun without making a murmur, and was none the worse. The next day at luncheon, I happened to say that Willy Herbert and George Clive *(cousins)* were nice schoolboys. "Oh," she said, "they are shockingly rude. I really dare not tell you what a rude play they did. They beat each other, not where their coats were, but where their trousers were!"

One day I was reading a story of a naughty boy who stole some red currant jelly. She said, "I think that was not the devil's, but his own naughtiness." I soon after said 'poor boy', at which she seemed annoyed and said, "Don't pity him. I never pity people that are naughty." Why? "Oh, I suppose it is because I am often naughty myself and there's nobody says 'poor' to me."

She now reads pretty fluently and has begun writing with a chalk on a slate. Her anxiety over forming the letters is very great – always aiming at perfection. She knows the countries of Europe, the counties of England and a good deal of Bible history, but lessons only occupy a very, very short time and her constitution seems to require such quantities of air and exercise that I don't know how she will get on when the real time of education comes.

This is where the journal seems to have a natural final paragraph. However, using a different pen and stronger ink in large letters Ellen writes two paragraphs.

"I love you and Geordina etc, but I love Papa best." Why ought you? "Oh, Aunty Nelly, you should not ask that; you know I ought, almost as if it was God"- with a very solemn whisper.

- a very interesting conversation on her remembrances of Hoylake to tell me the reasons why she was so unhappy at my leaving her there, and her feeling of gratitude to Marie Severne[8] was strongly expressed.

In enormous letters on a page at the back of the journal is a letter to Ellen:
My Dear Aunty, I saw such a lot of wild beasts yesterday - lions, tigers, and many monkeys. Papa, Captain and I gave them some biscuits and nuts to eat and I saw a lady riding on an elephant's back. Papa sends his love and Anne hopes you are all well. Your affectionate niece, M.C. Clive

On anther page :
Betley 1847 "Do not hug me so: you will spoil my cap."
"Well, Nelly, if I do, you can buy another cap but you cannot buy another love, you know."

Ellen's life afterwards

It seems that after Marianne's death, Ellen and Georgina spent considerable time in Welshpool, helping to raise Minny. A lengthy letter to Ellen by Lucy Herbert, the governess from Walcot, indicated that Ellen had been given the authority to appoint her, and also that Lucy took her duty very seriously.

My dear Ellen,

The visit of Minny to her Papa being now over, to the great regret of all who remain at Walcot, I think I cannot do better than to give you some account of it – the doing so will be an agreeable task to me, and I think I owe it to you from whom I first received the appointment of chief governess to the young lady during the period in question.

Of her health you will no doubt have heard from more experienced persons, and her ailments were scarcely sufficient to produce any effect perceptible to an unpractised eye, though Miss Saunders who evidently watches her with the greatest care, does not yet consider her quite well. Her spirits certainly were not affected and both cousin Clive and Miss Saunders considered her much better when we went away than when she came. I bore in mind your caution about over excitement and frequently questioned Miss Saunders as to whether she appeared over excited or over tired at night; or was at all put off her sleep. Miss S. always assured me that she was not the least so, but was on the contrary much the better for the visit.

The most exciting day was that on which our little cousin Jean Oakley Park came and saw Minny. In the course of five minutes she found a close friendship with Victoria, to whom she did the honours very prettily, embracing her about once in five minutes during the whole of the walk. On that one evening, and on that one alone, Miss Saunders said that she did lie awake a few minutes longer than usual. Minny's own account -I find that she likes to be considered as a bad sleeper - was that she lay awake a very long time – four or five minutes, I think!

She went up to rest every day between twelve and one, and we also left her to her Papa and Miss Saunders from five o'clock until she was dressed for the evening. And when we went to dinner, Harriet took her to bed.

The greater part of the morning and also part of the afternoon when she did not go out, was spent with Charlotte and myself and (for three days) Henrietta Clive, in the drawing room, where we drew. There she amused herself with painting, to which occupation she took a great fancy, and I encouraged this and such-like unexciting amusements. The grand racket of each day took place in the conservatory, where a little time was usually spent after breakfast or luncheon. ….and when her Papa was certainly not the most backward in joining in a game of play. I think I need hardly tell you, though I must not omit it either, that the dear little thing was as good as possible, obedient and good tempered, never attempting to do anything that she knew to be wrong and most scrupulously refusing any eatables, however innocent, of which she was not quite sure that Miss Saunders would approve. We were obliged to obtain authority from Miss Saunders for a piece of bun with the currants picked out, whose leave of absence was expiring.

Captain Justice is come back, looking very well, and at least as fond of his old friends……*(One sixth of this letter is missing)*

Pray give my love to Miss Tollet *(Penelope)* and to Georgina and will you give my best remembrances to Mr and Mrs Tollet. I'm afraid I am sending you a very untidy looking scrawl, but I hope you will be good enough to excuse it. I will, believe me, to remain
Very sincerely yours,/Lucy C. Herbert
P.S. Charlotte desires me to add that Minny's blue frock was very much admired. We all agreed that she looked extremely pretty in it.
(At the top of the letter near the address was another note.)
I ought to have mentioned Minny's deafness. It was very perceptible during the first few days, but was certainly better before she left us and Mamma is quite of the opinion that the best thing that can be done for it at present is to leave it alone. [1]

There were a few letters that Minny, written in enormous handwriting as a small child, had sent to Ellen. These were clearly treasured by her.

My dear Aunty,
I thank you for the very pretty sash you sent me. Papa thinks it is to dress up a doll for me. I dined at the castle yesterday and saw Mr Montgomery. I liked him very much… He wheeled me about upon the little wooden horse, and cousin Lucy gave me a ride on her rocking horse.
Your niece/ M.C.Clive

Another letter, which is not quite whole, bears the following words:
'The bantams are very well. We take them up every morning for Papa's breakfast. The calf is grown much since we were at Betley; the pony turns the calf away and then eats the calf's hay. I shall be glad to see you next spring and Deordina too. I do my lessons pretty well; I like my French. Cousin Lucy *(the former governess)* came here on Sunday. They are making a new thatch at the back of the arbour; the bunnies are well. I gave them food this morning. The Captain is not very well: he went out shooting with Lord Powis yesterday. Papa is a great deal better – he is downstairs. Your affectionate niece /M.C.C [2]

The social life of Ellen and Georgina, apart from their visits to Welshpool, resumed with visits to London and to Down to see Emma Darwin and former acquaintances. Ellen received a slightly humorous letter from Charles Darwin before 1850 in answer to a query. This was the first hint of any interest that Ellen had shown in geological specimens, although her late sister was reputed to be most knowledgeable on the subject.

Down, Farnborough, Kent
Tuesday

My dear Ellen,
The curiosity you sent me is, I believe, a comprolite for a fish or reptile, and coprolites are fossil guano. I took it up to ?G. and Son and showed it to two wise men; they thought it either a coprolite or a mere ?concoction i.e. an aggregation of foreign matter within another rock, through simple chemical attention often assumes perfectly unnatural and curious forms. An analysis for showing the presence of phosphate

of lime, would alone determine whether it was a coprolite. If the next time you see a chrysalis, you will look, I think you will find the ringed part at the tapering end, and not in the body at the other end - so much for the learned lecture.

I would have written sooner, had not Emma and myself been in London for a few days last week.

Thank you for sending the receipt *(recipe)* for pneumonia, which I shall carefully keep, though I have not heard of many deaths in the neighbourhood. I sincerely hope Mrs Tollet is better – pray give my kind and most respectful remembrances to Mr Tollet and believe me, dear Ellen, with our strong wishes to see you here.
Sincerely yours / C Darwin [3]

The friendship, which developed soon after Charles and Mary's wedding, between the Tollets and Wigleys continued over a long period of time. Ellen and Georgina visited Archer Clive's Rectory at Solihull in August 1844. The sisters were said to talk all day, Ellen in particular. However 'they are amusing and full of pursuits – drawing, architecture, schools, scandal. They allow that old maidism is a state of submission, that to be happy they want husband, children ...they don't yet despair though they are thirty-five and seven, I think, but they begin to think matters doubtful.'

5. Miss Dunscombe.

In fact Ellen would have been thirty-two. However thoughts of marriage must have still been at the forefront of her mind when she saw her friend, Annabella Crewe marry Mr Richard Monkton Milnes, (later the Marquis of Crewe). Ellen accompanied her friend, Miss Dunscombe, to Madeley Manor before proceeding, amid the celebrations of the villagers, to Madeley church.

In 1853, three years after her mother's death, Ellen and her father met Mrs Gaskell in London in 1854. Letters were exchanged mainly on society gossip. She accepted an invitation to visit Betley Hall the following year, and described some of its attractions, with its flower garden and lawns, sweeping down to the lake. She described Minny as a 'charming little granddaughter (mother dead) of thirteen, Minny Clive, who is the darling of everybody.'[4]

The early fifties must have been difficult for the Tollet daughters. After the death of George Tollet on 25th December 1855 there were many tributes to his work in the local area, describing him as an 'active, intelligent and impartial justice of the peace'.[5] His work as an agricultural reformer was known even before he changed his name to Tollet and came to this area in the 1790s. We have unfortunately seen no comments from his family until this tribute, found at the back of Ellen's first journal, written by Minny and her cousin, Mab.

> The recollections of Marianne Clive and Mary Elizabeth Wicksted of poor, dear, kind grandfather, who died on the twenty-fifth day of December 1855 and was born on the third of August 1767. Aged 88
>
> I remember going to church with him, in the old pony carriage and watching the old black pony 'Jipsy'. He was at Shakenhurst in the year 1851, and was interested in a cuckoo being found in a robin's nest. There is a colony of herons at Betley in the Old Wood, and Grandpa liked to watch them through a telescope and used to show them to us.
>
> After the sale of the fowls *(in January 1854)* and loss of the birds, he traced over on paper the genealogy of our blessed Lord from Adam – he did several copies and one for the use of the schoolmistress of the parish of Betley, so that she might refer to it without trouble. When we were very little we used to see him in the dining room till the last few years of his life, and he used to enjoy having us to dine with him on Sundays. I remember very well his being able to carve: his appetite

continued excellent till the last four days of his life. He enjoyed having letters from his grand children; he was delighted with any little drawings Charley or I did for him. Dear Grandpa used to watch us playing bagatelle in the ante-room, and sometimes he would play himself. He was very kind in coming to see the play house I made earlier under the sycamore trees in the flower garden, and sent for some clay on purpose for me to make hobs of it: there was a hollow under a Portugal laurel where he had a seat put for him and he called it Mab's arbour.

49. George Tollet IV

He took me in the new pony chair to see Madeley station *(which had been opened in 1837)* one summer's day about the year 1854, the very summer before he died. He walked with me and Beatrice Edwards to see a little well we had made – with his favourite Deordina. He sat for hours in the summer of 1855 on a bench in the flower garden watching the bees, which sipped the honey from the two beautiful flower beds in front of him, one of dark blue lobelia and the other of white and pink verbenas. He remarked that the bees preferred verbenas to the lobelias, and he repeated to me, "How doth the little busy bee improve each cheering hour." He was very anxious to have me at Betley when Papa was with Captain Justice.

He took a great fancy to Cochin and Shanghai fowls. All of us used very often to go and see them with him. A short time afterwards George and Charley caught him some little birds (which he put into an aviary) and several mountain finches, two of which he gave me in the summer of 1855. We used to cover ourselves with old shawls and go into the aviary with him, and he liked to sit quite still for fear of frightening the birds. He put an inner door to prevent us from letting them escape by accident. He took very great interest in the nests.

Dear Grandpapa walked at Grandma's funeral to church when he was eighty three years of age.

He spoke in a quite a strong voice. When I kissed him he said, "My blessing," and when I told him I was going to communicate with him he said, "I have been thinking of that....I try not to believe in transubstantiation," and also, "I feel very humble and yet I am perhaps too presumptuous. I never did trust in my own merits." We went to church at half past ten, and when we returned we heard that he had passed away without a struggle at eleven o'clock, and that he was sensible till the last ten minutes of his life, and now he sleeps in Jesus.

"A hoary head is a crown of glory."
Copied M.C.C. Feb 1857 [6]

Charles Wicksted inherited the Betley Hall Estate after his father's death. Like his siblings he returned to Betley for official functions in the village. For instance, there are records of Ellen laying the foundation stone of the new National School on land given by her father.[7] Charles lived mainly in Shakenhurst, the hall inherited by Mary Wigley, with the consequence that the social gaieties of former years ended until his son George Wicksted with his wife (née Blount) took up residence in Betley in the late seventies.[8] His second son, Charles Wigley Wicksted, inherited Shakenhurst from his mother.

50. Shakenhurst, the hall owned by Mary Wicksted and later her son Charles.

Ellen's correspondence with and visits to Emma Darwin's growing family continued after Emma left Maer to be married. The diaries of Emma Darwin reveal the frequency of their visits over the next decades. Both families had houses near each other in London, so that they were able to call on and dine together. At one stage in the 1860s they were all living in Queen Anne Street.

51. Charles and Emma Darwin.

Georgina must have been flattered by Charles Darwin when he asked her to proof read his major work, *'On the Origin of Species by Natural Selection'* (1859). He informed his publisher, John Murray, that as soon as he had read the manuscript to 'please send it by careful messenger and plainly directed to Miss G. Tollet, 14 Queen Anne Street, Cavendish Square.' She was regarded by him as an excellent judge of style who would 'look out for errors for me.' [9] On several occasions during visits, Georgina had made suggestions to Charles Darwin about his experiments and theories, some of which were noted by him. Later Georgina wrote to thank him for his book on orchids because her name appeared on the presentation list.[10]

In the letters between Ellen and Emma there were discussions about their families, the inevitable illnesses, religion, euthanasia, current literature, sharing two bushels of damsons, and just a little society gossip. The letters, of which there are more than forty, from 1861, were written by Emma Darwin and addressed to Ellen.[11] Mrs Gaskell was said to be intolerable, but more acceptable in her own house than elsewhere. Emma and Ellen have obviously discussed the merit of having a statue to Florence Nightingale in London. The former disliked the monument, and added that she preferred the old-fashioned way of life more than the emancipation of women – both ladies seemed to be singularly conditioned to accept their role in life.

From the census returns in 1861 it seems that all the surviving Tollet sisters made Queen Anne Street, London, their main home. The tie of Ellen and Georgina with Minny was very strong from her early days, and for a time their stays in Welshpool had been frequent. Both sisters hint that the happy relationship between Archdeacon Clive, their brother-in-law, and themselves had become strained for a short time. On being asked again to look over Charles Darwin's current work, Georgina wrote:

> My head is in too weak a state to read more than two or three pages at a time, but I enjoy these glimpses of the wonders you have discovered exceedingly. I much fear that I have no chance of talking it over with you this summer. Even if I were to get better before June 5th, that awful day will make me bad again. *(She was referring to the marriage on 5th June 1862 of her niece Marianne Clive to John Bridgeman.)*

I wonder if you ever saw a bird's nest built on top of another? In Lord Bradford's shrubbery there is a hedge sparrow's on the roof of a wren's. *(Lord Bradford lived in Weston Park and was the future father-in-law of Minny.)*[12]

However in 1862, at the age of 21, Minny was married in London to the Rev Hon John Robert Orlando Bridgeman, [13] the third son of the second Earl of Bradford. He was the rector of Weston from 1859-97. On returning from their honeymoon, they went back to Welshpool, where there was 'the liveliest enthusiasm for the young lady' by the townspeople. 'Arches of flowers and evergreens were erected throughout the town, the bells rang and great crowds lined the route from the station.' [14] The parishioners further celebrated the event with a dinner for two hundred and seventy children, when six sheep were roasted. Their son, William Clive Bridgeman, was born in December 1864.[15] When Lord Bradford died in 1865, the young couple left the vicarage and moved to Weston Park. About the same time William Clive resigned from his post and was appointed to a less onerous position in Blymhill as rector, near Weston - in the patronage of the earls of Bradford. He had been vicar of Welshpool since 1819, made archdeacon of Montgomery from 1844, and thus at the age of seventy deserved an easier life.[16]

A note from Emma Darwin in 1864 from Down to Ellen in Betley implied that the latter had been 'uprooted from Welshpool, a scene of almost maternal happiness for twenty-five years'. She wondered how the archdeacon could bring himself to it. The following year Emma stated she was glad Ellen was not going to Welshpool again because,

'the name will always be so odious to me henceforward.... you must tell the archdeacon I believe he never caused a more lively pang in the female heart than when I heard he was gone, as a friendly face would have been such a boon to me!

She further commented that the work of the Bridgeman's sister as being 'unamateurish'. However in 1861 Emma Darwin showed approval of Minny's future husband because her choice had 'all the moderation and sobriety which one might look for at a much further and advanced period – art, literature, evangelism, music.....' [17] These are real attributes indeed. Whatever the problem was between the Tollet sisters and their brother-in-law, it was soon resolved, as there were many letters sent by Ellen from Blymhill. Thus Minny's family was reunited.

With the birth of Minny's son, William, in 1864 Ellen's bond with Minny and the Bridgemans thrived. She loved this child and took a keen interest in his education.

There are a number of letters from Emma, in which she commiserated with Ellen and Georgina over Minny's loss of another child. In June 1869, Emma wrote that, 'Minny must ache through life with the irreparable loss.' She and Charles knew only too well the devastating loss of children. Of the Emma's ten children, three had died in childhood, and she knew that for her 'whatever God wills' was not best, that every death was so utterly 'hollow and unreal ' that she could 'never speak of this world as a place that it is better to get out of as soon as possible.' She continued, 'though we may believe noble spirits are taken away early to minister in some higher sphere, yet we cannot get comfort of that thought when we think of all that might have been here.' This was not Ellen's view after the death of her sister, Eliza, when she felt that mourning the death was inappropriate, as Eliza was in a better place with the angels. Perhaps Ellen's views changed after 1936. The same letter revealed that Minny was to be taken away for a holiday to help her recuperate. Emma commented that Ellen's 'separation from Minny would be a trial to you,' and she longed to hear that the journey had been 'successful to her.' In that same year Minny caused much anxiety to her aunts because she had had a bad fall down the stairs.

Old age brought the inevitable illness and loss. Ellen's sister, Frances, died in 1862. A hint in Emma's letters showed that Frances had been unwell for much of her life; however whilst she was in London she did join some of Ellen's social visits. Ellen's older sister, Penelope, who spent much of her life doing charitable works, was recorded as taking a holiday with her niece, Mab, in Llandudno in July 1864 and attending a dinner party at Doddington in 1871.[18] She died in 1882 aged seventy-nine. As before, Ellen, whilst she was fit, moved to friends and relations in the provinces.

Charles Wicksted had died in 1870 in Shakenhurst. Archer Clive described him as 'a kind, genial and most popular man' with the loudest voice ever heard, one that called for silence so loudly 'that the birds were frightened while the guns are on the other side of the field'. He was old fashioned, 'a type fast disappearing, a sportsman and yet a thorough gentleman, hospitable and kind to all, liking to have his friends and neighbours round him, but without the least ostentation.'[19] Emma Darwin had hoped that his family would be able to nurse him in his last illness, as he was unable 'to move in a way he had before.'[20]

Caroline Clive, the then well-known poet and novelist, who had become partly paralysed, died in a fire at her home in 1873, and her sister Mary Wicksted survived a few more years, almost blind.[21]

Throughout the last years of her life, Ellen sometimes revisited Betley. One occasion was the presentation of the choir desks by the Minny, (Hon Mrs Bridgeman) and the Archdeacon Clive after St Margaret's had had been restored. (It must have seemed a long time since William had preached a sermon there in 1836, when the church was in dire need of repair.)

52. The restored Betley church, showing the vicarage, the former home of Mr Turton.

Once Ellen was staying in Betley Hall with her nephew George Wicksted, the successor to the Betley estate. She wrote about going to the hunt at Woore, where The Empress of Austria was taking part. This lady was noted for her hour-glass figure: she had to be sewn into her riding habit to reveal her miniscule waist.

> Cartlick is splendid about the reception at Woore Hall where HM put on her habit; her manner, Mrs C. says was 'most queenly'. She is still a pretty looking woman with a fine figure and an awfully tight habit, so tight, she descended the stairs at Woore Hall sideways: she could not walk straight in her habit.

The Empress had a slight accident in Wrinehill involving Margaret Wicksted, George's wife, and she took 'the first opportunity to come up to apologise, talking English perfectly.' In the same letter Ellen commented that she had recovered from bronchitis and that there was a good report of Georgina. She added that, 'father and Willy too may be amused by this.'[22]

Living in the country and being closer to Minny and her family were important to Ellen. By late 1869 Ellen was making plans to move from Queen Anne Street. Emma Darwin was saddened by the news and showed just how close these former friends from Betley and Maer had become:

> The five o'clock teas with you on Sunday always came as something so light and cheering after the workhouse, I almost felt as if I could not return to my poor old people without that to look forward to .... I feel now I have lost a window into a home that had become so entwined with all my interests.'

When Ellen and Georgina were young they had discussed their retirement as old maids through rose- coloured spectacles. They had imagined a small house about two miles from Malvern, surrounded by objects of interest where they tended the sick, taught the poor, and were surrounded by young things – children, chickens, ducks in a garden of delicate flowers. This was a far cry from their present life. For the sake of Georgina, Ellen was spending considerable time in London and she must have become very sad, as Georgina, who had been handicapped by arthritis, became ill and her lifelong companion died in 1872, aged 64. In Emma's letter of condolence she talked of 'the intimacy of so many years, in which we have learnt to share so many interests..... something that no later friendship can replace.' She went on to add that for some part of the year she would look to the 'possibility of chance half hours with you as a real restful hope.' In later months Emma tried to console her by suggesting how, in the future, Ellen would be able to take pleasure in watching over William and his education. This she did. She had written to Emma about his ability to do maths at school; she had admired the clever way he managed to catch two sparrows,[23] and on his confirmation into the church, she gave him much spiritual advice.[24]

One of the letters amongst Ellen's private papers found after Georgina's death was a letter from Florence Nightingale from 35 South Street, Park Lane W on 6th November 1872:

> Oh my dear old friend, Ellen,
> How much you have to suffer! I have only just heard of your loss and ours. My dear old friend Georgina, and the old days! But, oh, my dearest, to those who have gone through so much as you and I have, though I know that to you there is but little more in this world without her, to whom you have had the brother's love, passing the love of women, yet when it pleases God to give her the reward of her patience sooner than the normal term of years. Who can doubt which would be for her, after all she had suffered, the better part?
>
> It is not as when a man Sidney Herbert is cut off in the very prime of his work and is found irreplaceable I am so driven. I think never in all my life (though it is eighteen years this week since I took charge in Scutari – and during those eighteen years I have but twice had one week's holiday) have I been so driven as these last few months. But you are always in my thoughts and prayers. God keep you -
>
> Emily Verny's death you knew. Had she lived she would have done better work than ever I have, 'But she is in her grave and oh, the difference to me!'
> Ever your old /Florence Nightingale [25]

Ellen was reputed to have helped Florence Nightingale in founding a London Hospital – the nature of that help is unclear.[26]

Country Conversations, the book by Georgina, had been privately circulated amongst friends for a number of years, probably because some of the Betley people mentioned were still alive. It was published posthumously in 1883. In the preface by W.C. Bridgeman, he noted that it was 'not a work of genius' but the writer 'had a quiet humour and keen powers of observation.' The book received good reports from a number of people in high places including Lord Rosebery, who had sent a copy to Gladstone. [27] It harks back to the years spent in Betley, when the daughters visited the ordinary people. Georgina had put together a number of short pieces of some of the ordinary folk living there. Here is a short extract about Mrs Harland:

> Though it is many months since Mary's wedding, it's not over with my sorrowing, Miss G. Our house has never been the same – everything was in the right place when Mary was here. The week before she was married I said I could not go through with it; but my husband and sons were both on Robert's side and the flys (sic) were ordered (and there were seven of them), so I was forced to give way; but I always will keep to it, Miss G, that I am as deserving of my daughter as any gentleman in all England. Before ever Robert took her in the church, I said to him, "Now, Robert, you go down on your knees and thank me for letting you have her;" and he went down as composed as could be. Mary was married in a bridal fall and wreath that was quite as cheap as a bonnet, and a worked muslin dress that I must own had been washed. She has left that behind for Hemily; but, indeed, I say we can have no more weddings at Bewley; indeed Hemily is disposed quite the other way, though there are two or three that would be glad to have her, especially since we got such a good price for our cheese.[28]

M. E. Gaskell (daughter of the novelist) wrote to Ellen Tollet in April 1881 expressing her joy at receiving a copy of the book:

> You can fancy with what a welcome I greeted *Country Conversations*. I have re-read nearly the whole book, and think it even more wonderfully entertaining than I did when I was hearing it - or reading it in M.S. Yes, I like the binding and printing very much indeed. It may be the guinea's stamp, yet I do think <u>outsides</u> matters of importance. …There are so many people that I am planning to lend it to – I can trust the previous volume out of my hands…..I am very much grieved to hear about your having been so ill. I think that a furious influenza is <u>the</u> most wretchedly form of illness. How I wish that I lived near you, I could often call in and see you, or at any rate enquire about you…..Ever your grateful and loving/ M.E. Gaskell.[29]

Francis Darwin, son of Emma, thanked Ellen for the copy of the book which he would have 'gorgeously bound'. He discussed the 'perfect naturalness of the whole book' and .. ..'the enjoyment of the humour', so that Ellen 'must feel like a queen with intriguing courtiers, begging for decorations for all their relations.'[30] There was a letter in a similar vein from Mrs Blanche Clough, widow of the poet, who commented that it was read with great delight particularly some of the dialect.[31]

Her great-nephew, William Clive Bridgeman, was very much in Ellen's thoughts. She wrote to him on Oct 5th 1880 from Blymhill:
> I was very glad to receive your letter and did not expect one sooner. You have a busy time beginning your work and furnishing too. I think you have made a good beginning with Mr Austen Leigh and I fully expect to hear that you and his other pupils give him good approbation – not unqualified, of course - that you can't expect. Your father and mother arrived last night. Mother to stay here for a few days and see the last of me, as I hope to be able to truant to Leamington on Thursday or Friday. If I get fully well …… I shall begin to hope to see you in Queen Anne St. I was awoken one night about one by Dandy barking at my window and I had to rouse the house to let him in. He had been out with the pony carriage and had played truant. He would have barked all night. Farewell dear boy/ EHT [32]

There was a reunion between Ellen and Emma in Leamington. The latter had saved up £20 in order to go to see her there. She hoped that Cox, Ellen's nurse, would 'be able to spare a room for her.' It appears that from the sixties Ellen had visited the Darwins at Down for several days each year and that they met frequently in London. Emma wrote from many different addresses – Dolgelly, Falmouth, Hopedene, Ravensbourne, Broadlands, Guildford, Chetham Hill, Manchester, Cumberland Place, Richmond, Queen Anne Street, Regent's Park and once when she was travelling on the great Western Railway.

From the seventies the common theme of the letters is their religion, the sorrow of old age, and the pleasure of their youthful days in Betley, a 'totally different life'. In 1871 Emma commented on the word 'Darwinism' for the first time' and discussed religion. 'What strange forms of religion there are in the world...... inquisitors would easily be found still.' Roman Catholicism came under scrutiny too:

> It seems to me Roman Catholicism is the only logical religion which grounds itself on any sort of Infallibility. All shades of Protestantism which try to keep a rigid outward test of truth seem to me inconsistent in comparison.

Emma sent a letter arranging to meet her adding, 'I suppose in most ways no two people can have had a more different part than you and I, but yet there is so much in yours that I fancy I can enter into.' They intended 'to read history together this winter unless it is too fatiguing.' She talked of the 'strong bond between women which is unusual between men.' When Ellen was ill in 1879, Emma sent a note with a request to visit her. She knew she was weak, but she knew she could say to her, "Hold your tongue," because they were friends. Charles Darwin died in 1882, leaving Emma with a number of children to support her. In the eighties the two friends must have found it increasingly difficult to arrange meetings. Their special relationship was well described by Emma:

> There seems to me in that Maer and Betley circle to have been a sort of affectionate light - heartedness, that I have never seen among our contemporaries, and I am sure our letters will give a hint of such a thing.

It was reported that Emma Darwin asked that a sentence about monkeys in *On the Origin of Species*... should be omitted in the next publication to avoid giving pain to father's religious friends - even those so liberal as Ellen Tollet'[33] - such were Ellen's strong religious views, witnessed in her journals earlier.

Meanwhile Ellen communicated with her great-nephew from her new address at 89 Harley Street:

> I have been wishing to write to you but have been ....and stupider than usual. Lady Farrer has sent me this. It is an address of a good French teacher at Paris – so take care of it as it may be useful, though Mr Austen Chamberlain's own English grammar is very faulty, his papa's speeches in Iceland have been capital......*she continued to refer to his acquaintances in Cambridge*..... Poor dear Mab is coming here next week. We must rest her and feed her and give her a little light reading. It is time for the migrating birds to fly south, I fear.
> Yrs aff / EHT [34]

Maer Hall.

53. Maer Hall, the former home of Emma Wedgwood.

The reference to Mab is to Mary Wigley Wicksted, her niece. Earlier Archer Clive, husband of Caroline, had commented that it was a pity Mab could not find a kind clergyman to marry because she was noted for her good works.[35] Instead she became a nun in the convent of St John the Baptist, a High Anglican Order.

William's grandfather, the archdeacon, died in 1883. His body was taken back by train to Welshpool to be buried with his wife, Marianne, who had died 42 years before. The townsfolk gave him due respect by muffling the bells and, no doubt, remembering the significant improvements he had helped to create there.

Ellen had a lively interest in the activities of her great-nephew's career: from Lower Park in September 1887 she wrote:

> My Dearest Willy,
> Your partridges are very tender and good and you must have had good sport at Leigh. Did Mr Lyttleton admire your mother's estate and manor – perhaps it is not a manor though? How glad you must be to be at home now that Father is poorly and you can be so useful. I think most of your affairs – I hear from those who know, that three months would be too short to speak and write French letters perfectly, also a private secretaryship leads only to political life, which I don't think

would really suit you, and my mind turns to Eton master's life as the happiest for you. It is the one for which you are already equipped. It has the advantages of London without the objections. It is within reach of the full tide of life and yet you are in the country......Your most loving/ E.H. Tollet.[36]

William did not follow his great-aunt's advice. Instead he entered politics, as a conservative MP, rose to be First Lord of the Admiralty in 1922 and was honoured with the title Viscount in 1929.

Towards the end of their lives Florence Nightingale wrote from 10 South Street on 13th March to sympathise with Ellen about her ill health. One letter had a long section on the power of prayer:

> Indeed I do pray for you, as I know you do for me. Don't say that your prayers are 'feeble' Perhaps the strongest prayers, the prayers our Heavenly Father loves, are ones which, scarcely more than a desire or will, but <u>one</u> in will with <u>His</u> will, are breathed to Him when, as our outward man decays and <u>is</u> as you say 'feeble'. He is standing so near us that there is 'nothing between', not even a prayer. At least St Paul thought so. His strength is made perfect in our weakness.........Dear Ellen, you say your prayers are 'feeble' – believe that they are strong with Him. The Holy Spirit prays – He prays <u>Himself</u> in us – and never prays more than when we are too feeble to pray. God in his Infinite Love give us both His infinite blessing, / Ever your loving / Old Flo.
>
> (PS) I know everything is a trial for you. Did you try peptonised cocoa? It is much recommended. Flo. [37]

Many letters to Ellen from Emma Darwin are written on the same theme after 1870.

It seems probable that Ellen's relocation to Harley Street was fortuitous, because Minny and her family also lived in the same street, when in town. Ellen died on 20th January 1890 in London, aged 77. George Wicksted, her nephew at Betley Hall was the executor of her will, and her worldly goods were bequeathed to Minny. Amongst these were her journals, which she had kept since 1835. In a philosophical moment when she was writing her journal she said she was glad to have a time 'which ought to be re-used for strengthening and refreshing the mind as well as body and endeavouring to prepare it for less peaceful days.' Let us hope she looked back over her journals to her happier moments. Some pages were faded, as though they had been left open for her to reminisce about her youth, nostalgically recording the happiest time of her life, probably spent in Malvern, or being rowed across the lake, listening to 'poetical effusions' from her young admirer.

Emma Darwin wrote of her life-long friend, 'I have been thinking that it is a great loss to be the youngest of a family and this death cuts off my last link with past life.'[38] After Emma died a few years later, her children were sorting through her belongings and found a water-colour by Ellen Tollet. It was thrown away because it was not thought to be of any value.[39]

54. A watercolour from the album.

Appendix

1 Some residents of Betley listed in White's *History, Gazetteer and Directory of Staffordshire*, 1834, page 617

Marked 1 are at Ravenshall, 2 Wrinehill, and the rest Betley.

Adams George, seedsman
Cockbane Mark, parish clerk
Fletcher Miss Anastesia, gentlewoman, Betley court
Harding Mrs. Eliz. gentwn.
2 Hewitt Mr. Benjamin
2 Hewitt Geo. master of Workhs.
Huxley George, clog maker
Jones Thomas, joiner
Meeke Thomas Wm. Smith, Esq.
Oakes Wm. Rawson, druggist
Robinson Christopher, gent,
Shufflebotham Wm. drpr. & grcr.
1 Swinnerton Wm. jun. grdnr. &c.
Tollet George, Esq. Betley hall
Turton Rev. Henry, Inc. curate
Twemlow Fras. Esq. Betley court
Wicksted Chas. Esq. Betley hall
Wilkinson Miss Mary

INNS AND TAVERNS.
Black Horse Inn, & excise office, Wm. Parks
1 Hand and Trumpet, Jph. Dean
2 Red Lion, John Timmis
Swan Inn, Joseph Warham
Three Anchors, Charles Leighton
Beer Houses.
Moore John
Redfern Wm.
Blacksmiths.
2 Summerfield Wm.

Moore John
1 Weaver Ralph
Butchers.
Latham Abm.
Mountford Geo.
Farmers.
1 Brassington George
Brassington Thos. Fields
Salmon Wm.
Bowsy wood
1 Swinnerton Wm. sen.
1 Timmis John
1 Wilson Thos.
Joiners.
Littler Jonth.
Wrench Thos. (and builder)
Maltsters.
Dean Thomas
1 Salt & Ward
1 Shufflebotham James
White Wm.
Boot and Shoe makers.
Brassington Joseph & Richard

Painters, Plumbers, &c.
Warham Chas.
Warham Jph.
Saddlers.
Redfern Wm.
Shaw Wm.
Schools.
Jones Mary National
Oakes W. R.
Adams M. A.
Shopkeepers.
Bowers John
Moore George
Morry P. (and cooper)
Surgeons.
Short Charles
Warburton Jno.
Tailors.
Gater Samuel
Gibbons Joseph
Wheelwrights.
Brassington Geo
Lindop Samuel

POST-OFFICE at the Black Horse Inn. Letters from all parts arrive at 6, and depart at 7 evng. CARRIER from the Black Horse, Mr. Rawlinson, from Newcastle to Nantwich and Chester, Thursdays, returns on Fridays.

Some residents of Betley mentioned in the journals

Mary Gater was the daughter of a poor widow from Balterley. After her education at Manchester she worked for George Tollet on his farm in the dairy. In 1861 she was living with her mother, Hannah, in Balterley Heath and together they were employed as washer-women. Hannah died in 1867, and

Mary aged 72 in 1900 in Tunstall Hollywell. I am indebted to Gregor Shufflebotham for some of this information.

Mary Southwell sat by Eliza's bedside in 1836; she was not at Mary Wicksted's confinement. Her husband, Joseph, danced with Mary Gater. The archivist from Betley, Gregor Shufflebotham, informed me that Mary Southwell (née Scott) was born in 1790 in Wrenbury and married Joseph Southwell, a gardener. Probably they were employed previously by George Tollet IV when he had rented Swynnerton Hall. In the 1841 census Mary Southwell is listed as the farmer in the Old Hall farm, and she had a periodic sale of stock at the Black Horse. She later lived on her own means with some of her family in the village, and died in 1862, aged 72.

Others: Billie Pollard, about 48 years old, danced with Ellen; it was Mrs Pollard, who went out leaving her door open. Old Wells was Charles Wicksted's keeper of the hounds. Mr Robinson, farmer Yoxall and his wife, Eliza, Mrs Wells, A Eardley, Mary Dod and Mrs Meek (almost blind) were all visited by Ellen. Moreton , a house-maid, went to Malvern. Hill gave a flowery discourse and was reprimanded. Tunnicliffe was a former housekeeper. Martha was a cook, whose husband had taken the pledge. Old Betsey, was spoken of with great affection, and was in the sick room where Anne cleaned the grate. Black kissed Mary Gater when she left the hall. In the poorhouse were S. Hawkins and George Wilding, Mrs Wettenhall was ill. Holding was a neighbour. Mr Short, was a doctor, probably living in Betley. (Charles Short was buried in Betley in 1843, but he lived in Chesterton.) Miss Short was engaged to marry Capt Mackenzie who died in 1835. Hannah Moore was mentioned with her dying child. Mr Lowe was present at the birth of George Wicksted. Mrs Wareham's child went to speak to the Tollets after church.

2 A short satirical sketch – untitled – by Ellen Tollet

Loose pages were found at the back of the first journal containing the scribbled version of a short story. It was signed EHT and dated 17th November 1835, just after Ellen has heard that Hugh Acland was rumoured to be attached to another lady. Did she intend to show or read it to amuse her sisters? It seems as though it was for family consumption, because 'Miss Georgi' was crossed out and replaced by 'Miss G.' and the Tollets did employ a servant called Old Betsey. It is very slight in execution, particularly with the change of the authorial point of view. However, it has some of the recurring themes of the journals – romance, social class, the role of women and drunkenness. Moreover the ending shows Ellen's feeling about the inequality of the sexes: man gains all. It is also reminiscent of Georgina's 'Country Conversations', written twenty years later, with a patronising attitude to the working class and a mockery of their speech, their dropping of aitches, and their bad grammar.

We were at one point of our lives enlightened by having a very amusing character in a maid servant. She first came into this family as upper housemaid, in which situation her straight and elegant figure and, it must be owned, her very affected manners always made her appear very much above the black lead and soap suds. Fortune which had endowed her with these charms, ordained that she should be placed in a situation more suited to display them, and on a vacancy occurring, she was, by the patronising influence of our old Betsey, raised to the august rank of the maid to the young ladies. Soon after this elevation, she was called upon to nurse G. through a very severe illness, when she acquitted herself in the most creditable manner, and was in consequence admitted to a higher degree of familiarity than is usual, and though always being very much attached to G., she certainly ruled us all pretty severely.

One day, having heard one of us speak to the other rather slightingly of the constancy etc of the other sex, she took occasion to make G. her confidant, and began by saying, "Well, Miss G., I'm sure I've no reason to say that man is inconstant, for I've had one for seven years and another fifteen."

She then proceeded to unfold her tale, how she had never truly and heartily loved but one, and he was a tailor, but after being loved for fifteen years (she was then only thirty), a quarrel took place. Both were too proud to bend and they parted.

In the meantime a shoemaker, named E. had been deeply struck by her charms. He had written to propose to her after not having seen her for several years.
"Well, S., what did she do?"
"Well, Ma'am, she did not wish then to marry, nor did she like entirely to refuse him, so she said, 'I wrote back to him, not giving a direct answer, but asking him what his faults were, naming those which I thought the most objectionable, like drunkenness etc.' Since that time there had been a perpetual coquetting on her part and languishing on his. She had just now received two most distressing letters, one from himself in which he described himself as

"dying, stretched on his sofa, gazing on her picture," (a hideous block she had sent him) and concluding with a quotation from Byron.

> All my feelings have been shaken
> Pride that not a world could *bow*
> Bowing to thee, by thee forsaken' etc.

This is a slight misquotation, which we may expect from a shoemaker! It should be: 'Every feeling hath been shaken:/ Pride which not a world could bow, Bows to thee - by thee forsaken,/ Even my soul forsakes me now.' From 'Fare Thee Well'.

The other letter was from his sister in which was the following paragraph. "Picture yourself a man in a large and increasing way of business in an excellent house, the comforts of which only make your loss the greater. Added to this, two apprentices who sadly want a mistress to make the most of them. Surely after this you cannot be impernaturbable.? *(A deliberate misspelling! Does she mean 'imperturbable'?)*" These letters caused great uneasiness and G. begged her to be decided one way or the other, as she was using the man very ill, but this she would never allow, always saying, "Oh, Ma'am, things are quite different with us to what they are with the ladies."

She then proceeded to confess there was yet another young man in her chains, one who after dancing with her at the New Year's Ball, wrote to beg he might see more of her, and with him she was now keeping company, and that she really believed she liked him the best *(better)* of the two.

Some time after this conversation, one sad day who should come from N. but Anne, the shoemaker's sister, in order to urge her brother's suit. The coquette was in great trouble: the friend was so anxious and set before her so strongly the superiority of her town–bred brother over the village lover, whom she most unluckily met on a walk. Though her heart was so far more in B. than N., the poor Abigail *(the name for a 'maid servant')* was so much overcome that on parting with her friend she exclaimed, "Well I suppose you must have it your own way."

The consequence of this permission was shown in a few days by the personal appearance of Mr E. himself, who positively *(could)* take no denial, nor leave the place till she promised to marry him. No sooner was he gone than bitter repentances seized her and she began to move Heaven and Earth to get out of the scrape, so she wrote to her mother, (who she knew disliked the shoemaker) for her advice. The mother told her she thought him drunken, and that "cruel were the tender mercies of a drunkard," upon which she sent after him a final abandonment and rejection!!

For months after this she was most miserable, for the village lover was so affronted by his rival's visit, that he would take no notice of her, in spite of many little arts, such as her appearing in mourning at church, the Sunday after his mother's funeral, and notwithstanding that he was now become the landlord of the public house, and of course needed a wife to make the most of it. At this period affairs were a serious aspect and anyone who did not know how all conquering, how miserably inconsolable, she was, might have supposed the coquette in great danger of being an old maid.

But even now there was one who sought her hand - a most ill-tempered, disagreeable butler, whom she and all the other servants hated and persecuted without pity. – even he when he left his place left also a note for her beginning, "The efection *(affection)* I have for you, I wish to make none *(known)* to you. I have saved £300 and wish to keep a turnpike gate, and if you approve there is no-one I should think well of so much so as you." To this effusion she with great dignity returned no answer. He wrote once more and she sent back his letter. Her spirits continued for some time much depressed.

The publican's show of resentment had raised his consequence in her eyes and she was dying to bring him back again. At length fortune again favoured her. Another dance offered her the opportunity of again opening the battery of her charms upon him. He surrendered and she received his renewed homage with apparent dignity and secret triumph and soon announced that she believed she had now promised to help poor J. out of his troubles.

G. wished her much happiness, but enquired whether she thought him good tempered as well as sober and industrious, "Well, Ma'am," she replied, "poor J. is a comical sort of a creature, but I believe he is more sulky and obstinate than regular vicious, and I do like him and there's the truth." She frequently regretted his awkward manners saying, "He has no hease *(ease)* in company."

At last the happy day was fixed for the ending of poor J.'s troubles, and it was to be feared the beginning of hers - amid many tears the elegant bride, clad in

purple, with a white bonnet was led through the flower garden and down the drive to the church, and then after, partaking of roast goose and veal pie at the farm house, the elegant, the admired, delicate Miss K settled down into the hardworking, ale-drawing, gin-measuring mistress of a public house.'
EHT

3. Family tree

Tollet Family Tree

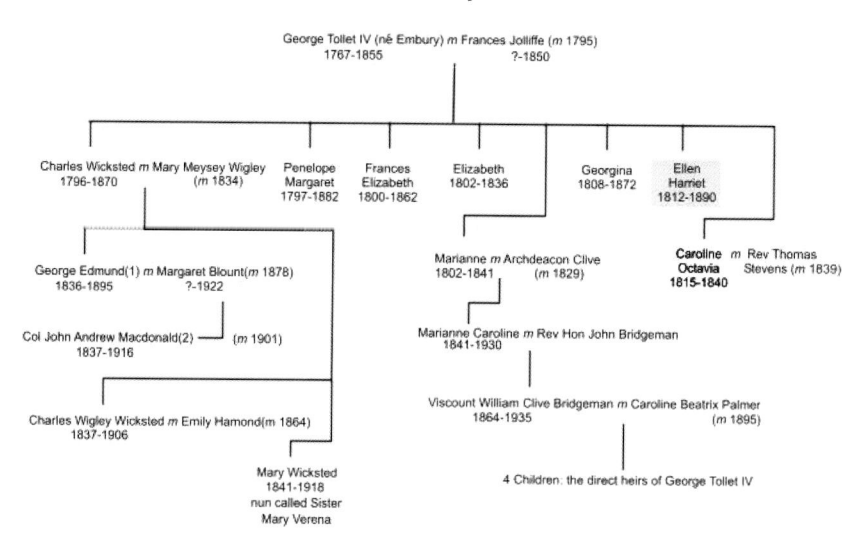

George Tollet IV (né Embury) *m* Frances Jolliffe (*m* 1795)
1767-1855 ?-1850

- Charles Wicksted *m* Mary Meysey Wigley
  1796-1870 (*m* 1834)
    - George Edmund(1) *m* Margaret Blount(*m* 1878)
      1836-1895 ?-1922
        - Col John Andrew Macdonald(2) — (*m* 1901)
          1837-1916
    - Charles Wigley Wicksted *m* Emily Hamond(m 1864)
      1837-1906
        - Mary Wicksted
          1841-1918
          nun called Sister
          Mary Verena
- Penelope Margaret
  1797-1882
- Frances Elizabeth
  1800-1862
- Elizabeth
  1802-1836
    - Marianne *m* Archdeacon Clive
      1802-1841 (*m* 1829)
        - Marianne Caroline *m* Rev Hon John Bridgeman
          1841-1930
            - Viscount William Clive Bridgeman *m* Caroline Beatrix Palmer
              1864-1935 (*m* 1895)
                - 4 Children: the direct heirs of George Tollet IV
- Georgina
  1808-1872
- Ellen Harriet
  1812-1890
    - Caroline Octavia *m* Rev Thomas Stevens (*m* 1839)
      1815-1840

4. Local halls visited in 1835-6

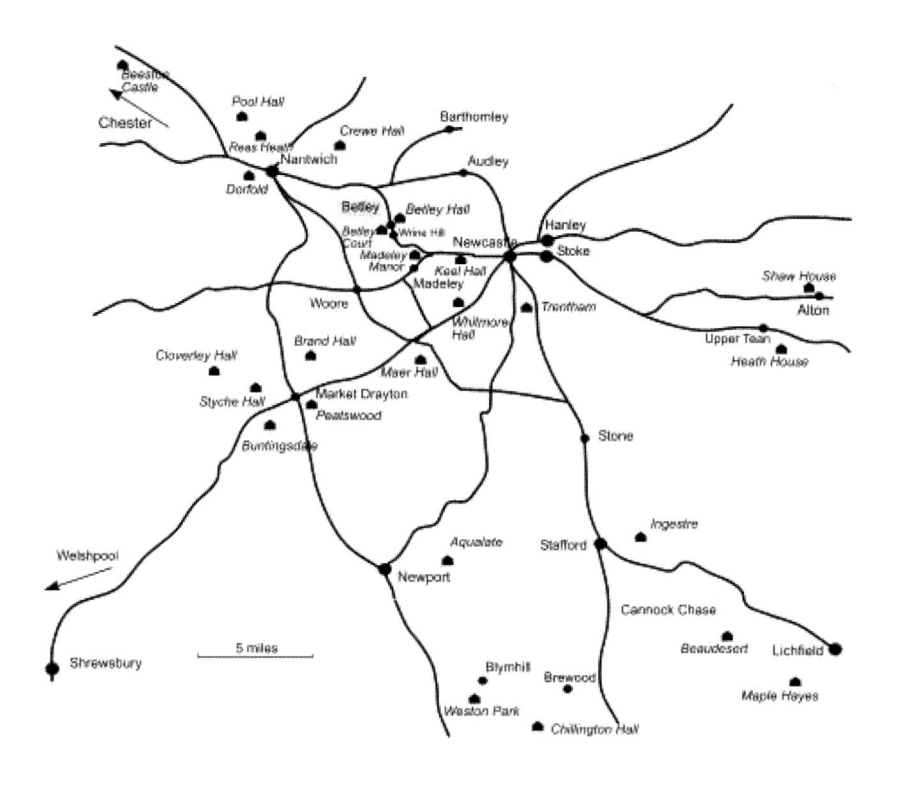

5. Betley in the 1830s

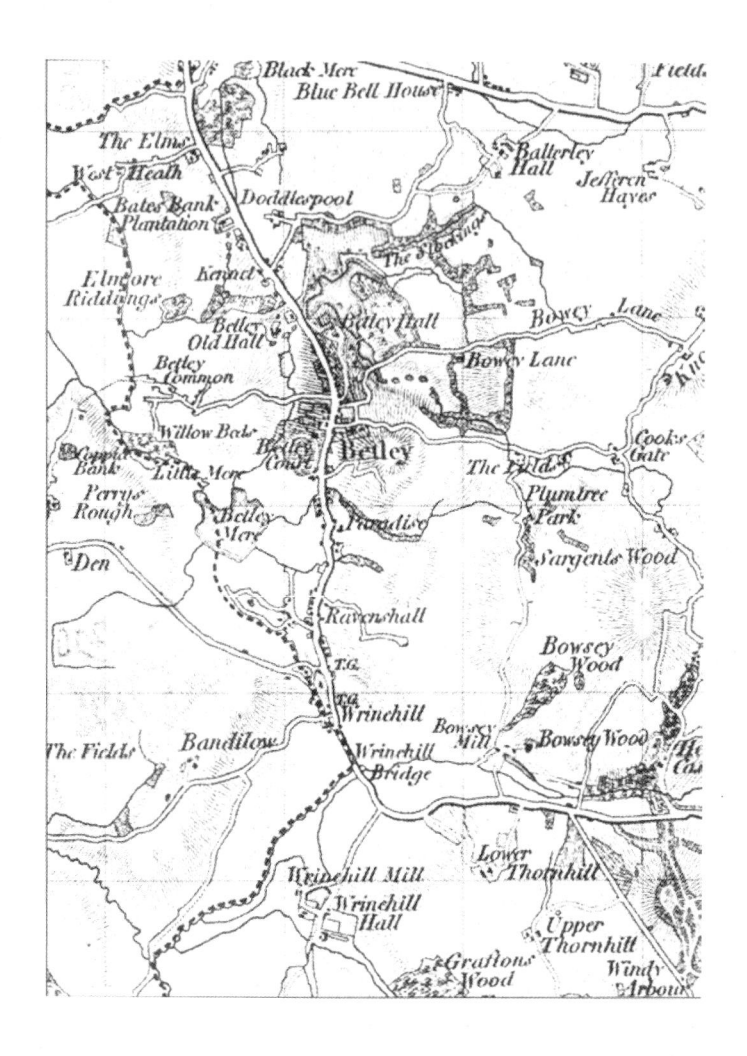

Notes and References

General

Cox Michael *The Concise Oxford Chronology of English Literature* Oxford University Press (2004)
Clive Mary *Caroline Clive from the diary and family papers of Mrs Archer Clive* Bodley Head London (1948) 287pp
Litchfield Henrietta *Emma Darwin Letters* John Murray(1915)   p147 from January 30 1823

[SRO is the abbreviation for Shropshire Record Office and WM   the Wedgwood Mosely Collection at Keele University.]

Background

[1] Smith M.E. *The Tollet Family of Betley Hall* (2005) p12
[2] Litchfield Henrietta *Emma Darwin Letters* (1915) John Murray p147 January 30 1823
[3] Clive Mary *Caroline Clive* from the diary and family papers of Mrs Archer Clive Bodley Head London (1948) p186
[4] Blagg C. J. (1902) *A history of the North Staffordshire Hounds1825 -1902* London Quiller Press pp 6,7 .
[5] Fergusson Gordon (1993) *The Green Collars: Tarporley Hunt Club and Cheshire Hunting History,* London Quiller Press pp 458, 459
[6] Betley Local History Archives.
[7] London Gazette 22nd April 1831. The Yeomanry were a volunteer force of cavalry enlisted as a result of the threat of invasion from France.
[8] Litchfield ibid p 361
[9] Brown Roger and Phyllis *The clergy and people of Welshpool* (2003) Tair Eglwys Press, Welshpool p31 William Clive was appointed at a very early age to the post in Welshpool, probably because of his family connections. In his lifetime in Welshpool he encouraged the education of the poor and education generally. Many of the town's institutions gained his support - the reading room, savings bank and temperance movement, to name but a few. He was also instrumental in increasing the accommodation in his church, St Mary's. By 1844 he was made archdeacon of Montgomery. Styche Hall, north-west of Market Drayton, was the family home of Henry, Edward and Robert Clive.

10 O'Malley I.B. (1931) *Florence Nightingale 1820-1856* Thornton Butterworth
11 Burkhardt F. and Smith S. Editors *The correspondence of Charles Darwin* Volume I April 11 1826
12 W/M 181
13 Staffordshire Record Office *Formula No 1 Population Enquiry 1831* D689/PC/5 18
14 *History, Gazetteer, and Directory of Staffordshire and the city and County by William White* (1834) p 617
15 Clive ibid p186
16 *Emma Darwin's Diaries Online* within *The complete works of Charles Darwin Online*
17 Litchfield ibid Vol 1 p 39

Journal 1   SRO 4629/11/1 /1

1 Reported in Smith ibid p 27
2 Wallop was the home of Mary's older sister, Anna, who was married to Mr Serverne, sheriff of Montgomery in 1824 and of Northamptonshire in 1828. It stood on the south-eastern slope of the Long Mountain. *Shropshire Houses Past and Present.* Stanley Leighton (1901) Chiswick Press p 7.
3 Dr Robert Waring Darwin was the father of Charles. He had married Susannah, daughter of Josiah Wedgwood. Marianne had gone to Shrewsbury for her confinement with the hope that this time the baby would survive under his care.
4 Mrs Tayleur lived in Buntingsdale near Market Drayton. The Tayleurs were wealthy landowners with strong connections in Liverpool. They were very friendly with the Tollets. The house which still exists was rebuilt about 1730 and bought by William Tayleur. He was a sheriff of Shropshire in 1797, as was his grandson John in 1827, who was also MP for Bridgewater in 1833. *Shropshire Houses past and present* Stanley Leighton.(1901) Chiswick Press p 30.
5 Peatswood is near Market Drayton. Charles was staying at the home of the Twemlows, related to the Twemlows of Betley Court. The arrangements for the daughters to stay with Marianne to keep her company must have been elaborately planned by Mrs Tollet. At this time the girls would not travel unaccompanied, and distances between nightly rests for the horses carefully controlled.

[6] Hugh Acland was a student at Oxford. His full name was Hugh Woodhouse Acland, born in Killerton, Devon in 1818. He died in March 1851, having married Mary Edwards in 1841. His mother, Ellen Jane Woodhouse, came from Lichfield. Her first husband was Rev William Robinson, rector of Swynnerton until 1812. It seems probable that she would have met the Tollets when they were renting the hall there, before they took up residence in Betley Hall. Her second husband, Hugh Dyke Acland, was a well known translator of French History. There is a memorial to his honour above the door of the north transept in Lichfield Cathedral.

[7] Aqualate Hall was built for Sir John Boughey by John Nash in 1808.

[8] Old Wells was Charles Wicksted's famous kennel huntsman. He was reputed to have broken every bone in his body in pursuing the sport. Charles had excellent hounds; he was proud of one in particular called Harlequin, and he once sold a pair for seventy guineas. Old Wells lived in the cottage called The Kennel, about two hundred yards along the main road from Betley Hall. He was mentioned by Egerton Warburton (1877) in *Hunting Songs*.

[9] Joseph Sykes, probably born in 1811, was a writer using his initials, J.S. He was interested in French literature and wrote on *The Restoration of the Bourbons to the Fall of Louis Philippe*.

[10] Madeley Manor was owned by the Crewe family in the nearby village, about two miles from Betley. It was rented by the Egertons of Egerton and Oulton Park.

[11] This could have been 'Caller Herrin', a poem by Lady Nairne, written about 1821, and set to music.

[12] This was a game originating in France with rhymes that seemed impossible because of their disparate meanings.

[13] Ellen is referring here to the first Lord Crewe who died in 1829. He was succeeded by the second Baron who died in December 1835. The Jacobean house was later destroyed by fire and the modern Crewe Hall remodelled by Barry.

[14] Maer Hall is about four miles south-east of Betley and the home of Emma Wedgwood.

[15] Whitmore Hall is about three miles from Betley, occupied by the Mainwarings.

[16] Dorfold Hall is about one mile west of Nantwich, owned by the Tomkinsons.

[17] Keele Hall is the home of the Sneyds about three miles from Betley.

[18] Sir Robert Peel's resignation took place on the 8th April 1835. In November 1834 King William IV dismissed the Whig government and appointed Sir Robert Peel as Prime Minister. After a general election Peel pledged his acceptance of the 1832 Reform Act and argued for moderate reforms. He gained more supporters, though the Whigs still outnumbered the Tories in the House of Commons. The king asked him to form a new government with the support of the Whigs. Peel's Government passed the Dissenters' Marriage Bill and the English Tithe Bill. But Peel was out-voted on some occasions and thus resigned from office. It has taken only one day for the news to reach them.

[19] Mr Butt, the vicar of Trentham, lived at the large house near the present mausoleum. He would have known George Tollet, as both men were prominent in North Staffordshire and raised awareness of the need for a local hospital. Mr Edwards also was a clergyman in Trentham at that time.

[20] Anne Brady died on 25th April - *Manchester Times and Gazette*. No. 340 2.05.1835

[21] Joseph Locke (1805-1860) was a significant civil engineer, who had successfully planned many lines of the Grand Junction Railway. He had suggested Crewe for the site of the locomotive and rolling stock works.

[22] The Trentham estate, owned by the Duke of Sutherland, was having landscaping alterations.

[23] A light, open two wheel carriage.

[24] Ingestre Hall, about three miles east of Stafford, was the Jacobean home of the earls of Stafford.

[25] *The Minute Book* and information about the Branch of the Manchester School for the Deaf and Dumb is held in the Wedgwood Mosley Collection at Keele University W/M 1070. I am indebted to Dr Alun Davies who informed me of the whereabouts of this archive.

[26] This is a reference to the Mary Malpas murder, the subject of much commentary in the Betley Local History Society and elsewhere. It is unusual because the memorial stone actually names the supposed murderer. Its fame was such that Peploe Wood, who did the painting of the church, also did a painting of the memorial stone.

[27] Chillington Hall is a large impressive classical style house, owned by the Gifford family.

[28] Maple Hayes Hall is one mile west of Lichfield and former home of Dr Erasmus Darwin, grandfather of Charles. He had an attractive garden.

²⁹ A britzka is a horse drawn carriage with four wheels pulled by two horses. It had a folding top over the rear seat and the rear-facing front seat. It was possible to lie in it.

³⁰ Beaudesert Hall with its Park was the seat of the Marquis of Anglesey. It had been rebuilt from 1771 to include many neo-gothic features, and was famous for its paintings.

³¹ Letter from Georgina to Emma Wedgwood. W/M 181.

³² Pevsner N *The Buildings of Staffordshire* Penguin Books (1974). Heath House was built for John Philips. This is the first time in this journal that Ellen has crossed the Potteries.

³³ The Savings Bank, part of the Tollet estate, is in the middle of Betley. It was a branch of the Stone Bank, normally opened once a month. The school was here too with a library of 200 books. Its current name is the Reading Room.

³⁴ Morrisons Pills did exist and were used to cure liver complaints.

³⁵William Gilpin was a well known landscape gardener who had written a book on the subject in 1835. His work is still remembered because he landscaped Westonbirt.

³⁶The Wolverhampton riots took place after elections in May 1835. Magistrates called in the military after the Riot Act had been read. Three people were injured and one man had his leg amputated after a gunshot wound to the knee. Captain Manning was the officer in command. *Hansard* Vol XXV III 1835

³⁷Brand Hall is a sizeable house just outside Norton-in-Hales.

³⁸G.Tollet's thoughts on the opening of the Manchester- Liverpool Railway, June 1830 Staffordshire Record Office D 240 /M Gb /viii.

³⁹Speake Robert *Betley in old picture postcards* Zaltbommel/ Netherlands(1984) No 55 states that the house has been 'a barracks, a workhouse and a shop'. White's Gazetteer refers to the workhouse Master as Mr Hewitt, living in Wrinehill. It was probably the stunning house currently known as The Summer House, holding a dominant site in Wrinehill, and formerly the Hunting Lodge of the Egertons. Earlier George Tollet had built two cottages for the poor of the parish, probably on the Common. He was a Trustee of William Palmer's Charity. Staffordshire Record Office D 689/PC/31.

⁴⁰ When the library of Betley Hall was sold in 1923 there was a first edition of Bacon's *'Essays'* in the library which fetched at auction £470.

⁴¹Mary Gater must have made an impression during the interview for entry to the School for the Deaf and Dumb.

⁴² Brown's shop in Chester is a large departmental store, one of the first of its kind, and still exists.

⁴³ There were many machines which produced electrical shocks to illustrate new science of electricity.

⁴⁴ Arnott Neil *Elements of Physics* (1788-1874), an eminent physician.

⁴⁵ Betley was adequately served with a daily collection by the Post Office at northern end of the former inn, The Black Horse. The Penny Post was introduced in 1839 by Rowland Hill. To avoid direct payment of postage by some government officials and MPs, a method of franking was used. The letters were signed on the outside, so that the post office could check that there was no required payment. What Ellen was doing for Hungerford Crewe was mysterious. Was she simply putting letters in envelopes?

⁴⁶The Egertons lived at Shawe Hall, near Manchester.

Journal 2   SRO 4629/11/1/2

¹ A translation of this : Delphine was weeping ' I'm going to look ugly' she thought. 'I'll go and look after my father. I won't leave his bedside.'
Ah, now you're like the person I wanted you to be!' exclaimed Rastignac.
The heart of a sister is a pure diamond, an abyss of tenderness.
I am indebted to Mary Ball for the transcription and translation.

²Archdeacon Jebb was an Irish Roman Catholic priest who attempted to pacify differing religious views in the 1820s.

³Mrs John Wedgwood was born in 1771, née Louisa Jane Allen, and married to John Wedgwood, the banker. Earlier George Tollet had helped John Wedgwood when he had major financial difficulties by letting the family take one of his properties in Betley. Thus the Maer Wedgwoods were able to visit the two families at the same time. John Wedgwood was one of the founder members of the Royal Horticultural Society.

⁴ Jameson Anna (1794 -1860) was an early art historian.

⁵ It was a painting by Raphael (1519), then in the Dresden Museum.

⁶ Macaulay reviewed Croker's edition of Boswell, written in 1831 saying it was 'ill compiled, ill arranged, ill written and ill printed,' with too many blunders. Obviously Ellen disapproved too.

⁷*In Navarre and the Basque Provinces* by C.F. Henningsen

⁸ W /M 1068

[9] *The Picture of Liverpool or Stranger's Guide,* published by Thomas Taylor (1835) p 173. Presumably the crossing of the Mersey by boat would have been rather rough even on a steam ferry. It would be safer to stay indoors when it was very rough. Steam Navigation had been introduced for passengers to Dublin by 1815.

[10] Caldwell Anne Marsh was a local writer from Talke, born in 1791. Her second book was 'Tales of the Woods and Trees' (1836). Earlier in the century The Tollets and the Caldwells mixed socially - see *Diaries of James Caldwell Online.*

[11] Ellen and her sisters were used to teaching children at the Sunday school in Betley.

[12] Gibson John (1790- 1866) was a Welsh sculptor, encouraged by Roscoe, a Liverpool banker. After leaving Liverpool, he received wider acclaim.

[13] W/M 1068 *'Regulations for the School for the Deaf and Dumb in Manchester.'*

[14] Powis Castle stands above the town of Welshpool as a grand fortress in a wonderful garden and park. In 1784 Lord Powis' daughter, Lady Henrietta Herbert, married Edward Clive. The marriage led to the union of the of the Powis and Clive estates in 1801.

[15] Birmingham Town Hall was completed in 1834 designed by Joseph Hansom and Edward Welch.

[16] Barry's new school was probably King Edward's school on New Street.

[17] The Warwick vase was excavated in Italy by Gavin Hamilton and later owned by Lord Hamilton.

[18] Smith ibid p 6

[19] The diorama was devised by Daguerre and Bouton to give a naturalistic illusion for the audience. It was contained in a large building with the audience seated in the middle and a large display of architectural and landscape scenery often 70 × 45 feet, arranged and lighted in a specific way so that the front picture could be seen by direct, reflected light, and varied amounts and colours transmitted from the back revealed parts of the rear painting. What is more the audience, numbering up to 360 people, was slowly moved around by some machinery below so that an illusion of reality was given. The Diorama in Regent's Park was housed in a building by Morgan and Pugin, costing £10,000 to build.

[20] The National Gallery dates back to the 1820s, although the first part of the building was started in 1832 in the area now known as Trafalgar Square. There was some confusion about the name. 'The National Gallery' was not finalised

until 1839. (Only two hundred well dressed visitors were allowed in the gallery each day)
[21] Healey Edna *Emma Darwin* Headline (2001) p 99
[22]The Zoological Gardens were founded in 1826.
[23] Clive Mary ibid p 125
[24] A one horse hackney carriage.
[25]This could be Robert Justice, who later becomes ill.
[26] The Cartoons by Raphael are part of the Royal Collection in Hampton Court Palace. Strawberry Hill was the Gothic home of Horace Walpole, sold later in 1842.
[27]*The Belle's Stratagem* is a comedy by Mrs H. Cowley (1780).

The years between 1836 and 1841
[1] Wedgwood Mosley Collection.*The Minute Book for the Manchester School for the Deaf and Dumb* W/M 28599
[2] Letters W/M 1070 Correspondence 1836-46
[3] SRO   At the back of the Diary 1 SRO 4629
[4] W/M 1070
[5] Clive ibid p 22
[6] Clive ibid p196
[7] Burkhardt and Smith ibid vol 2 p 446-7
[8]Litchfield ibid 25th November 1838
[9]W/M 181
[10] Clive ibid p 22
[11] W/M 291

Journal 3 1841 -1846   SRO 4629 11/1/3

[1] *Eddowes Salop Journal* Vol 76.
[2]The implication is that the ceilings of Betley Hall were elaborately decorated with classical themes. Cupid and Psyche were personifications of Love and the Soul.
[3] Calomel is mercury chloride - a purgative.
[4] Charles and Mary's daughter was about the same age as Minny. She was called Mary, but nick-named Mab.

[5] Walcot Park, 5 miles SE of Welshpool, was the home of Edward Clive, the first Earl of Powis, and Henrietta Clive. It had been rebuilt and furnished by Robert's father, Clive of India.
[6] The Rev Turton had married Amelia St George Smyth in 1838 at Richmond Surrey. She died in 1892, her husband in 1861. There were four children by his first wife, Francis, Julia, Henrietta, Henry (Ellen's Godson), and five by his second wife, Ralph Lancelot (presumably Larry), Amelia, Harriet, Frances and Charles.
[7] F.Willbraham was probably the vicar's wife in Audley.
[8] Eli- Elijah
[9] Marie Severne - a relative of Mary Wicksted's sister, Anna.

Ellen's life afterwards
[1] SRO 4629/1/1881/115
[2] SRO 4629
[3] SRO 4629/ 11/2/1
[4] Chapple J.A.V.and Pollard A. editors (1966) ibid
[5] *Staffordshire Advertiser*
[6] SRO 4629
[7] Smith ibid p 29
[8] Smith. ibid p26
[9] Burkhardt and Smith ibid Vol 7.p 470
[10] Burkhardt and Smith ibid Vol 10 p 206
[11] W/M 401
[12] Burkhardt and Smith Ibid Vol 10 p 206
[13] Burke's *Landed Gentry*. Marianne Clive, the granddaughter of George Tollet, was born in 1841 and died in Feb 1930.
[14] *Eddowes Salop Journal* Vol 76 p10
[15] Burke's *Peerage* Born Dec 1864 William Clive Bridgeman, Ist Viscount Bridgeman,was educated at Eton and Trinity College Cambridge. He became Conservative MP, Rose to be Lord of the Treasury 1915 -16, Secretary of State for Home Affairs 1822-24, First Lord of the Admiralty 1924-29. Made Viscount in 1929 and died in 1935.
[16] Brown Roger and Phyllis *The clergy and people of Welshpool* p 32
[17] W/M 401
[18] *John Sneyd's Diary 1815-1871* by P. Inder and M. Aldis (1998) Leek Churnet Valley Books

[19] Clive ibid p 281
[20] W/M 401
[21] Caroline Clive (1801-1873), sister of Mary Wicksted, often used the nom de plume, 'V'. She wrote a considerable amount of poetry and five novels, the most famous of which was *Paul Ferroll* (1855), reputed to be one of the first detective novels. It may still be bought today.
[22] SRO 4629 /1/1881/29
[23] W/M 401
[24] SRO 4629/1/1881/43
[25] SRO 4629/1/1881/15 Emma Verny was a relative of Florence Nightingale's older sister; Sidney Herbert was the first Baron of Lea (1810-1861); the quotation is from Wordsworth.
[26] Healey Edna p 217
[27] Litchfield ibid p 68, 69
[28] Tollet G. *Country Conversations* p 45
[29] 4629/ 1 /1881/29
[30] SRO 4629/1/1881/49
[31] SRO 4629/1/1884/59
[32] SRO 4629/1/1884/160
[33] Healey ibid p217
[34] SRO 4629/1/1887/54
[35] Clive ibid p 286
[36] SRO 4629 /1 /1887/53
[37] SRO 4629/ 1888/115 To peptonize means to make soluble by partial digestion.
[38] Litchfield Vol 2 p 287
[39] Healey Edna ibid p 343

Index

Inevitably in a diary, members of the family, friends, local clergy and frequent visitors can have many entries in an index. To make the index more usable, not all references to individuals and events, where they occur, have been included, but have been restricted to the more important occasions. Note also that spellings of names are not always consistent.

Ackland, Hugh Woodhouse 16, 22, 52-59, 77, 81, 85, 93, 98, 100-103, 185, 188
Betty (Hinckley) Mrs 23, 34, 185
Adbaston 124
Alington 151, 156, 180, 181
Allen,
   Launcelot Baugh 17, 113-117, 125, 177, 187
   Jessie (Sisimondi) 28
   Josiah 153
Aqualate 23, 28, 29
Armistead, Rev. John 88

Bache, Lady de 175
Bagot, Mr 29, 37, 39, 49, 82, 86
Bayton 19
Beaudesert Hall 59
Beeston Castle 40
Betley Church 152, 157, 222
Betley Court 13, 15, 32, 44, 68, 81, 82, 107, 119, 122, 139
Betley Hall 9, 12, 48, 217
   Library 13
   Map 238
   residents (1834) 231
Betley Old Hall (Farm) 13, 86
Birmingham 57, 174
Birthdays
   Carry 145
   Eliza 165
   Ellen 43, 157
   Georgina 27, 114
   Marianne 85
Births 84, 192
   Clive, Marianne Caroline (Minny) 193
   Clive, William 221
   Wicksted, George 110
Bloomfield, 57, 82
   Georgina 51-52, 92, 152
   Lady 42, 50-51
   Lord 64, 92, 187
Blymhill 221
Boughey, Sir T and Lady 68, 88
bouts rimés 26, 27
Bowhill 49

Brady, Dr 14, 34, 38-40, 42, 63, 96, 99-153
Brand Hall 80, 89, 129, 154, 158, 167

Bridgeman,
   John R. O., Rev. Hon. 220, 226
   William Clive, Viscount (Willy) 220, 224, 226, 228, 229
British Gallery 175
Buntingsdale 21, 49, 73, 167
Bury, (C)aroline 37, 175
Butt, Mr 36, 39, 68, 94, 96-97, 120, 186

Cannock Chase 59
Card, Dr 52, 62
charades 23, 27, 85, 97, 103, 125
Cheadle ball 86
Chester 11, 100
Cholmondley castle 40
Clive,
   Caroline (see Wigley, Caroline)
   Henry 16, 20, 30, 104, 174
   Marianne (see Marianne Tollet)
   Marianne Caroline (Minny) (Bridgeman) 193-200, 213, 215, 220, 221, 22
   Robert, Lord 16, 42, 43, 44, 104, 197
   William, Rev. 11, 22, 41, 42, 44, 131, 142-143, 146-147, 151, 154, 171, 174, 180, 193-210, 206, 222, 228
Cloverley Hall 79
coaches
   britzka 59, 174
   curricle 40
   fly 177
   fly-cart 63
   gig 124
   phaeton 27, 43, 120
   pony driving 74, 100, 114, 118, 216

Coape, Miss 74-77, 175
Corbet(t) 45, 146, 171, 173
Covent Garden Market 176
Crewe,
   Annabel 76, 83, 108, 174, 177, 178, 215

Fanny 49, 77, 102
Henrietta 33
Hungerford, Lord 16, 41, 60, 65, 70, 76-77, 91, 116, 118, 120-122, 185
Willoughby 119
Crewe Hall 27, 41

dance, servants 27
Darwin,
  Caroline 17
  Catherine 11, 17, 20, 46
  Charles 11, 16, 113, 189, 213-214, 218, 219, 227
  Dr (Robert) 11, 16, 20, 36
  Emma (see Wedgwood, Emma)
  Susan 17, 28, 46
Deaf and Dumb School (Manchester) 45, 159-160, 168, 183
Deaf and Dumb Institute (Liverpool) 162-163
deaths,
  Brady, Mrs 38
  Clive, Caroline 194
  Clive, Marianne 194
  Crewe, Lord 27
  Daughter of Marianne Clive 22
  Davenport, Henry 85
  Egerton, Fanny 23
  Eglantine, Lady 57
  Eliza 150
  Mackenzie, Capt 25
  Salisbury, Marchioness 90
  Tollet, Caroline (Carry) 191
  Tollet, Ellen 229
  Tollet, Frances 221
  Tollet, Georgina 223
  Tollet, Penelope 221
  Turton, Harriet 20
  Wicksted, Charles 222
diorama 175

Dodsworth, Mrs 178
Dorfold 17, 24, 30, 31, 38, 83, 98, 105, 122
drawing 25, 27-28, 38, 52-53, 56, 62, 68, 74, 76, 100, 113, 172, 179, 214
Dunscombe, Miss 214

Egerton (of Madeley),
  Col. 46
  Eglantine, Lady 17, 26, 40, 41, 44, 57, 68, 134
  J(ohn) 17, 32, 45
  Lady 26, 30, 44, 66, 68, 71

Mary-Anne 17, 26, 30, 32, 38, 41, 43, 45, 66, 68, 70, 71, 109
R. 40
William 17, 37, 49, 99, 125
electrifying machine 101
Embury, George (see Tollet, George) 9

family tree 236
Fenton, Julia
Fletcher,
  Miss 13, 17, 26, 88, 139, 152
  T.F., Sir 13
food 14
  beef 95, 223
  brandy cherries 32
  damsons 36, 219
  fowl 109, 189
  goose and veal pie 236
  gruel 145
  mince pies 95
  mutton, raw 14, 124
  oysters 14
  partridge 14, 80, 228
  tea 14, 178, 223
funeral
  Eliza Tollet 152
  Marianne Clive 194

Gater, Mary 45, 62, 65-92, 99, 112, 119, 159-169, 180, 183, 185
gardening, 39, 41, 43, 47, 159, 161
  flowers 40, 166, 167
  geraniums 159, 165
  pansies 37, 41
Gaskell, Mrs 215
Gilpin, Mr (landscape gardener) 78

Hadens 50-51
  Mrs 178
Heath House 70
Heleigh castle 27
Hill, Mr D. 33
Hinckley, Mrs B(etty) 38, 43, 58, 81
Humberston 100-104, 113
  Mary 147
  Mrs 33, 34
  Sophie (Sophy) 33-36, 147
hunting 10, 25, 27, 29, 84, 121-123, 136, 139

Ingestre 44, 76

Justice,
    Captain 17, 20, 88, 171, 173, 176, 179, 180, 210, 212, 217
    John 45
    R 178

Keel(e) 18, 160, 169
Keele Hall 169
Kew Gardens 179
Kingscote, Mrs 50-51, 62, 64, 82, 91, 153
Knutsford ball 84

Langton,
    Mr 49
    Charlotte 61, 152
Lawrence, J(ane) 24, 30, 37, 44, 71, 106, 119, 163-165
Le(i)gh, Mr 30, 37, 71, 142, 149, 155
Lichfield 73
    Cathedral 58-59
Lister,
    Harriet 19, 33, 38, 105
    Isobel 19
    Mrs 19, 31, 33, 34, 175
Liverpool 12, 161-166
Locke Mr 39, 81, 100, 108, 183
London 14, 174-180, 193
Ludlow 82, 89, 133, 141

Madeley 24, 30, 31, 32, 40, 44, 68, 134
    station 216
Maer Hall 28, 48, 49, 66, 90, 114-116, 123-124, 223, 228
Mainwaring,
    H. 32
    Miss 34, 114
Malpas, Mary 49
Malvern 14, 46, 47, 50-60, 63, 81, 98
Maple Hayes 57-58, 73
marriages,
    Bridgeman, Rev. Hon. J. R. O. and Minny 220
    Charles and Mary 18
    Eccles, Capt and Sophy Humberston 147
    Hinckley, Mr and Mrs Acland 34
    Tomkinson, Major and Susan Torleton 109
    Stevens, Rev T and Caroline Wedgwood, R. and Fanny Crewe 49
    Wilson, Dr and Mary Ann Northen 78

Massie, Charlotte, 32, 37, 105
medical diseases and treatments,
    bleeding 14, 110
    blistering 14, 36, 143
    cholera, Asiatic 20
    cow pox 168
    dentist (Georgina) 162
    lancing 196
    leeches 14, 36, 143
    measles 168
    scarlet fever 153
    tooth drawn 28
    whooping cough 168
Minny, (see Clive Marianne Caroline)

Nantwich 34, 88
Newcastle 36, 43, 160
    Ball 74, 95
Nickill, Mrs 176, 177, 179, 203
Nightingale, Florence 10, 11, 224, 229
Northen, 39, 44, 49, 67, 78
    Dr 20, 24, 28, 33, 36
    Fanny 24, 66, 69
    Harriet 17, 19, 20, 66
    M(ary) A(nn) (Wilson) 24, 106, 110, 120, 124, 145, 185
    Mrs 33, 66

Old Wood 62, 83
Oxford 174

Peatswood 22, 45, 55, 121
Perkins 57, 77
Philips, Mr 70
Pinkorn, Miss 52, 77, 85
Pool Hall 105
Powis, Lord 16
Powis Castle 147, 173, 195, 207, 209
Pryor (or Prior), 92, 100, 104, 119, 122, 126
Psyche (Joe Sykes) 29

railway 84, 88, 183, 185, 194
reading room 14, 73
    savings bank 14, 72, 73
Rease Heath 104
Roebuck 94, 181

Saunderson, Mr 34, 81, 134, 137
School 14
    Sunday (Ellen) 33, 40, 50, 64, 71
Schoolmaster (Mr Oakes) 95, 101
Severne,
    Anna 10, 16

Mr 10, 71-72
Mrs 110-114
Shakenhurst 10, 18, 19, 38, 43, 192, 217, 218, 222
Shaw House 92
Short,
    Miss 23, 26, 28
    Mr 99, 107
Shrewsbury 11, 19, 25, 98
Sismondi, Jessie 9, 17, 28, 114
Southwell, Mary 119, 131
Sneyd,
    Miss Sneyd 32
    Mr 32, 35, 68
Styche 11, 28, 80, 197, 198
Summer House 87
Sutcliffe, Mr 25, 27, 31, 39, 42, 74, 107
Sutherland (Duke and Duchess) 39, 74, 90, 175
Sutton Park 57
Swynnerton Hall 15
Sykes,
    Joseph (Psyche) 17-29, 53-57, 117, 121-137, 185, 188
    Mr Sykes 53-57
    Mrs 52-57, 174, 176

Tarleton (Torleton),
    Mr and Mrs 30
    Susan 109
Tayleurs (of Buntingsdale) 17, 27, 43, 44, 49, 72, 96, 104, 125-126, 159, 160, 167
    Harriet 119
    Miss E. 43
    Mrs 22, 27
Temperance society 76, 79
Thrupp, Mr 52-57
Tollemache, Mr and Mrs 24, 32, 40, 100
Tollet,
    Caroline (Carry) 11, 12, 16, 18, 30, 31, 34, 46, 52, 68, 108, 170, 191
    Charles 9, 13, 15
    Elizabeth (Eliza) 11, 16, 18, 30, 36, 41, 46, 47, 49, 50, 52, 66, 68, 98-156
    Frances (Fanny, daughter) 11, 16, 35, 36, 51, 52, 68, 81, 221
    Frances (mother) 9, 15, 16, 18, 27, 36, 40, 42, 45, 48, 50, 62, 66, 71, 81, 110, 125, 142, 171, 215, 217
    George (papa) 9, 10, 16, 22, 27, 34, 40, 44, 45, 50, 68, 81, 86, 117, 152, 165, 171, 181, 183, 187, 215, 216

Georgina (Georgy) 11, 12, 16, 25, 97, (diary 97-154), 170, 219, 223
Marianne (Clive) 11, 16, 19-22, 35, 36-44, 49, 52, 121, 131, 140, 146, 148, 153-154, 171, 174-181, 186, 187, 192, 197
Penelope 11, 16, 29, 34, 42, 44, 64, 66, 71, 88, 90, 103, 115, 118, 182, 184, 187, 188, 212, 221
Tomkinsons of Dorfold Hall 17, 82
    Fanny 129
    Henry 26, 119, 129
    Julia 65
    Major 17, 90, 109, 113, 122, 188
    Mr 36, 37, 63, 70, 91
    Mrs 32, 37, 65, 67, 84, 113
Tomlinson, Mr F. 30, 69, 95, 116
Trentham 94-95
Turton,
    children 24, 33, 36, 39, 47, 50, 63, 77, 107, 201
    Harriet (Northen) 17, 19, 20
    Henry, Rev. 13, 17, 24, 25, 39, 41, 49, 62, 66, 67, 77, 87, 99, 111, 123, 125, 132-136, 222
    Mary Ann 17
    Mrs (second wife) 205
Twemlow 26, 32, 48, 55, 88, 107
    Francis 17, 152, 183
    M. A. 73-74, 89, 91, 101, 122
    Mrs 37, 45, 68, 125
    Thomas 37, 67, 68

Walcot 198, 199, 211
Wallop 19, 173
Wedgwood, 17
    Allen 75, 95
    Burslem (Hensleigh) 47
    Catherine 97, 121
    Charlotte 49
    Col. 30
    Elizabeth 9, 45, 116-117, 150, 152, 158
    Emma (Darwin) 12, 15, 17, 28, 29, 33, 39, 41, 61, 90, 103, 121, 124-125, 185, 189, 213, 218, 220, 221, 223, 226, 229, 230
    Henry 66
    Jessie 146, 150, 152, 160, 162
    John 68, 152
    Josiah 15, 39, 90, 95, 96
    Mary 146
    Mrs (John) 143

Robert 17, 49, 72, 77, 102, 146, 153, 159
Wedgwoods, Hensleigh 47
Wells, William 24
Welshpool 11, 31, 33, 64, 83, 86, 129, 146, 158, 170-173, 194-210, 220, 228
  vicarage 202
Westminster Abbey 17
Weston Park 220
White(Whyte), Anthony 69
Whitmore Hall 29, 43, 48, 76, 100
Wicksted,
  Charles (Tollet) 9, 10, 16-37, 41, 53, 66, 70-89, 93, 110, 117, 127, 133, 136, 142, 154-155, 161, 170, 176, 187, 217, 222
  Charles Wigley (son) 187, 217
  George 110-133, 158, 161, 170, 222, 229
  Mary 10, 16-37, 46, 48, 53-54, 78, 108, 133, 154, 158, 161, 170, 176, 186, 187, 192, 222

Mary (Mab) 197, 207, 208, 215, 221
Mrs (Nantwich) 38
R. (Nantwich) 42, 43
Wilson, Dr 78, 107, 124, 185
Wigley,
  Anna 10
  Caroline 10, 16, 28, 55, 86, 187, 222
  Mary Meysey (Wicksted) 10, 16, 18
  Mrs (mother) 25, 27, 28, 138, 143
Woodhouse, W. 100-101
Wrinehill 18, 77, 119, 122
  Workhouse 14, 30, 38, 87-88, 170

yeomanry 10, 18
  Ball 73

zoological gardens 176